From shodo—"the Way of calligraphy"—to budo—"the martial Way"—the Japanese have succeeded in designing their traditional arts and crafts as paths to meditation. The names of these skills frequently end with the word Do, also pronounced Michi, which equals the "Way." When practicing a Way, we unearth universal principles that go beyond a specific discipline, relating to the art of living itself. Featuring the books of H. E. Davey and other select writers, works by **Michi Publishing** center on these Do forms. Michi Publishing's focus is on classical Asian arts, spirituality, and meditation, benefitting all cultures.

The
Teachings of Tempu

PRACTICAL MEDITATION FOR DAILY LIFE

H. E. Davey

Michi Publishing • Albany, California

NOTE TO READERS

Shin-shin-toitsu-do, or Japanese yoga, involves the movement of both mind and body. As with any method of physical training or psychological practice, if the techniques depicted in this book are misused, misinterpreted, or incorrectly practiced, injuries and other problems may result. The author and publisher will not be held responsible in any manner for any injuries or damage of any kind that may occur as the result of following the directions presented in this book. No claims regarding the suitability of any of the techniques described or illustrated in this book for the treatment of any physical or psychological disorder are made or should be inferred. Readers are encouraged to seek appropriate medical and psychological advice before undertaking the practice of Japanese yoga or any of the procedures presented in this book. Readers are also advised to practice the methods outlined in this book only under the direct guidance of a qualified instructor.

Published by Michi Publishing
michipublishing@yahoo.com
All photography by Megan Martin.

Printed in the United States of America.

CONTENTS

FOREWORD

"I think that we can distinguish the West to have considered being as the ground of reality, the East to have taken nothingness as its ground. I will call them reality as form and reality as the formless, respectively."* Thus wrote the modern Japanese philosopher, Nishida Kitaro (1870-1945). Likewise, H. E. Davey, in this important book about Nakamura Tempu and his methods of meditation, makes it abundantly clear that Nakamura placed "nothingness" at the center of his teachings about the universe and our place in it. Nothingness is the ultimate foundation of the universe, and it is also to be found deep within each of us. Davey recounts a scene where Saburo (Tempu's name before enlightenment), when talking to his Indian meditation teacher Kaliapa, is told of hearing the Voice of Heaven. Sceptical about the heavens having a voice at all, Saburo asks his teacher if he has ever heard this voice. Kaliapa cheerily responds that he hears it all the time. After countless days of meditating and listening, Saburo tells his teacher that "I was watching the clouds, and suddenly my thoughts about myself disappeared ... just a vast void, brimming with energy. It's indescribable, but I didn't hear any voice." This was what Kaliapa was waiting to hear from Saburo. The soundless sound, or voiceless voice, was, in fact, the Voice of Heaven, the voice of the universe itself. Once the ego is out of the way, and the noise of the discriminating mind is silenced, one may then be able to hear the silence of nothingness.

Nishida tells us that we will come to see that all things are "lined" with nothingness, as a kimono is lined with precious silk. But the lining itself is unseen, and one only knows it is there by the "hang" of the garment, if deftly tailored. Each and every thing in the universe, including ourselves, is lined with this creative energy that is nothingness. It is our very source, that from which all things come and that to which all things return. As Kaliapa concluded, "From this moment your life will be guided by, and filled with, the immeasurable energy of the universe." It is this energy which Nakamura and Davey provide instruction for manifesting and controlling.

This energy is called "ki" in Japanese, which Davey aptly characterizes as "the universal essence that permeates and gives life." Ki manifests through both mind and body. Ki, Davey reminds us, is the universal spirit, or God, or whatever a religion designates this universal and primary life-giving energy source. Ki is, in fact, this nothingness, and it is our lining, if we only could become aware of this elemental and voiceless presence. Once we do, we can learn to work with it, rather than against it in destructive ways. We can enhance this energy in us, unblock its flow, and direct its expression in creative and meaningful ways. This is what "practical meditation" is all about, and this is why the principles and experiments described so clearly here by Davey are so important. To begin to follow the steps outlined in *The Teachings of Tempu: Practical Meditation for Daily Life* is to begin the process of unifying our mind and body. Just as a baby displays remarkable strength when it takes your finger in its tiny hand, so one who follows this path will also begin to display remarkable energy and power. We are born unified, but then we lose it, for we are regularly taught that mind and body are radically distinct and separate, and increasingly we allow them to function separately and in an uncoordinated fashion. The so-called "father of modern Western philosophy," Rene Descartes (1596-1650), taught that mind is never body, and body is never mind; they are two distinct substances. The mind is not spatial, and the body does not think. His great problem—and ours since his time—has been to show how the one can possibly influence the other, the mind/body problem. By way of contrast, in much of Eastern thought (although by no means all of it), the two were never thought of as separated. Such Japanese arts and practices as aikido, flower arranging, the way of tea, Zen landscape gardening, and Tempu Sensei's teachings are paths to enlightenment that allow us to perceive not only the oneness of our own mind and body, but indeed the oneness of all things. As H. E. Davey succinctly puts it, speaking of all those who understand this truth, "My associates and I have the same purpose as people practicing Indian yoga: to be one with the universe. It's a significant tradition to share."

And this is why this book and its message are so important: from it one can learn how to gain personal power and health, to be more positive in one's outlook and in dealing with others, to focus the mind-body in whatever one is called upon to do, and if one persists long enough, to glimpse the oneness of all things … to hear the voiceless Voice of Heaven itself!

Robert E. Carter, Ph.D.
Professor Emeritus (Philosophy)
Trent University
Peterborough, Canada

ABOUT ROBERT E. CARTER: With degrees from Harvard and the University of Toronto, Robert Carter is regarded by many as the world's foremost Western authority on the thinking of Nishida Kitaro, one of Japan's leading modern philosophers. Aside from his writings about Nishida Sensei, Dr. Carter is the author of numerous works on Japanese spirituality and meditation, including *The Japanese Arts & Self-Cultivation*, *Encounter with Enlightenment: A Study of Japanese Ethics*, and *Becoming Bamboo: Western and Eastern Explorations of the Meaning of Life*. He was also a visiting professor at Kansai Gaidai University in Japan. Robert E. Carter has spent a lifetime, in and out of Japan, researching classical Japanese art forms and methods of meditation.

INTRODUCTION

I'm honored to write the Introduction to H. E. Davey's latest book, and there are numerous reasons why I believe Davey Sensei is the most qualified person to write about the teachings of Nakamura Tempu, the founder of Shin-shin-toitsu-do ("The Way of Mind and Body Unification"). Davey Sensei has not only practiced the methods of mind and body unification that comprise this art since an early age, but he's also taught them to Americans for many years. Combine this lengthy training with his experience as an author and journalist, and you have a potent combination of attributes.

He has learned from four students of Nakamura Sensei. Shin-shin-toitsu-do is little-known outside Japan, and it's rare for a Western person to study under even one advanced disciple of the founder, let alone four direct pupils. I'm happy to count myself as one of Davey Sensei's teachers.

Beyond Shin-shin-toitsu-do, he has a broad perspective on meditative disciplines from studying Indian yoga, Chinese philosophy, and Japanese Zen Buddhism. This broad understanding of Asian spirituality is important because yoga meditation, Chinese philosophy, and Zen all influenced Nakamura Sensei.

I'd like to tell you more about Davey Sensei and how I met him. Understanding authors' personalities makes their books more interesting and easier to comprehend. Davey Sensei is qualified to write about and teach all aspects of Shin-shin-toitsu-do because he began learning these teachings when he was just a junior-high student. Before that he had studied Japanese martial arts from the time he was quite young, yet chronic illness and lack of confidence prevented him from advancing. Once he was introduced to Shin-shin-toitsu-do his health recovered within two years. He started showing remarkable talent in judo and also aiki-jujutsu, a martial art he learned from his father, who studied jujutsu in the USA and Japan. Davey Sensei eventually learned aikido as well. He started teaching martial arts when only in high school.

He eventually settled in California and founded the Sennin Foundation Center for Japanese Cultural Arts in 1981, where he teaches Shin-shin-toitsu-do, healing arts, martial arts, and calligraphy. He has over 30 years of teaching experience in California alone, and in his dojo (training hall) are awards given to him by students and associations grateful for having learned from him.

He has written many books, including works on Nakamura Sensei's Japanese yoga, *shodo* (calligraphy), *budo* (martial arts), and *kado* (flower arrangement). You can appreciate his adept writing if you read *Japanese Yoga: The Way of Dynamic Meditation*. In this book he doesn't quote from what Nakamura Sensei wrote but rather introduces Shin-shin-toitsu-do philosophy and methods using his own explanations. In Japan even senior-ranking students of Nakamura Sensei have rarely attempted such a feat, let alone pulled it off to critical acclaim.

His firsthand sources are all Japanese teachers, who were closely instructed by Nakamura Sensei. Davey Sensei has often trained in Japan, too. He's studied all the books and materials relating to these teachings, even reading difficult books on meditation written in Japanese by my late teacher. (Some of these books are hard for Japanese intellectuals to understand.) Davey Sensei's library is vast allowing him to also study Indian yoga, Lao Tsu's Taoist thought, along with Buddhism and Zen meditation. This wide experience also helps him explain Nakamura Sensei's ideas, which cannot be fully understood if you don't know the cultural mix from which they arose. This point shouldn't be lightly dismissed. Nakamura Sensei experienced a profound spiritual realization during nearly three years of intensive practice in India, but his unique yogic meditation was presented in the context of Japanese culture.

Davey Sensei has visited Japan numerous times with his late father and his Japanese-American wife, Ann, a Japanese flower arrangement specialist. This has given him a deep understanding of the cultural background influencing Nakamura Sensei. Davey Sensei's pursuit of Japanese calligraphy and ink painting also aided him in this direction. He's won prizes at international shodo competitions and received an advanced teaching license in this art.

There are important similarities between Davey Sensei and Nakamura Sensei. Both are masters of shodo and budo. When Nakamura Sensei was younger he was a great martial artist and outdoor activist. His image was far removed from a man holding a calligraphy brush quietly indoors, but at around age 60 he began brushing calligraphy, progressing to a level that amazed even experts. He applied Shin-shin-toitsu-do methods of concentration to shodo, and countless people in Japan treasure his brush writing and *sumi-e* ("ink painting"). Years later, Davey Sensei applied the same principles to shodo and sumi-e. His calligraphy is also powerful, showing unusual strength in the brushed lines, combined with profound concentration, which is reminiscent of my teacher.

Nakamura Sensei also excelled at judo as well as *kendo* and *iaido* (forms of swordsmanship). He was captain of the judo club at Shuyukan high school. He served in the Russo-Japanese War, and once he drew his sword nobody could match him; he was a lethal weapon (who would eventually become a pacifist). This is why he was a bodyguard for Sun Yat Sen during the Xinhai Geming Revolution in China in 1911. He served in the same capacity for Rash Bihari Bose when Bose was exiled to Japan. Bose was an activist in the Independence Movement of India with Gandhi.

While Nakamura Sensei was trained in judo, he only practiced swordsmanship later in life, primarily as solo moving meditation. His best martial art was an ancient form of iaido. I witnessed his sword demonstrations several times, and I was awed. He instantly drew his razor-sharp blade, waving it about his head so swiftly spectators couldn't follow its movement. In the next moment, he sheathed his sword with a pleasant clink. Audiences were always impressed by the beauty of his performance.

It's dangerous to do lightening fast iaido. Some students begged him to refrain from it, because he could cut off a finger or put the sword into his stomach. But Nakamura Sensei said, "I never think of failure, so I can do this iaido. Whatever you are engaged in, you must have confidence . . . but true iaido must ultimately come from deep inspiration. Never do iaido; never imitate me, unless you can touch the true source of inspiration at any time." He continued his sword feats until he was about 90 years old.

Davey Sensei's father was one of the first Americans to extensively study martial arts. In the 1920s, he learned jujutsu from Japanese teachers in the U.S. and continued this practice for several years in Japan. He also studied judo and aikido, obtaining black belts in each field. He eventually received the advanced rank of *Nihon Jujutsu Kyoshi* from Tokyo's Kokusai Budoin martial arts association; this classical title equals sixth- to eighth-degree black belt. H. E. Davey later received the same rank and a seventh-degree black belt from this group. Davey Sensei is also very good at swordsmanship, another connection to my teacher.

Through budo he met a judo practitioner who studied Shin-shin-toitsu-do under Hirata Yoshihiko Sensei, a student of Nakamura Sensei. Although Hirata Sensei lived several hundred miles away, a young Davey Sensei regularly visited him to learn mind and body unification. Judging from this book his early determination paid off. He later met Tohei Koichi Sensei, another advanced student of Nakamura Sensei, who eventually developed his own versions of Shin-shin-toitsu-do and aikido. Eventually, Hirata Sensei passed away, and Tohei Sensei was much less actively teaching.

Subsequently in the early 1980s he found a new teacher: Hashimoto Tetsuichi

Sensei, a professor in Tokyo and a disciple of Nakamura Sensei. Hashimoto Sensei taught his university classes in English, so he and Davey Sensei could easily write to each other, and Davey Sensei began visiting him for additional instruction. Hashimoto Sensei knew his other teachers and became a senior advisor for Davey Sensei's dojo.

In 2001, Davey Sensei's book *Japanese Yoga* was published. I admired what he wrote so much that I went to see him in the San Francisco area. I was impressed by his character, intelligence, and passion for truth. I accepted the honor of becoming a senior advisor to his Sennin Foundation Center in 2004.

After many years of teaching Davey Sensei is experimenting with what he learned from his teachers, which I believe is a natural and correct outgrowth of his development through meditation. Some of his reworking also comes from adapting a Japanese art to America. But make no mistake, at this time his books and classes represent the only source outside of Japan for learning the authentic Shin-shin-toitsu-do of Nakamura Sensei.

One outstanding characteristic of Nakamura Sensei's teachings is their universality. This broad international vision is due to him having studied medicine in the USA, psychology and philosophy in Europe, and yoga in India, where he reached spiritual realization. He brought the bare bones of yogic meditation and philosophy to Japan, analyzing and explaining them in plain language. He updated ancient ideas so modern people educated in the scientific method could accept, understand, and practice them. He served in military intelligence in China and Mongolia, giving him a broader perspective on life and multiculturalism, which further contributed to the universality of his message. His experience abroad was unusual for Japanese at this time, and it helped him create something genuinely universal and cosmopolitan.

Describing eternal and universal truths isn't easy, and Nakamura Sensei struggled to make his realization understandable to average people. To aid him, he studied how German philosopher Immanuel Kant explained his theory of knowledge. Nakamura Sensei also investigated how Chinese philosophers and Zen Buddhists elucidated their principles for living. He didn't copy these approaches, but they were a catalyst for his unique teaching approach. They also lead to his global viewpoint.

This worldview prompted him to present his teachings for all humankind. They form a road anyone from any culture can walk on to keep their health. He prayed for world peace and stood against nationalism and racism, even during an era when it was dangerous to espouse such convictions. When few dared speak out, he was boldly against

World War II. He was arrested and imprisoned. A brave man with deep convictions, upon his release he continued to insist at public lectures that Japanese involvement in the war was not right. History proved him correct.

I began studying directly under Nakamura Sensei when I was 18. I was his student for 12 years. I knew him from the age of 81 until he passed away. When I entered university, I fell seriously ill. Despite the efforts of many doctors I couldn't cure my sickness. Filled with despair, I stopped attending classes. Thinking my illness might kill me, I read about Buddhism and Christianity, trying to discover what becomes of a human being after death. I thought constantly about life's purpose; my conclusion amounted to nihilism. I felt completely lost. Just then, I attended a lecture by Nakamura Sensei and met him afterward. I started learning coordination of mind and body from him; I felt awakened by the truths he taught. My questions were answered, and I overcame my nihilistic despair and what was probably a psychosomatic illness.

Inspired, I began writing poems galvanized by Nakamura Sensei's teachings, which were noticed and translated by American poets and appeared in magazines and an anthology in the USA. Shin-shin-toitsu-do helped me become an accomplished poet. Aside from Shin-shin-toitsu-do and poetry, I studied English at Kyoto University and Rutgers University. I accepted a position as a university lecturer of English in Kyoto, where I taught for 34 years. As for Shin-shin-toitsu-do, I became Nakamura Sensei's assistant and received the highest teaching credential in this art.

The teachings of Nakamura Sensei can give you mental and physical power, while they maintain your health and lead to happiness. We're all looking for this, so Nakamura Sensei's message is as useful to Western people as it is to Japanese. Unlike some approaches to these subjects Shin-shin-toitsu-do offers simple and concrete methods to accomplish your life's goals. It's possible for any Westerner to practice them, even without knowledge of the esoteric concepts that gave birth to Shin-shin-toitsu-do.

Scientific and spiritual ideas were inextricably entwined in Nakamura Sensei's personality, but he wasn't a religious teacher nor did he follow any particular religion. Due to his background in Western science and education it's easy for Americans and Europeans, whose schooling has been influenced by science, to understand him. More exactly, his teachings illustrate related universal truths he found in science, religion, and philosophy.

Unfortunately today many religions are at odds, while other religious viewpoints demand rejecting scientific thought. Since several religions are old, they use myths to explain their teachings. Some followers embrace these stories as literal truth, while others that are influenced by science find it hard to accept them as more than unverifiable legends or allegories. This has led the public to believe they must choose between spirituality and science.

Since Nakamura Sensei's teachings aren't based on accounts of ancient episodes but rather logical principles, people don't have to decide if such stories are fact or fiction. You can study Shin-shin-toitsu-do and embrace science.

While Nakamura Sensei's ideas are a universal spirituality, they are not a religion. Unlike most religions, Shin-shin-toitsu-do includes physical exercises tied to its spiritual components. This is important as numerous teachings are one-sided. Religious people and philosophers are sometimes too busy dealing with metaphysical problems to care for their physical wellbeing; some teachers of physical education are so partial to exercise that they ignore problems of the mind. Rarely in Western culture has anyone offered methods that equally emphasize, train, and coordinate the mind and body. This has resulted in a "mind-body split." Shin-shin-toitsu-do can help Westerners heal unneeded imbalances and conflicts between the mind and body.

This is the central aspect of Nakamura Sensei's ideas. He taught that if you unify mind and body, you can be united with the universe and filled with its life energy, which we call ki in Japan. If you coordinate mind and body you can bring profound concentration to whatever you're doing.

Beginning in the 1920s, American Napoleon Hill wrote of the power of positive thinking. Hill suggested using short affirmations to encourage success. My late teacher also stressed positive thoughts. Through books like those by Hill and Dale Carnegie this concept is acknowledged in the West.

Hill's affirmation theory is useful as autosuggestion utilizing the power of words, but if this is our sole means of altering our habits and subconscious, it's limited in effectiveness. It's not easy to succeed in the world with only positive affirmations. Nakamura Sensei discovered what I think are more effective ways to motivate positive thinking by more directly altering our subconscious. There are several methods, aside from affirmations, and they're expertly explained in this book. Nakamura Sensei also helped people to discover a positive mental state with newly devised forms of meditation.

He created a unique and simple meditation based on his studies of Karma yoga and Raja yoga. He called it Anjo Daza Ho. (Karma and Raja yoga focus on philosophy and meditation, as opposed to Hatha yoga which is more physical in nature.) Anjo Daza Ho can be rapidly understood and it's marvelously effective. His invention was to quickly concentrate the mind by focusing on a bell or a buzzer. He also created a related meditation called Muga Ichi-nen Ho, in which the mind is easily focused by watching a small object. You can learn both methods in *The Teachings of Tempu*, and they differ from other forms of meditation with difficult theories that take years to master.

Some say reaching satori (spiritual realization) is as hard as jumping to the top of a tower without any staircase, so Nakamura Sensei emphasized an intermediary "staircase," which is concentration. Concentrating on a sound or object encourages attention, a stepping stone to satori, and learning to concentrate is vital for experiencing satori.

I clearly remember my first impression of Nakamura Sensei at a lecture in Kyoto. I was in a big hall waiting for him to appear when his assistant charged with preparing for his lecture made a mess around the rostrum. Suddenly an old man appeared behind him. He briefly scolded the assistant with a voice like a lion's roar. I thought he was angry, but in the next instant he beamed a big, warm-hearted smile at all assembled. It was Nakamura Sensei.

I didn't expect a lecturer to have such a happy, composed, and confident face just before speaking to a huge audience. Most speakers are a little nervous, but he looked cheerful and full of youthful energy, although the rumor was that he was over 80. His cheeks were shining pink.

I was already impressed by his cheerful, strong voice. It sounded like a heavy iron bell. I was a college freshman, lost in nihilistic despair. While he lectured he seemed filled with an unusual amount of ki, surpassing the stamina of healthy men in their twenties. Though some people wrote of him being as handsome as a film star, he was more than handsome. He appeared to me like a majestic snow-capped mountain. In my memories Nakamura Sensei always seemed inspired and inspiring.

Several years later I was chosen as his assistant. There was an event in Kyoto and about 200 students gathered in a big restaurant to have lunch with him. I was honored to sit next to him. There were many dignitaries among the students—famous politicians, great scholars, doctors, and company presidents—so I was given an unusual honor. To my surprise, Nakamura Sensei was somewhat different from when I saw him lecture. He was nonchalant, quiet, and innocent like a child. In time I realized that he was a genuinely humble and down-to-earth person.

He was at once incredibly sensitive to his environment, but still simple, modest, and pragmatic. An extremely powerful and disciplined man, he was also always smiling and compassionate. Exceedingly blunt and forthright in speaking, he nevertheless went out of his way to help others in need. Deeply spiritual, he simultaneously had little tolerance for occultism or superstition. Despite his interest in American and European culture, as well as his espousal of world peace and cultural exchange, he never left Japan again after founding Shin-shin-toitsu-do. Yet he hoped Shin-shin-toitsu-do would reach the West.

Nakamura Tempu Sensei passed away in 1968, but he would have been happy to see my colleague's new book and moved that many English-speaking people will be reading *The Teachings of Tempu*.

Sawai Atsuhiro
Kyoto, Japan

ABOUT SAWAI ATSUHIRO: Sawai Atsuhiro Sensei was born in 1939 in Japan. He met Nakamura Tempu Sensei in the 1950's, eventually becoming one of his closest students and obtaining the highest teaching credential in Shin-shin-toitsu-do. Professionally, Sawai Sensei was a full professor of English at Kyoto Sangyo University. He became Professor Emeritus of English in 2004. Since his retirement he has had several top-selling books on Nakamura Sensei's teachings published in Japan. He is also the Chief Instructor of the acclaimed Wakuwaku Honshin Juku, a school devoted to meditation in the tradition of Nakamura Sensei, and he is the President of the Kokusai Nihon Yoga Renmei (International Japanese Yoga Association) that promotes inexpensive instruction in Shin-shin-toitsu-do around the world.

PREFACE

In 2001, I wrote the first book in English on the Shin-shin-toitsu-do system of Japanese yoga, an art founded by Nakamura Tempu. Titled *Japanese Yoga: The Way of Dynamic Meditation*, it received favorable reviews in *Yoga Journal*, *Tempu* magazine, and other publications. It was also later translated into Portuguese as *Yoga Japonesa: O Caminho da Meditacao Dinamica*. As a result, a significant number of people were introduced to a popular and important system of meditation and health maintenance that was for decades largely invisible to the Western eye. Many readers wrote to tell me how *Japanese Yoga* helped them realize deeper calmness, concentration, willpower, and positive thinking.

This, in turn, flooded my home and computer with letters and e-mail from around the globe. Usually readers want to learn more about Shin-shin-toitsu-do, if there's a training center near them, and where they can read more. I also received very specific questions about practicing forms of meditation in my book. I appreciate the positive response to *Japanese Yoga*, and while I personally answer each e-mail and question, my answers are often the same.

I inform readers that no other English books about the original form of Shin-shin-toitsu-do exist, that I believe I'm the only member of Tempu-Kai ("The Tempu Society") offering ongoing, in-depth training in English, and that the Sennin Foundation Center for Japanese Cultural Arts doesn't presently have other branches. I also attempt to answer the aforementioned "very specific questions" about Shin-shin-toitsu-do via lengthy e-mail replies. And all of this has resulted in my being so slow to get through daily e-mail that friends have sometimes given up on this avenue of communication, resorting to phone calls if they have anything to discuss.

So, for my readers, for people interested in meditation, and especially for my frustrated e-mail correspondents, I've written *The Teachings of Tempu: Practical Meditation for Daily Life*.

Before we begin . . .

I primarily teach and write about meditation or traditional arts practiced as moving meditation (such as Japanese calligraphy and martial arts). For anyone in my position there's the danger that the public may see them as a "spiritual master" or an unimpeachable authority. I doubt such beings exist, and as we begin I want to note I'm nothing of the sort.

You've probably heard the joke that people become psychologists because they think they're crazy, and they want to know for sure. Fine, except this is no joke to various psychologists who have studied with me. Many in this field have told me that, in their case, the joke was more or less true. The same can be said, unapologetically, for people who teach meditation—including myself. We don't get involved in disciplines like Shin-shin-toitsu-do because our lives are perfect. We begin as a way to see through our own suffering, like many of you reading this book. In essence, we're still learning about the meaning of our existence and how to live well . . . the same as most people.

As a child I had severe asthma, a disease from which I nearly died twice before adolescence. I was overweight, uncoordinated, unpopular, and shy. While starting martial arts at age five was helpful, a bit later I discovered Shin-shin-toitsu-do's meditation, breathing exercises, and mind-body unification principles. My young life dramatically changed for the better. My asthma disappeared rapidly, along with quite a few other problems. In books on personal growth or meditation such statements may be expected or even viewed as cliché, but it's true nevertheless in my case.

Although I've practiced Shin-shin-toitsu-do since childhood and taught the art throughout the USA, I'm still a student (just like all teachers of meditation). I haven't completely mastered the activities I teach, and due to their depth I doubt full mastery is possible. Not a bad thing as my writings and practice will keep me busy, interested, and growing spiritually for the years to come.

Thus, I believe no author is entirely qualified to write about any Japanese art. In a sense we're always unready to write about any *Do* form ("Way") such as shodo—calligraphy, budo—martial arts, or Shin-shin-toitsu-do—"The Way of Mind and Body Unification." Nevertheless, if everyone with advanced experience waited until they could write the perfect manuscript, no books would appear. And numerous people, who first learned of an art from a book, would be that much poorer.

Universal Principles

Most Japanese Do forms involve examining ourselves in detail—and our relationship with everything around us—through the penetrating study of a single art such as tea ceremony or flower arrangement. Through in-depth examination of a particular art enthusiasts discover principles transcending preparing tea or sculpting flowers. To reach advanced levels students unearth concepts or cultivate character traits which ultimately relate to all of life: universal principles.

But Shin-shin-toitsu-do, in its absolute sense, is unlike these other Ways. It isn't the study of a particular activity that expands to include universal life principles. *Shin-shin-toitsu-do works directly with universal principles from the moment we are first exposed to it.* Therefore it's not just the study of stretching exercises, breathing methods, and meditation as often believed. Rather, it is the direct investigation of universal principles for living, and its different physical disciplines and outward forms are just a means to personally feel the effects of these principles. By understanding such principles innumerable aspects of our lives are transformed.

The Teachings of Tempu focuses primarily on these principles. Although Nakamura Tempu's Shin-shin-toitsu-do features a huge variety of stretching exercises, physical training methods, seated and moving meditation, healing arts, breathing exercises, and autosuggestion, in this book I've written largely about Shin-shin-toitsu-do's principles for living and its forms of meditation. I also explore Nakamura Tempu's life in Japan and India, using his actual experiences to introduce meditation and mind-body unification principles. (For Shin-shin-toitsu-do self-healing, stretching, and physical training consult *Japanese Yoga: The Way of Dynamic Meditation.*)

Beyond Copying, Beyond Theoretical Understanding

Looking at the principles underlying life's essence—the Way of the universe—can become abstract and arduous. So people have a powerful propensity to merely memorize concepts they read about. This is noticeably strong when reading about matters of this nature, and numerous "spiritual leaders" encourage their followers in this direction. Since I don't fall into the spiritual leader category, I don't do this and neither did Nakamura Tempu.

Memorizing a definition of the truth isn't personally seeing the truth. It is second-hand understanding. It's neither your experience nor your knowledge. Regardless how much material is remembered, and no matter how eloquently we speak about remembered information, we're devoted to a description of something that's not ours. Besides, the description is never the item itself. Clinging to our impression of particular descriptions or teachings, we're often unable to see the real thing when it's right before our eyes. Our eyes are conditioned by our memorization of, and convictions about, topics we've never seen for ourselves. This is prevalent enough as to be the rule.

When ongoing Shin-shin-toitsu-do practice is conducted in a group it is easier to dodge this trap, in that skilled teachers will immediately notice and clarify misunderstandings. But a reference work is different, so I'm addressing this subject straight away in *The Teachings of Tempu*. I've also used experiments to illustrate Shin-shin-toitsu-do's principles of mind and body unification. By experimenting, the reader is encouraged to look at him or herself and what's taking place at the moment. Using such experiments Nakamura Tempu hoped individuals would sense these principles firsthand and consequently have authentic understanding of them.

Shin-shin-toitsu-do holds that the mind and body are one. Real understanding takes place through personal experience and manifests as real ability. If we haven't actually felt topics addressed in this book, we don't know them. And to know something is to be able to use this knowledge in life. For Nakamura Tempu, theoretical understanding didn't exist.

Mind and body are one—*shin shin ichi nyo*—and this will be discussed in varying ways in this book. To genuinely understand equals a deep, life-changing unity of knowledge and ability, perception and response.

Learning Directly from Life Itself

Nakamura Tempu's principles stem from his clear perception of the universe. He felt we're all capable of directly perceiving the nature of life as he did. While he acknowledged that he'd learned exercises and techniques from others, he believed each individual must genuinely experience the innate unity of mind, body, and the universe for themselves. Such experiences cannot be copied or given to us by another, although the right exercises and forms of meditation can help us to personally discover this state of harmony.

Looking to another person, living or dead, for the truth is bypassing the Way of the universe right before us. It's trying to look through the eyes of another; and it results in delusion. Followers believe they've seen the truth, but they've seen a representation of the truth at best. In spite of that many still elect to follow, because searching for the truth involves leaping alone into the unknown.

To my knowledge Nakamura Tempu didn't teach students *what to do* with their lives. Instead, he offered them a medium to discover *how to do it*. This is important because the reverse is a kind of "spiritual dictatorship," which I hope you want no part of.

This same point is equally important for an author. It's not my place (or anyone else's) to tell you how to live. Simply put, I'm not up to the job, and I question if anyone else is either. My aim in *The Teachings of Tempu* is sharing meaningful ideas with others, not manufacturing a tract on what we should do with our lives. Each person must determine that privately.

About The Teachings of Tempu

I've learned a great deal writing this book. I hope the ideas and methods in the book will also be a catalyst for your growth. To help you achieve this, I've arranged the topics logically. I start with this Preface and proceed to Nakamura Sensei's life story in the first chapter. (Sensei is an honorific term meaning "teacher." To avoid insult, it is always placed after a teacher's name, but in Chapter One it's not attached to Nakamura Sensei's name until after the founding of Shin-shin-toitsu-do, since only at this point did he become a teacher.)

From there, we'll examine principles of mind and body coordination. Be sure to read about these principles before proceeding further. Everything in The Teachings of Tempu is based on them. In describing these principles, I've included fun mind-body experiments; don't think this section is dry, philosophical dialogue.

Then we'll study principles for developing a positive attitude, methods for cultivating concentration, techniques to alter subconscious habits, forms of meditation, and integrating Nakamura Sensei's ideas into life. Last is advice about continuing practice. A glossary and references section is located in the back of my book.

This publication is for the average person, eschewing complex medical, anatomical, and psychological terminology. I've employed commonplace wording, putting descriptions in laymen's terms whenever workable. Simultaneously, to preserve the cultural soul of Shin-shin-toitsu-do, I've used Japanese words to depict singular aspects of this Way; a literal English equivalent wasn't always feasible. In other instances I deliberately utilized Japanese words unfamiliar to Western readers, thereby avoiding preconceived ideas.

Numerous quotes in this book are from Nakamura Sensei's books and lectures. This is the first time his translated writings have appeared in English. The quotes, nevertheless, aren't word for word translations, and they've been condensed a bit in some cases. This isn't to suggest, however, that they aren't accurate. It simply takes into account that literal translations of Japanese don't always work well for Western readers.

Moreover, in his books Nakamura Sensei frequently referred to a life energy that animates the universe, which he often called ki, itself a fairly common word in Japan. Nonetheless, he sometimes used a variety of other Japanese terms to describe this universal energy. For the sake of consistency and to make matters simple for people not familiar with Japanese, I usually rendered all these terms as "ki" in this book.

It wasn't feasible to detail every aspect of Shin-shin-toitsu-do. Readers shouldn't take my book as a complete description of this remarkably diverse spiritual path.

Additionally, since Nakamura Sensei passed away in the late 1960s more than one interpretation of Shin-shin-toitsu-do was created by his students. I've studied the original version and modern, modified renderings of this art. The material in my book reflects that fact. And like numerous books, *The Teachings of Tempu* bears the footprints of its author. This project isn't the "official version" of anything, except perhaps what we're presently working with at the Sennin Foundation Center for Japanese Cultural Arts. Plus, even within Shin-shin-toitsu-do groups in Japan different teachers sometimes have notably different approaches to identical disciplines.

At the same time, all of the principles and exercises in this book stem directly from the traditional Shin-shin-toitsu-do of Nakamura Sensei. Some readers of *Japanese Yoga* wondered about this point, so I want to clarify that while I've studied offshoots of classical Shin-shin-toitsu-do everything in *Japanese Yoga* and *The Teachings of Tempu* is my interpretation of Nakamura Sensei's original methods. What's more, since I wrote *Japanese Yoga* additional research into the life of Nakamura Sensei has allowed me to correct a handful of historical errors found in *Japanese Yoga* in this new work.

Nakamura Sensei sometimes used exercises well-known to people studying Indian yoga, but I've focused on explanations of mind and body coordination not ubiquitously found in Indian yoga books. There are several excellent works which reveal such traditional Indian methods. I don't want to restate the efforts of others.

In the USA at least, the term "yoga" has become rather generic for disciplines aiming at harmony. It's not unusual to see books about, for instance, "Taoist yoga." American and Japanese Shin-shin-toitsu-do enthusiasts also occasionally use Japanese yoga to broadly characterize their study because of Nakamura Sensei's past training, to recognize the use of "yoga" in a non-specific sense, and because the Sanskrit designation "yoga" suggests achieving harmony—the objective of Shin-shin-toitsu-do. In short, my associates and I have the same purpose as people practicing Indian yoga: to be one with the universe. It's a significant tradition to share.

What is Japanese Yoga?

Shin-shin-toitsu-do is sometimes characterized as "Japanese yoga," and people often telephone the Sennin Foundation Center wondering about the distinction between

Japanese yoga and "regular yoga." By regular yoga, they frequently mean Indian yoga. By Indian yoga, most callers really mean Hatha yoga, the most broadly practiced style in the West.

Hatha yoga is just one version of Indian yoga; it specializes in physical training and yoga "postures" (*asana*). *Pranayama* breathing drills are also sometimes covered. However, several other forms of yoga exist in India, from methods emphasizing meditation, to methods which are largely devotional religious practices.

Readers should realize I am in no way appropriating a significant Indian cultural property by writing this book. In fact, the label "Japanese yoga" declares Nakamura Sensei's debt to the spiritual traditions of India. This is sometimes missed by people who equate all yoga with Hatha yoga and are dismayed that Shin-shin-toitsu-do doesn't largely focus on asana training.

This shouldn't be surprising, since Nakamura Sensei didn't have in-depth training in Hatha yoga. It appears he primarily studied Raja yoga—the yoga of meditation—and Pranayama breathing exercises. There's no universally acknowledged version of Raja yoga or Pranayama in India. Rather these arts take various forms, according to teacher and system, some quite different from others.

In contrast to Raja yoga, Shin-shin-toitsu-do is a much more diverse Way, although I feel the objective of both practices is alike. Shin-shin-toitsu-do contains an extensive medley of stretching practices, breathing techniques, sitting and active meditation, massage-like healing, autosuggestion, mind-body coordination exercises, as well as principles for the union of mind and body. These principles of mind and body coordination, the aforementioned universal laws, reveal the workings of nature in human existence. As such they correlate to boundless commonplace activities. It's customary in studying Japanese yoga, i.e. Shin-shin-toitsu-do, to experience classes dealing with using universal principles in office work, marketing, business administration, sports, art, and other subjects. Learning to utilize rules of mind and body integration to grasp our full potential in any action is the intent. The exercises cited above are based on identical principles, connecting ingeniously a variety of activities. More than this, the varied disciplines work as mediums for grasping and refining mind-body coordination principles. These principles can be applied immediately, unobtrusively, and directly in life.

Although stretching and breathing methods may heighten relaxation, in lots of situations when we get upset, we can't employ such procedures. Descending to the concrete to stretch while riding a motorcycle, or trying to lecture while doing deep breathing, is impractical. But applying a principle is different.

Subtly changing your posture and centering mental and physical energy in the lower abdomen (as depicted in future chapters) can be accomplished anywhere and anytime. This results in coordination of mind and body—self-harmony. It likewise leads to tranquility. Applying principles of mind and body integration not only lets us comprehend the exercises comprising Shin-shin-toitsu-do more easily, the same principles can be practiced outside of these disciplines. They aren't contingent on the exercises themselves.

The diversity of subjects in Shin-shin-toitsu-do is due to Nakamura Sensei's globetrotting quest to cure his tuberculosis. While Nakamura Sensei investigated yoga in India, this nation was the final stop on his international search. Preceding yoga, he was absorbed in Japanese martial arts and spiritual methodologies. He studied psychology in Europe and medicine in the USA. His descriptions of yogic ideas and his teachings were affected by Japanese meditation and martial arts, not to mention psychiatry and medicine. Nakamura Sensei viewed his Japanese yoga as a union of psychology and physical education which transformed both subjects. While aspects of Shin-shin-toitsu-do can be detected in other disciplines, the art is unique unto itself. Shin-shin-toitsu-do, due to Nakamura Sensei's studies outside of Japan, represents one of history's earliest successful mergers of Eastern and Western educational approaches. From the East is an emphasis on intuitive understanding via direct practice and constant repetition of basic exercises. Western education's influence can be seen in Nakamura Sensei's point by point lectures, well thought out explanations, and use of controlled experimentation.

These are but a small number of ways in which Shin-shin-toitsu-do uniquely fuses Asian and Western techniques of mind/body coordination, with yoga concepts and exercises constituting a backbone for this multi-limbed creature. The above descriptions are merely offered to contrast Japanese and Indian yoga. They aren't motivated out of rivalry with Indian yoga, an art Nakamura Sensei and I both honor.

When Nakamura Sensei returned from India to Japan in the early 1900s he was regarded in some circles as the "father of yoga in Japan." Regardless, over time Shin-shin-toitsu-do became less connected to Indian yoga and more its own Way. Due to his instruction in India Nakamura Sensei naturally drew parallels between what he taught and Indian traditions, but present-day Shin-shin-toitsu-do has evolved into a *Japanese* kind of yogic meditation. Practitioners of Indian meditation shouldn't be puzzled if some techniques and terminology utilized in this book don't coincide with what they've previously experienced. This needn't be an obstacle if we understand genuine learning only takes place in the face of the unexplored.

Though I draw parallels between Shin-shin-toitsu-do and Indian forms of meditation, I haven't stringently backed up my general remarks about Indian teachings, mentioned sources, or offered explicit data about the history and outlook of Indian techniques. This is beyond the reach of this work, which is specifically devoted to a Japanese descendant of yogic meditation. Besides, a number of teachers are more competent to write about Indian yoga and meditation than I am.

Acknowledging Teachers, Students, and Scientists

I wouldn't be practicing Shin-shin-toitsu-do, if I hadn't trained in the original Shin-shin-toitsu-do and its modern derivatives under extraordinary teachers. I am indebted to the late Hirata Yoshihiko Sensei, the late Tohei Koichi Sensei, Hashimoto Tetsuichi Sensei, and Sawai Atsuhiro Sensei, all direct and senior students of Nakamura Tempu. Hashimoto Sensei and Sawai Sensei, both leaders in Shin-shin-toitsu-do in Japan, serve as Senior Advisors to the Sennin Foundation Center.

In particular, I owe a huge dept to Sawai Sensei, who worked unselfishly for months helping me translate Nakamura Sensei's writings and providing me with rare photos of him from his collection. Much of the historical information about Nakamura Sensei which comprises Chapter One is derived from Sawai Sensei's unpublished article *The Life of Nakamura Tempu*, which I helped edit and translate. Large sections of this book wouldn't have been possible without his assistance.

I'd been practicing and teaching Shin-shin-toitsu-do for most of my life when I met Sawai Sensei. He'd read my book *Japanese Yoga*, and he wrote me a letter calling it an "epic work," telling me how happy he was to see the teachings of Shin-shin-toitsu-do available in English, his second language. Sawai Sensei later favorably reviewed *Japanese Yoga* for the Japanese magazine *Tempu*.

Despite his lofty position within Shin-shin-toitsu-do and his years of study under the founder of Shin-shin-toitsu-do, he treated me as an equal and fellow teacher of this art. After he visited my dojo (training hall) in California, I treated him as my sensei. Although he speaks more directly than some Japanese teachers and holds strong opinions, he's one of the most open-minded and humble people I've met. I am tremendously indebted to him.

I'm likewise indebted to my teacher Hashimoto Sensei. He was a source of support during the writing of this book, urging me to create simple explanations for Nakamura Sensei's teachings; while he encouraged me to write what I felt was most true and valuable for Western readers. Hashimoto Sensei's son Koji also helped me research Shin-shin-toitsu-do's connections to India. Koji-san is not only a serious practitioner of this art; he's a good friend as well.

I also appreciate the Foreword by Dr. Robert Carter, author of highly regarded books on Japanese spirituality and meditation. More than this, I appreciate his friendship.

Likewise, I'm grateful to my students, particularly Kevin Heard Sensei, who has studied Shin-shin-toitsu-do as well as Japanese healing arts and martial arts with me for over 25 years. His assistance with my dojo and with www.senninfoundation.com is greatly appreciated.

Nakamura Sensei had a background in Western medical theory, and he drew parallels between his teachings and medicine, biology, quantum physics, and other sciences. I, however, studied art in college. Luckily I'm a capable researcher, and I received assistance from accomplished scientists in writing *The Teachings of Tempu*. Their reviews of my manuscript were helpful, and they lend scientific credibility to this work.

My student Kyle Kurpinski Sensei provided me with anatomical, physiological, and medical information that helped support many of Nakamura Sensei's ideas about Shin-shin-toitsu-do and the mind, body, and nervous system. Dr. Kurpinski holds a joint PhD in Bioengineering from the College of Engineering at the University of California Berkeley and the School of Medicine at U. C. San Francisco; he also holds a Master of Science degree in Biomedical Engineering from the University of Michigan. He's the coauthor of *How to Defeat Your Own Clone: And Other Tips for Surviving the Biotech Revolution*, and the Executive Director for the joint Master of Translational Medicine Program between U. C. Berkeley and U. C. San Francisco.

Wesley Keppel-Henry Sensei, another of my students, has a degree in biology from U. C. Berkeley; I appreciate her advice regarding human physiology, science, and Shin-shin-toitsu-do. Her advanced anatomical knowledge helped me to make this book scientifically accurate, and her editing skill made it easier to understand.

My student Srinivasan Sethuraman also reviewed the scientific references in this work, in particular my discussions of quantum physics and its relationship to Shin-shin-toitsu-do. Mr. Sethuraman holds a Masters degree in physics from Stanford University. His contributions to the scientific authenticity of this work and his informal commentary about the culture of India are much appreciated.

Boris Faybishenko, another of my students, similarly reviewed my statements about the relationship between science and Shin-shin-toitsu-do. Born in the Ukraine, Mr. Faybishenko holds PhD and Doctor of Science degrees from Moscow State University and Kiev State University in earth science. Specializing in hydrogeology, he's an author and authority in environmental and ecological fields.

In Osaka, Dr. Imagawa Tokonosuke responded to my questions about Shin-shin-toitsu-do theories for cultivating the body via air, water, soil, sunlight, diet, and other means. He's not only a prominent medical doctor in Japan, he's one of the original students of Nakamura Sensei, and I'm grateful for his help.

My friend Stephen Fabian in New Jersey has a Ph.D. in cultural anthropology and he's received the following honors: Fulbright Scholar, Phi Beta Kappa, and Magna Cum Laude. Dr. Fabian has taught at various esteemed universities, including Princeton, and I appreciate consulting with him about my explanations of the philosophy of science and scientific theory.

My wife Ann Kameoka also studied anthropology and graduated Phi Beta Kappa from U. C. Berkeley. She has helped me to more intelligently discuss science and its connection to Nakamura Sensei's teachings. I'm also indebted to her for proofreading this book and for her assistance with almost every other aspect of my life. In turn, I'll do a better job of applying Shin-shin-toitsu-do to cleaning the house and taking out the garbage.

Several of my advanced students posed for illustrations in this book. I'd like to acknowledge Wesley Keppel-Henry Sensei, Kyle Kurpinski Sensei, and Troy Swenson Sensei.

Megan Martin took the photographs that illustrate the various experiments and exercises in *The Teachings of Tempu*. I'm appreciative of her top-notch photographic skills.

Linda Ronan laid out *The Teachings of Tempu* and designed the cover. I appreciate her artistry and her ongoing help with my books.

Finally, I'm grateful to the readers of my six other books on traditional Japanese art forms. Even if my books went unread and unpublished, I'd still benefit from writing them. But it sure is nice when someone buys a copy or two! I hope you get as much out of reading them as I do from writing them.

This book is dedicated with love to my mother Elaine Davey (1916-2001).

H. E. Davey
Green Valley, California

PRONUNCIATION GUIDELINES

Japanese is the accepted vernacular of the Japanese cultural arts and forms of meditation. Japanese expressions can have different meanings depending on context. It is commonly preferable to employ Japanese terms, rather than substitute English words that may not communicate the full significance of the original wording.

Shin-shin-toitsu-do isn't simply a set of healthy exercises and meditation. It is a Japanese cultural art. For this reason, a modest comprehension of Japanese can open doors, leading to a deeper awareness of Japan and making the study of it's cultural activities more worthwhile. This insight allows Western enthusiasts to interact with Japanese teachers without fear of embarrassment.

It's possible to pronounce the Japanese terms in this book by following this formula:

A is pronounced "ah" as in father
I is pronounced "ee" as in police
U is pronounced "oo" as in tune
E is pronounced "eh" as in Edward
O is pronounced "oh" as in oats

Double consonants such as *gakko* ("school") are verbalized with a very short break between syllables as in gak'ko. R in Japanese is pronounced between an "r" and an "l."

It's traditional in Japan to put the family (last) name first and the given (first) name last as in Nakamura Tempu. This practice has been followed in my books. *Sensei*, a title of respect that means "instructor," is placed after a teacher's family name as in Nakamura Sensei. It is employed like the honorific expression -*san*.

Chapter 1

AWAKING FROM THE WANDERING DREAM— THE LIFE OF NAKAMURA TEMPU

Now I am completely awakened from the wandering dream, and I stand at the entrance to a new, enlightened existence. My eyes are open to see a brilliant life in the future. My heart is filled with inexpressible and infinite joy.
— *Nakamura Tempu*[1]

Since the early 1920s a unique spiritual path has existed in Japan. This distinctly Japanese version of yoga is called Shin-shin-toitsu-do, and it combines seated meditation, moving meditation, breathing exercises, and other disciplines to help practitioners realize unification of mind and body. Besides yoga, it is a synthesis of methods, influenced by Japanese meditation, healing arts, and martial arts; along with Western psychology, medicine, and science. Shin-shin-toitsu-do is widely practiced throughout Japan, although it is almost unknown in other countries. Through its principles of mind and body coordination people have an opportunity to realize their full potential in everyday life.

A remarkable man created this path, and he led an equally remarkable life. He was known in Japan as Nakamura Tempu Sensei, and this is his story.

The Birth of Nakamura Saburo

His father, Sukeoki, was a samurai and a son of a prominent feudal lord in Kyushu. Descended from the Tachibana family of the Yanagawa Clan, Sukeoki was a progressive man who introduced European ideas into his country. Chou, Nakamura's mother, was born in Tokyo.

For much of Japanese history, the Emperor reigned without actually ruling. A feudal military regime, lead by the bushi (samurai) caste, governed Japan with an iron fist. Then, in the late 1800s, Emperor Meiji and his followers wrenched Japan from the hold of the bushi in a bloody civil war. After the Meiji Restoration in 1868 the bushi were no longer in power, and their class, with its special rights and privileges, was abolished. Nakamura's ex-bushi father was given a high-ranking post in Tokyo with the Department of the Mint in the Finance Ministry. While working for the Mint he invented an exceptionally strong paper made of silk and traditional Japanese paper, which was used to manufacture the new government's bank notes. The family lived well in a Tokyo suburb not far from the paper factory. Nakamura was born in this house in 1876 and originally named Nakamura Saburo.

A British engineer who specialized in printing was employed by the Mint. He lived near the Nakamura household, and his family was fond of Saburo. They taught him conversational English on a daily basis. Saburo excelled in English, a skill that would serve him well during his later travels in the USA, Europe, and India.

He was a wild child. Hoping that some discipline would settle little Saburo down, he was registered in martial arts classes at age six. It didn't work. Once during a schoolyard fight, he became so furious that he broke a child's fingers and tore off another's earlobe. This is quite a contrast with the gentle person he became, a respected spiritual teacher who espoused world peace.

At 13, he enrolled in a middle and high school called Shuyukan where English was taught on a regular basis. In this school, Saburo led the school judo club as team captain. So, when his squad defeated another school in a tournament the losers bore a grudge against him. They ambushed him as he was coming home from school; ten of the boys beat him severely.

The next morning Saburo visited each of their homes and confronted them. Apologies were forcefully extracted. Finally, he visited the house of the losing team's leader and upon entering the residence found the teenager. Fearing for his life, the boy rushed into his kitchen, grabbed a knife, and attacked Saburo. They grappled and the knife ended up in his adversary's belly. The boy died, and Nakamura went to prison. He was subsequently released after it was declared that he acted in self-defense.

While Nakamura later regretted the violent episodes of his childhood, he eventually felt that his youthful determination to never be overcome by others or life events helped him rise above several difficulties that arose in his life. In time, this inclination mutated into a search for excellence that caused him to take immense satisfaction in doing anything and everything thoroughly. Still later, as a teacher his thoroughness could be seen in his quest for genuine truth through science and philosophy.

A Secret Agent is Born and Nearly Dies

Nakamura Saburo played an active role as a military intelligence agent in the Sino-Japanese War (1894-95). He engaged in secret service activities in Manchuria and China a few months before this war broke out. As part of his military service, he studied Chinese intensely for one year.

During the Russo-Japanese War (1904-05) he got a job as an undercover agent. Nakamura was chosen because his history indicated that he was courageous and because he excelled at judo, kendo, and *Zuihen Ryu batto-jutsu*, an ancient form of swordsmanship. (His political ties also likely helped during the selection process.) Training for this elite army unit wasn't the same as graduating. The vast majority of trainees dropped out of the program because they couldn't handle the physical and psychological pressure.

Nakamura soon shipped out to Manchuria, which was essentially under Russian control. He worked as a spy there with his Japanese partner Hashizume Wataru. Hashizume was born in Manchuria, and he spoke and looked Chinese. During the Russo-Japanese War their team fought with bandits, with both sides using swords. Nakamura was lethal with a sword in his hands. During his time in Manchuria he even acquired a bit of Russian language skill, adding it to his linguistic lexicon.

Nakamura and his subordinates blew up bridges and railways, and even slipped into a Russian army headquarters to eavesdrop and steal documents. Despite his espionage skill he was captured by a Cossack cavalry, interrogated for a month, and finally sentenced to die. He later wrote that, to his surprise, he wasn't afraid to face death. In fact, he had a sound night's sleep before his scheduled execution. That morning he was served a substantial Russian breakfast, which he ate to his heart's content. The official who was to observe the execution joined him at breakfast. Impressed by Nakamura's composure he said, "You look like a young boy. I'm sorry I have to execute you. Do you have anything to say before you die?"

"No, nothing."

"Strange, you don't look sad or frightened. Why?"

Nakamura said, "I'm not sad, but I do regret something."

"What do you regret?"

"My mother can't see me now."

The Russian official exclaimed, "I don't understand Japanese people! Would your mother be happy to see you die?"

"No, but she'd be proud that I'm dying for my country and that I'm facing adversity with dignity."

Before he was to be executed, Nakamura refused a blindfold. Tied to a wooden post, he told the three gunmen, "I want to see where your bullets hit me. Don't miss my heart and leave the job half done."

When the gunmen were about to fire, a hand grenade exploded marking the timely arrival of Nakamura's partner Hashizume. The commotion caused by the explosion allowed them to flee. It was a narrow escape. In the 1930s, this incident became a popular play performed in Japanese theaters.

Tuberculosis and the Search for a New Life

Japan won the Russo-Japanese War. However, Nakamura's life in Manchuria was less than wonderful. He drank polluted water, ate rotten food, and worked in disguise, wearing old laborer's clothes. At 29 years old he returned to his parents' house in Tokyo. (He was one of only nine people that returned home alive out of his group of 113.) After his return, Chairman Nezu Kaichiro asked him to join the Dai Nippon Flour Mill as an executive.

His employment was cut short when he began coughing frequently. After vomiting blood, he was diagnosed with severe tuberculosis, which he probably contracted during the war. Death was advancing and there was no cure in those days. The doctor who made this diagnosis gave him only six months to live.

Despite Nakamura's knowledge of Japanese healing methods his tuberculosis advanced, leading to an existential crisis that was worse than the illness. When he'd been sentenced to die he wasn't afraid, but this time it was different. Feeling his physical and emotional deterioration, he grew angry with himself. Unable to work, he began reading voraciously about religion and philosophy, constantly pondering the meaning of life. He met with Christian and Zen Buddhist authorities, but none of them could help him find peace of mind.

Nakamura Sensei in Osaka with his student Takagi Teruko. (Circa 1926 and about age 49)

Looking for clear, pragmatic principles or methods that could guide him, he didn't find them in organized religion. What he did find, he subsequently recalled, were people preaching certain ideas that they couldn't actually teach. Remembering his illness, when Nakamura became the meditation teacher Tempu his first priority was helping people by inventing easily understood principles and techniques of mind-body unification.

Even with modern transportation, most people wouldn't travel internationally while seriously ill, but in 1909 Nakamura visited the United States to meet Orison Swett Marden, a Harvard trained doctor and author of books on personal growth. Marden's popular writings promoted the idea that faith and inspired visualization were as effective for curing disease as medical intervention, a concept that motivated Nakamura to leave Japan. Nakamura eventually succeeded in contacting Marden, who is considered by some to be the founder of the modern human potential movement in the USA. Marden's first work, *Pushing to the Front*, published in 1894, sold well in the U.S. and Japan. His numerous books express the need for optimism and self-assurance. Despite his prolific and pioneering efforts in psychosomatic healing, Marden's method provided no cure for

Nakamura's disease. Marden's only real advice was to keep reading his books until Na-kamura had memorized them.

While in the U.S. Nakamura received Western medical care, which initially seemed to cure him. Nakamura also studied medicine at Columbia University. His illness returned, however. Nakamura was crushed. After the long journey by ship, crossing the Pacific Ocean to seek answers about human mortality, he was coughing up blood again.

Despite his training in Japanese spiritual paths, since his tuberculosis diagnosis he'd become completely preoccupied with his body. Eventually realizing this, he contin-ued investigating the mind as a mechanism of healing. Encouraged by Thomas Edison's assertion that his famous discoveries weren't due to what he'd learned in school but came instead from conscientiously observing ordinary events, Nakamura thought a remedy might lie within his psyche and be unearthed in daily life.

After medical training in New York, he felt the secrets of life weren't confined to Japanese approaches. Nakamura then heard of a metaphysician who'd successfully treated an ailment of Edison's with psychosomatic medicine. None of it worked for him, but from these mind-body theories he developed a spiritual outlook and non-materialistic attitude that influenced him for the remainder of his days.

In 1911, he sailed across the Atlantic to Britain, where he attended a psychology seminar lead by H. Addington Bruce called "Mental Activities and the Nervous System." Bruce authored copious articles and books about psychology. Unlike more materialistic premises adopted by various academic psychologists, Bruce's emphasis on the signifi-cance of environmental and spiritual factors in psychology lent scientific credence to new psychological approaches. It foretold psychology's change in the 1920s towards a greater stress on the effects of one's environment on the mind and a greater concern with the unconscious.

At the conference, Bruce concluded, "If you have an illness, forget it. That's the secret to curing a disease." Nakamura wasn't satisfied with Bruce's explanation, so he visited him.

"I'm at a loss. I can't seem to forget my illness. Please show me how to forget it."

"Well, you just need to keep trying," the seminar leader said.

"I've tried many times, but . . . ."

Bruce didn't have another answer. The two quarreled and Nakamura left in a huff. He later recalled thinking that lecturing people without first showing them how to do what you're asking of them was as effective as not speaking at all. This experience became a catalyst for his practical approach to teaching mind-body unification.

While in Europe he resolved to keep investigating the young European science of psychology, common themes from which he later adapted to his teachings. His research into psychology and philosophy spread across France, Germany, and Belgium—with tuberculosis haunting his every step.

Encounters with Celebrities and Philosophers

Shortly after Bruce's seminar, an acquaintance gave him a letter of introduction to the famous actress Sarah Bernhardt (1844-1923). Bernhardt wasn't only a great artist but an ardent student of philosophy as well. When he visited her Parisian mansion he expect-ed an old woman, but Bernhardt looked to be only in her late 20s. She was, in fact, over 60.

"You look very young. Are you really Sarah Bernhardt?"

"Yes, there's no age for an actress," she said smiling. Nakamura received his first lesson in the effects of attitude on aging, which he would later reference in his classes. He stayed a few months at her home, where stunning actresses and celebrities visited her salon. He often heard genuinely happy laughter, and he began to realize the impact of laughter on health and mind set, one of his major teachings. (One of my teachers of Shin-shin-toitsu-do, Hirata Yoshihiko Sensei, sometimes started classes by leading us in three successive belly laughs, a procedure inherited from Nakamura.)

Through Bernhardt, he learned of Immanuel Kant, a German philosopher who had an incurable disease from childhood. Kant endured immense pain and relentlessly complained to his parents, but his physician finally advised, "Your illness, I'm sorry to say, cannot be cured. Your body's suffering, but your mind is healthy and needn't suffer. If you don't think about your body, your mind will do what you want it to do and your physical suffering may lessen." Kant took his doctor's words to heart, and they produced positive results. Kant then realized how he'd live his life—he would follow the inclina-tion of his mind to do what he most wanted, which was to study philosophy. Nakamura was moved by this tale and its suggestion that people needn't let an illness dominate every part of our lives. It was a message that was subsequently reflected in his Shin-shin-toitsu-do, "The Way of Mind and Body Unification."

While in Paris he visited Lyon University through an introduction from Bern-hardt. He studied with a French psychologist, who taught a method of autosuggestion using a mirror. (You'll learn Nakamura's version of this important habit-altering tool in Chapter Six.)

Nakamura left France to meet Hans Adolf Eduard Driesch (1867–1941). Driesch

Nakamura Sensei lecturing at the Akasaka Prince Hotel in Tokyo in 1963. He was about 87. In the audience were two members of the Japanese Imperial Family, the Governor of Tokyo, and the Chairman of the Japanese Senate.

was a prominent German biologist-turned-philosopher. He discovered that a segment of an early sea urchin embryo could develop into a living being. This challenged prevailing mechanistic outlooks and led to Driesch's theory of "vitalism," explaining organic systems in terms of an enigmatic self-determining law instead of in purely physical or chemical terms. Essentially, he wrote of an unseen vital force that served as an animating agent behind all life. (Nakamura encountered this same idea previously in Japan and China.)

Nakamura asked Driesch about the relationship between body, mind, and disease as well as how to make his mind stronger. The philosopher replied, "This is an age-old mystery. I'll think about it, and you'll think about it. If either of us finds the answer it will be a vast contribution to humanity." Driesch's comments were honest but not encouraging. Nakamura years after told students, "I thought if I opened this door, there'd be a garden of beautiful flowers. I found an immense ravine of despair."

Nakamura lost all hope. In May of 1911, he decided to return to Japan to see his mother and die a disappointed man. At Marseilles he boarded a cargo ship for China. He wondered if he would die on the way home.

When the vessel neared the Suez Canal they received a report that an Italian gunboat ran aground at the Canal, and that they'd have to wait in Egypt for several days. They dropped anchor in Alexandria at the mouth of the Nile River. A boiler man onboard from the Philippines befriended Nakamura. "You and I are the only Asians on this boat. Why don't we become friends and go see the pyramids?"

Nakamura wasn't in the mood, but he went with him to Cairo, where they stayed at a hotel. The following morning Nakamura vomited a hefty quantity of blood into the washbasin. Feeling dizzy, he couldn't stand so he lay lifelessly in bed. His companion saw the pyramids alone.

A Mysterious Stranger

Eventually an African hotel worker noticed him and said, "If you continue to go without eating, you'll die." A huge man, he carried an emaciated Nakamura in his arms to the hotel restaurant. Nakamura noticed a small gentleman with a long white beard dressed in a dark purple gown, worn atop brilliant white Indian clothing. Sitting five or six tables away, his skin was brown, and he looked about sixty years old. He was closer to 100. Two young men stood near him, and one cooled him with an immense feather fan.

"Maybe he's a chieftain somewhere," Nakamura thought.

The stranger looked at Nakamura and smiled. Nakamura, strangely moved by the man's gaze, grinned back weakly. The old man commanded, "Come here!"

In an instant Nakamura found himself standing before him. He felt as if he was pulled by a strong magnet. They chatted casually while the gentleman watched him intently for several minutes. Then the stranger spoke in English.

"You have a serious illness, and you've given up on life. But my eyes tell me you're not destined to die yet. Come with me tomorrow."

"Certainly," Nakamura answered without thinking. He was surprised by his own words.

The next morning he went to the riverbank behind the hotel. Onboard the ship was his new benefactor, who simply said, "You're saved."

Nakamura didn't ask who he was, where they were going, or even how he could save him. He recalled, "My silence seemed to interest and delight the gentleman in purple."

At the Foot of the Himalayas

The mysterious man was a guru, a yoga expert named Kaliapa (a.k.a. Kaliappa). He told Nakamura that a branch of the British Royal Family invited him and his tiny entourage annually to England, and Nakamura met him by chance in Cairo on his way back to India.

Their journey to India took three long months. They passed through the Suez and then down to the Red Sea. From there, their voyage took them around the Arabian horn, where they sailed along the Arabian and Persian coastline. They moored at seaports along their way. When they arrived at Karachi they left their ship and drifted up the Indus River on a barge pulled from the shoreline using camels. Next, Kaliapa and Nakamura headed east, riding camels through the Rajasthan and the Hindustani Plain, eventually stopping in Calcutta. Then they trekked to the north to Darjeeling.

Much of the time Nakamura rode awkwardly atop camels and donkeys, which he found arduous in his weakened condition. They eventually reached a village in Nepal called Gorkhe, which was at the foot of Mt. Kanchenjunga in the Himalayas. At 28,146 feet, Kanchenjunga is the third highest mountain in the world. Yogis came to Gorkhe to practice under the guidance of Kaliapa, who was their guru[2]. Kaliapa's retreat, situated in a sharply sloped gorge, was an independent rural community comprised of diminutive cabins. In this yoga village an elderly man was assigned to care for Nakamura, who was offered a simple hut. His roommate was a goat. He was given a pale azure cloth to wear around his waist, an Indian garment known as a *dhoti*.

Every morning the guru gave an audience to his students. Nakamura and others prostrated themselves on the ground and were forbidden to look up. Days passed in this way, but Kaliapa didn't teach him anything. He assumed his guru would call him immediately for instruction, but more than a month passed with no training. Had Kaliapa forgotten his promise at the Cairo hotel? Nakamura couldn't wait any longer, and one day when the guru came his way he stood up suddenly and blurted, "I have a question!"

Kaliapa smiled broadly. Nakamura knew then that he hadn't forgotten his pledge.

"You told me in Cairo that you'd teach me. When will you do it?"

"I'm prepared to start anytime, but you're not ready yet."

"I am ready! I've come here for no other reason."

"You don't look ready. Let me explain. Bring me a pot of cold water."

Earthen pots of water were lying here and there. Nakamura brought one to his guru. Next Kaliapa ordered him to bring a pot of hot water. "Pour this hot water into the cold pot," the teacher said, even though the pot was already full.

"The water will overflow, if I do," said Nakamura.

"How do you know that?"

"Why, it's an easy thing to see," Nakamura stated indignantly.

"The same can be said of you. Your mind is full of other things. You're thinking, 'I've studied medicine in America, I'm from a developed country, and I've read a lot of philosophy books.' You're filled with pride. If you're not empty, whatever I say won't enter your mind. Right?"

40

Nakamura was taken aback.

"You seem to understand me now. All right. I'll teach you from tomorrow morning. Come to my room with a mind like a newborn baby's."

First Steps on the Path

At last Nakamura began yoga training. He studied various methods, with an emphasis on meditation and breathing exercises. But more than this, Kaliapa got Nakamura to stop searching for revelations in books, ideologies, or the beliefs of others. Kaliapa, using psychological approaches that Nakamura remembered as severe, energized him to seek firsthand awareness, which wasn't reliant on any master or method.

Kaliapa taught him that the universe and human beings are one. We're thus endowed with the energy of the universe (ki in Japanese, prana in Sanskrit). Consequently he felt that we can learn from nature itself.

He informed Nakamura that his illness was a blessing in disguise because it compelled him to contemplate the nature of his being. Nonetheless, to progress further in life, it was time to forget about dying. Kaliapa observed that since it was impossible to predict the time of death, he should cease agonizing about dying and live every day fully.

Kaliapa also noted that the body mirrors the brain and feelings. Figuratively, the mind is the origin of a stream, and the body is like the downstream flow. Kaliapa stressed that if the body falls sick the mind must stay positive or the body further weakens. He even indicated the condition of specific organs was a sign of associated emotional difficulties.

He taught Nakamura that an important step for maintaining a positive condition in the mind, body, and organs was understanding kumbhaka; a mental and physical state he said was akin to a spiritual body, which could endure hardships in the harsh Himalayan Mountains. His teacher only gave hints about how to accomplish this: "Keep your body like a bottle full of water with even pressure around it. This is kumbhaka."

Yogis entered a shallow stream and sat in the water in meditation to grasp kumbhaka. Gorkhe's elevation is 4,094 feet, and the water was icy, coming from melted Himalayan snow. With the lower body in the torrent, they attempted to adopt a posture utilizing kumbhaka, which let them endure extreme cold and which will be fully detailed in upcoming chapters. Once a day, Nakamura practiced this with the other yogis. His guru told him an old man, then nearly 90, had been doing it for years, but he still couldn't remain composed in the frigid conditions. Nakamura, however, after some weeks could tolerate the ice-cold stream.

"You're getting it!" Kaliapa shouted as Nakamura sat in the water. Kaliapa said happily, "Now you have it. You're the fastest to master kumbhaka."

Although Nakamura was happy about his progress, he wasn't too excited about what he was eating. He felt meals were meager at the yoga village—sometimes just millet or barnyard grass dipped in water and served on fig leaves. One day he complained to his teacher, "I'm suffering from tuberculosis. When I was in Europe I ate nutritious food like meat and eggs every day. Meals are poor here. Can they sustain my body?"

Kaliapa indicated that a vegetarian diet was more than acceptable for maintaining health, commenting that his companions were all vegetarians and rarely fell ill. Nakamura in time realized how important this statement was. After some months he stopped vomiting blood, his chronic fever dropped, and he gained weight. At first he thought, "This clean, fresh air must be good for me." Years later he decided the vegetarian food improved his health. Throughout his life he encouraged his students to follow a semi-vegetarian or vegetarian diet.

Once he understood kumbhaka his guru began taking him to a waterfall deep in the mountain to meditate. Kaliapa riding a donkey and Nakamura on foot went up the mountain daily. There was a flat rock near the basin of the waterfall. On their first visit Kaliapa pointed at the rock and said, "Sit there and think about why you were born." Once he was in the lotus position (his guru's favored seated meditation posture) Kaliapa left.

Nakamura sat and thought for hours. In the evening his teacher abruptly appeared and asked for an answer to the question. His answer was wrong. Kaliapa suddenly struck him.

At that shocking instant, Nakamura realized that we're born with a great mission to work in unison with the universe. He later remembered feeling at one with the universe and receiving its wisdom. Nakamura's realization ultimately led him to declare that people are "lords of creation," since only humankind is conscious of being born and the certainty that we'll pass away. Humanity has reflexes shared with plants and emotions similar to animals, but we're different from plants and beasts because our ability to use logic. This capacity for rational thought is seldom duplicated by animals. While it can usher people away from their natural condition, it also gives us the ability to consciously grasp our intrinsic harmony with the universe, a faculty that Nakamura called *uchu-rei*, the "universal mind," or *reiseishin*, the "spiritual mind" of a genuine human being.

He told this to Kaliapa. And this time his teacher replied, "Well done."

Nakamura Sensei, at age 87, performs a traditional Japanese dance.

The Voice of Heaven

Despite his realization Nakamura and Kaliapa continued visiting the waterfall for meditation. At first Nakamura was annoyed by the thundering cascade, complaining to his teacher, "That sound's terrible and deafening; it drives me crazy. Can I sit somewhere more peaceful?"

Kaliapa replied, "I've thought deeply about this, and I've chosen that flat rock for your meditation."

"Why?"

"To help you hear the Voice of Heaven."

"The Voice of Heaven?"

"Yes."

"The heavens have a voice?"

Nakamura respected his guru, but he had doubts about this "Voice of Heaven" idea. Coming from a more urbane, educated society, he thought he was in a less sophisticated country. He asked cynically, "Have *you* ever heard the Voice of Heaven?"

"Yes, all the time. I'm hearing it even as we speak."

This made no sense to Nakamura. Kaliapa elaborated, "If you're disturbed by the waterfall you can't hear the Voice. Nor can you hear the Voices of the Earth."

"You mean there are Voices of the Earth, too?"

Kaliapa explained, "Beasts howling, insects chirping, birds singing, the sound of the wind—these are all Voices of the Earth."

"I already hear them."

"Can you hear them by the waterfall's basin?"

Nakamura blurted, "No, it's impossible. Near that overpowering sound, you can't hear anything."

"Think negatively and you really can't hear them. Try to hear the Voices of the Earth today. Actually try first and then see whether you hear them or not."

He tried, but the roar thundered over him, and he couldn't listen to a thing. Yet a few hours later, as he was closing his eyes and sitting calmly on his rock, he faintly heard chirping, "Twee, twee, twee." He opened his eyes to see little colorful birds flying from one stone to another. It seemed like a hallucination, but suddenly he clearly heard a bird singing in unison with the movement of its hooked beak. After that he noticed whenever he strained to listen to them he couldn't hear the birds. But when he did nothing his mind grew unruffled and empty, and he could eavesdrop on their twittering. (This was a key realization, an insight that's actually valuable to anyone studying meditation, and one that will be explored in upcoming chapters. In short, the more a person tries to calm the mind, the more they unsettle it.)

After days of sitting alone, motionless by the Himalayan cascade, Nakamura perceived cicadas chirping, the wind rustling foliage, and even the howls of leopards and wolves deep in the woods. He happily reported this to Kaliapa.

"That's wonderful. Now also listen for the Voice of Heaven."

Nakamura tried hard to perceive this Voice. However, he couldn't hear anything. He didn't have a single clue to go on so he eventually asked Kaliapa, "What does the Voice sound like?"

"Did you also hear the Voices of the Earth when you tried to hear the Voice of the Heaven?"

"What?"

Kaliapa clarified, "You can naturally hear the Voice of Heaven if you're not attached to the Voices of the Earth that enter your ears."

Nakamura was puzzled but kept struggling to notice the Voice of Heaven. "I'll really ignore the Voices of the Earth," he thought. Yet the more he tried the more the natural sounds stuck in his mind. Nakamura then understood if we strain to not think about something, *we are thinking about it*. Real meditation involves *doing nothing* and resting in complete naturalness.

Day after day he listened for the Voice of Heaven to no avail. He was irritated, but his ego wouldn't let him ask Kaliapa another question. Frustration mounting, he began grinding his teeth. He sat statue-like for long hours, absolutely motionless in meditation, beside the falls. And each day he experienced immense pain in his legs and back, to say little of his psychological torment. Once, he contemplated throwing himself into the basin of water at the bottom of the falls. "How many days have passed like this?" he wondered.

One day, sitting with his eyes closed, he felt something lick his knee. He opened his eyes and saw an animal the size of a large dog. Nakamura quickly realized this was no oversized puppy. It was an Indian leopard, an animal resembling a black panther.

Nakamura stared at the leopard. The leopard stared at Nakamura.

Looking into its glaring eyes his mind emptied itself just as when he first heard the Voices of the Earth during meditation. He did nothing, and the big cat leisurely wandered down to a stream. After it departed Kaliapa appeared and rushed to him, "Did you see the leopard?"

"Yes, I did."

"Are you all right?"

"Yes, I am, sir."

Nakamura was told Himalayan black leopards are the world's most fierce and dangerous. On the way back home that evening his guru asked, "Did you feel fear when you met the leopard?"

"No, not at all."

"Then you'll hear the Voice of Heaven soon. When your eyes and the leopard's met you did and thought nothing. That natural, unforced, innocent feeling is extremely important. Don't forget that feeling."

Three more months passed, but Heaven wasn't talking. He told Kaliapa, "It's really hard to hear this Voice."

"If you think negatively it is hard. Right now birds and cicadas are singing. When you listen to me your mind perceives them, yet it isn't attached to them or distracted by them. You can only truly hear me when you aren't mentally stuck on the other sounds in your environment. That's why you can listen to me, right? That's it. It's the same thing. It's simple."

Nakamura tried again and again to hear the Voice of Heaven, and it nearly drove him insane. Humiliated, his burden was nearing its limit.

"No more! I'm done. I give up."

He stood up shouting, "What's the use? I've lived my whole life without hearing that Voice. The hell with it!"

He threw himself face up on the grass. Opening his eyes halfway, he gently looked

Nakamura Sensei and students in Nagoya in 1963.

at the sky. Flecks of clouds floated by, and he was slowly attracted to the changing form of each cloud. Although he still heard the sounds around him, unconsciously he found himself, once again, doing and thinking nothing.

Instantly he experienced a state beyond thought, beyond personal ego, beyond suffering. He later wrote at that split second, in a moment outside of time, he penetrated deeply into the ultimate nature of life.

Kaliapa ambled up to the waterfall aboard his faithful donkey. He found a transformed student. Nakamura said to him as they left the mountain, "I was watching the clouds, and suddenly my thoughts about myself disappeared. Just a vast void, brimming with energy. It's indescribable, but I didn't hear any Voice."

"You've heard it at last!"

"What do you mean?"

"The Voice of Heaven is the Voice of the Universe. It's a voiceless voice, a soundless sound—absolute stillness."

"I see . . . well, I have another question. What will happen now that I've heard the Voice?"

Kaliapa answered, "From this moment your life will be guided by, and filled with, the immeasurable energy of the universe."

"Energy of the universe?"

"Soon the signs of its presence will be clearly evident to you."

Tears welled up in Nakamura's eyes. He thought, "I studied medicine at Columbia, but I couldn't see this truth. Now the universe, trying to save a fool like me, whispers its secrets through this old man." He cried in joy.

It was 1912. At 36 years old he experienced satori, or spiritual realization. His illness was long gone. It never came back.

After approximately three years in India and Nepal he returned to Japan, where he achieved success in the world of business. He became President of the Tokyo Bank of Business & Savings and served on the Board of Directors of the Dai Nihon Seifun Milling Company. He also profitably managed several companies, becoming quite wealthy. After several years of playing a leading role in the Japanese business community, he had a powerful vision that he was to teach what he'd realized in India. He abandoned his social status, businesses, and fortune. At 43 he began teaching the public on June 8, 1919.

The Wind of Heaven

Nakamura Sensei dropped Saburo, renaming himself Tempu, "the Wind of Heaven."[3] He taught a combination of the different arts and forms of meditation he'd learned, at first in private, then gradually more openly. Every morning he presented free training in Shin-shin-toitsu-do in Tokyo at Hibiya and Ueno parks. Nakamura Sensei stressed the union of mind and body, which he christened *Shin* ("mind")-*shin* ("body")-*toitsu* ("unification")-*do* ("Way"). At times the names *Shin-shin-toitsu* ("Mind and Body Unification"), *Shin-shin-toitsu-ho* ("The Art of Mind and Body Unification"), and *Toitsu-do* ("The Way of Unification") were, and occasionally still are, used by practitioners. The authentic spirit of the teaching cannot be limited by a name.

He founded the Toitsu-Kai ("Association for Unification"), with the word "toitsu" being an approximation of the term "yoga," meaning union and harmony in Sanskrit. In September of 1919, the Toitsu-Kai became the Toitsu Tetsui Gakkai, the "Unification Philosophy and Medical Research Society," dedicated to improving mental and physical health. It was a nonprofit educational organization as opposed to a church or temple. Nakamura Sensei insisted that Shin-shin-toitsu-do is an inquiry into the core of spirituality not an organized religion.

Well-known people in political and financial circles attended his lectures. Through a recommendation from a member of the Imperial Family, Nakamura Sensei taught Shin-shin-toitsu-do to three princes (Higashikuni, Kitashirakawa, and Takeda).

From 1925 on numerous branches of the Toitsu Tetsui Gakkai were established in Kyoto, Nagoya, Kobe, and Otaru, Hokkaido. In January 1940, the Toitsu Tetsui Gakkai was renamed Tempu-Kai (the "Tempu Society"). Seminars and activities were held nationwide until the start of World War II.

In October 1947, at the age of 71, Nakamura Sensei taught Shin-shin-toitsu-do for three days to an audience of about 250 officials of the U.S. Army General Headquarters. The millionaire John D. Rockefeller III happened to be in the audience. Impressed by the teachings of Japanese yoga, he offered to bring Nakamura Sensei to the USA to teach. Nakamura Sensei declined stating that his first priority was re-establishing the health of war-torn Japan.

Among the past and present students of Shin-shin-toitsu-do are members of the Japanese Imperial Family, government officials, business leaders, famous scholars, Japanese Order of Culture recipients, Olympic gold medalists, well-known actors, and celebrated novelists. Nakamura Sensei never directly advertised for students. He preferred to share the Way of the universe with people who found him through the natural course of their spiritual evolution. New students joined via the introduction of senior members of his group.

While Nakamura Sensei did teach specific methods of mind-body coordination, meditation, and health improvement, they merely served as techniques for living well. These techniques, while useful, cannot mysteriously produce enlightenment. No technique can. Correct techniques can, nonetheless, greatly improve our health and under the right circumstances aid in giving birth to an environment within which meditation can occur. It's within meditation, not within a copied method, that the opportunity for spiritual realization exists.

Indian Influences

Various historical influences can be seen in Shin-shin-toitsu-do. Nakamura Sensei practiced unique versions of Raja yoga and Karma yoga with Kaliapa, with an emphasis on Raja yoga. These yoga forms had a major influence on his teachings, and Karma yoga is the yoga of action, cultivating awareness of our actions and their aftereffects. Karma yoga is also the yoga of selfless service (*seva* in Sanskrit); recognizing that since we're all one with the universe to help others is to help ourselves. Nakamura Sensei's writings, indeed every one of his actions after returning from India, were examples of his Karma yoga path.

Raja yoga is often thought of as "classical yoga," the yoga of meditation outlined in Patanjali's *Yoga Sutras*, the two-thousand-year-old seminal work on this subject. In the *Yoga Sutras* a course of meditation involving both mind and body is explained as a Way to spiritual liberation through union with the universe. Patanjali taught an eight-limbed path, one of the oldest and most respected interpretations of yoga in India. While several types of yoga have evolved since the *Yoga Sutras* were written the eight-aspect form that follows is considered by many to be most representative of ancient and traditional yoga:

1. *Yama*—The five outward characteristics of spirituality:
   a. *Aparigraha*—Contentedness and not being materialistic
   b. *Asteya*—Respect other's property and boundaries; to not steal
   c. *Ahimsa*—Nonviolence in thought, word, and deed
   d. *Brahmacharya*—Transcend lust
   e. *Satya*—Sincerity and integrity
2. *Niyama*—The five internal characteristics of self-mastery:
   a. *Samtosa*—Satisfaction in the present moment
   b. *Tapas*—A burning determination
   c. *Saucha*—Purity of mind and body
   d. *Svadhyaya*—Self-awareness and introspection
   e. *Ishvara Pranidhana*—Surrendering to the universe
3. *Asana*—Posture, which refers more to correct postures for seated meditation than to the postures of physical training practiced today in Hatha yoga
4. *Pranayama*—Breathing practices to balance, purify, and strengthen the mind and body
5. *Pratiyahara*—Nonattachment to the fleeting aspects of life; transcending the senses
6. *Dharana*—Methods of concentration that fix the mind on a single point
7. *Dhyana*—Meditation that progresses from dharana
8. *Samadhi*—An ecstatic state of union with the universe that is the goal of meditation

Nakamura Sensei's teachings parallel the eight aspects of classical Raja yoga. His worldview embodied yama and niyama. The lotus posture he advocated for meditation is similar to one of the postures espoused in the *Yoga Sutras*. He also promoted pranayama breathing for health. In his book *Anjo Daza Kosho (A Booklet on Anjo Daza Meditation)*, Nakamura Sensei explained the advantages of not being attached to the relative world of fleeting phenomena (pratiyahara). He likewise indicated that in meditation we transcend our five senses to "hear a soundless sound" that's the quintessence of the universe, also an expression of pratiyahara. Nakamura Sensei further indicated his methods of meditation stem from concentration that leads to meditation. All of this culminates in what he called *zanmai*, the Japanese conception of samadhi. His Shin-shin-toitsu-do shows the clear influence of classical yoga. True, it isn't aligned with the Hatha yoga often popularized in the West, with its emphasis on physical training and body sculpting. It does, however, have numerous similarities to the ancient Raja yoga outlined in the *Yoga Sutras*.

Although Nakamura Sensei's teachings don't represent Hatha yoga, or really any of the other forms of traditional Indian yoga, it's wrong to think they're only slightly related to genuine Indian yogic traditions. They are deeply connected to the time-honored meditative practices of Raja yoga. Nonetheless, his teachings aren't a mere copy of what he learned in India. They are, rather, a new way of explaining ancient truths, truths that transcend cultures and divisions. Drawing on medicine, psychology, and science, he sought a different, easier way of presenting these teachings to modern people. Even so it's a mistake to think that Shin-shin-toitsu-do has no present association with Indian meditation, just as it's also erroneous to assume that it's simply a Japanese translation of the original Raja yoga.

Both Anjo Daza Ho and Muga Ichi-nen Ho meditations, which we'll delve into soon, were shaped by yogic meditation. Since Nakamura Sensei had limited training in Hatha yoga, it was natural for him to evolve new stretching exercises and physical education based on the philosophy of Kaliapa, Japanese martial arts, and his own insights. Still, he sporadically taught a handful of asana, or Hatha yoga postures. And even though he created new breathing techniques, some traditional Pranayama exercises were also covered. I've made a point, however, in *The Teachings of Tempu* to avoid offering material readily available in scores of books on Indian yoga.

Western and Eastern Influences

Nakamura Sensei's stress on experimentation and comprehension through direct insight echoes his background in Western science and medicine. He supervised experiments to study the effects of Shin-shin-toitsu-do. His processes of autosuggestion, which you'll also read about later, are borrowed from his study of psychology in Europe.

Practices like autosuggestion were in vogue during Nakamura Sensei's time in the USA and Europe, where they were popularized via New Thought philosophy. Some

Nakamura Sensei at a party at the Shinagawa Prince Hotel in 1965.

New Thought groups emphasized 19th-century semi-scientific theories such as mesmerism, while others promoted the autosuggestion, affirmations, and self-help methods of Émile Coué. Some advocated meditation, while others taught positive thinking as a jumping off point for teaching the "law of attraction," bringing about personal/financial success by visualizing these conditions. Some stressed vegetarianism, others taught the significance of willpower and directed thoughts, and still others focused on psychophysical healing and affirmative prayer.

Despite "New Thought" being an umbrella term for various occasionally diverging movements and philosophies, it has certain universally accepted principles. A primary tenet is that thinking itself creates one's experience of the world. A philosophy of idealism and optimism, New Thought professes the central role of the mind in relation to experiencing the physical world and emphasizes positive thinking, affirmations, and meditation. These methods are commonly taught using books and courses.

New Thought's proponents birthed various self-development, self-empowerment, and self-help offshoot philosophies, such as those advocated by writers Napolean Hill and Charles F. Haanel, with their focus on training willpower for success. One prominent New Thought influenced author was Orison Swett Marden, who Nakamura Sensei met and some of whose teachings are clearly echoed in Shin-shin-toitsu-do. In researching this book, it became clear that the New Thought movement had a profound effect on Shin-shin-toitsu-do, much more than is sometimes acknowledged in Japan.

Unquestionably Japanese influences can also be discerned in Nakamura Sensei's teachings. Shinto, the native Japanese faith, underscores purity and union with nature; it infused every aspect of Japanese civilization. Similarly, Zen Buddhism made an impression on Japan with its appearance from China. Since Nakamura Sensei grew up in Japan, which has been tinged for hundred years by Zen and Shinto, ambient aspects and aesthetics of these doctrines are detected in what and how he taught.

He enjoyed the books of Dogen, a famous Zen monk. Even if he dismissed most of the religious trappings, rituals, and regulations Dogen mentioned, he found a like mind in Dogen's spiritual insight and concept of meditation. When Nakamura Sensei's students indicated that the wording of these texts was different from his (and for loads of people incomprehensible as well), he was unabashed. He explained he identified not with the writing as much as the spirit behind it, adding that yoga and Zen sprang from the same Indian soil. He felt the meditation of Kaliapa and the Zen of Dogen lead to the same place, but he was also clear about wanting to create new explanations for both Indian meditation and Japanese Zen, to which modern people could more easily relate.

Chinese Taoism originally stressed existing in harmony with the universe. Over time it evolved meditations and health practices aiming at not just wisdom but also long life and in some sects even outright deathlessness. Hundreds of years ago these teachings shifted to Japan. Advanced Taoist mystics, who'd accomplished elevated spirituality and physical health, and according to ancient legends eternal life as well, were called *Hsien* in China and *Sennin* in Japan. Although modern Japanese often fail to distinguish between man and myth when they think of the Sennin, real life Sennin mystics practiced *Sennin-do*, the Japanese version of Taoist yoga, which underscores developing life energy via mind-body exercises. The Sennin have been characterized as Japanese equivalents to the yogi, and several of their techniques are comparable to methods found in Shin-shin-toitsu-do, which some believe is also a form of Sennin-do. Nakamura Sensei mentioned the Sennin and Sennin-do (a.k.a. *Senjutsu*) in his books, and his methods of self-healing and some of his breathing practices are too close to esoteric Taoist disciplines to be mere coincidence.

Shin-shin-toitsu-do isn't a martial art, but Japanese budo (martial Ways) also made an impression on Shin-shin-toitsu-do. Nakamura Sensei was exceptional at Zuihen Ryu swordsmanship, and the power of the martial arts can be felt in forms of moving meditation taught in Shin-shin-toitsu-do. It can likewise be witnessed in the vigorous and disciplined atmosphere in Shin-shin-toitsu-do classes.

During the Russo-Japanese War he utilized his sword in combat, which years later earned him the somewhat dubious handle "Man-Cutting Tempu." However after returning from India, he stressed compassion for all living things and during World War II earned the ire of Japan's government by speaking against war of any kind. While he drilled solo sword exercises throughout his life, he imagined no adversary when using a sword for mobile meditation. His ability, nonetheless, remained intact. He could easily slice through fat sections of bamboo, and he could do it using a wooden sword.

Inspiring? Certainly, but more inspiring still was the fact that the bamboo was suspended horizontally from holes cut in two vertical ribbons of paper. These paper strips were in turn hung from two upturned knives clutched by two assistants. The bamboo would be split without ripping the suspending top and bottom holes in these paper ribbons. (When bamboo is carved in half with enormous speed, the middle part drops, permitting the outer ends to slide from the holes without disturbing the paper.) Nakamura Sensei, using mind and body coordination principles, even taught average folks with no swordsmanship training to accomplish the same feat. He also taught students to slice through a pair of chopsticks with a business card or postcard by visualizing ki energy passing through the utensils. Such is the power of mind and body unification.

Moving from the *shita hara*, a natural abdominal center, and concentration in the same region has a heritage in Zen, martial arts, and Shin-shin-toitsu-do. Nakamura Sensei never formally practiced Zen, but he was a martial artist, with a background in judo and swordsmanship. Not surprisingly, his teachings also place a heavy emphasis on the role of the shita hara in mind and body unification.

The idea that the shita hara is important for wellbeing didn't originate with Nakamura Sensei, and it permeates many aspects of traditional Japanese culture. But he did teach a simpler and more logical way of using this natural center in the lower abdomen than is often experienced in other Japanese disciplines. Nakamura Sensei's creative methodology for concentrating mental and physical power in the shita hara will be fully detailed in subsequent chapters.

In several movements found in *Sekkyoku Taiso*, his series of moving drills for mind-body health, we can notice imprints of judo as well. Because Nakamura Sensei was friends with the originator of aikido and had important aikido instructors as students, we can observe aikido influences in Shin-shin-toitsu-do, especially in the art's contemporary spin-offs. In short, the Japanese martial arts influenced Shin-shin-toitsu-do, and Shin-shin-toitsu-do since its inception has influenced at least some well-known martial arts and martial artists.

All of these disciplines relate to Shin-shin-toitsu-do, but they aren't Shin-shin-toit-

Nakamura Sensei, at age 89, speaks to one of his American students.

su-do. A respected exponent of this art once criticized part of my history of Nakamura Sensei in *Japanese Yoga: The Way of Dynamic Meditation* by saying Shin-shin-toitsu-do was the creation of Nakamura Sensei and that it shouldn't be related to other disciplines. I agree . . . up to a point.

Shin-shin-toitsu-do is undoubtedly an outgrowth of the creativity of Nakamura Sensei. Even so, everything comes from something. Nothing just spontaneously appears, and to imply that Shin-shin-toitsu-do evolved solely from the mind of its founder—with no historical ties to other cultures and meditative disciplines—won't go over with readers versed in Asian culture and spirituality. For people like myself, who've spent their lives researching Asian religion, culture, art, and meditation, it isn't difficult to see that yoga, Zen, Shinto, Taoism, martial arts, and Western sciences relate to Shin-shin-toitsu-do. However, I'm not suggesting that blending the disparate elements above culminated in Shin-shin-toitsu-do. We could repeat everything Nakamura Sensei did and still not attain realization or even arrive at identical practices. He studied a plethora of methods before traveling to India. It didn't help him much. In truth, it was only when he stopped shopping for a fresh remedy or discipline that he could behold the Way of the universe.

Shin-shin-toitsu-do Today

Nakamura Sensei taught for about 50 years. He gradually created exercises and mind-body unification principles that encapsulated his realization in India, and his teachings transformed countless people. He directly taught more than a hundred thousand students.

One of his favorite pupils, Sawai Atsuhiro Sensei, remembers him having the vigor of a twenty-something in his late eighties. Sawai Sensei often comments on how even as he aged his extraordinary intelligence and acutely heightened senses never dimmed. But shortly before his death he noticeably weakened. Physicians were consulted, yet no cause could be determined. His clarity of consciousness, however, never paled.

According to his advanced students and relatives, at 92 years of age, on December 1, 1968, he called them together. Sensing the end was near, or perhaps consciously deciding to leave, he said in a clear and calm voice, "Thank you. I'll see you all again." With that, like the fading note of an immense and ancient bell, he closed his eyes and merged with the universe.

It's Nakamura Sensei's unadorned perception of existence that made him beneficial to others. To reveal his insight, he employed different practices with which he was well versed; but this is nearly incidental. Every individual he moved with his statements was inspired more by the strength of his link with ultimate reality than by anything else. It's futile to only mimic the original methods he studied, to accumulate a compilation of such arts ourselves, or to blindly copy what he developed. Instead, we should personally perceive the truth as he did.

After his death attempts were made to preserve and consolidate his teachings, creating official versions of exercises and methods. Easier said than done as Nakamura Sensei taught "according to the person," meaning different students sometimes learned different things, with exercises performed in different ways. Because he wasn't promoting a dogma or religious tradition, when he was alive his teaching was not fixed, and "official versions" were in flux. He continued learning and growing, which caused the way he taught and practiced various exercises to change as well. Thus, early students learned different approaches than people studying Shin-shin-toitsu-do later in Nakamura Sensei's life. Likewise, people in Kyoto didn't always get identical instruction as individuals in Osaka or Tokyo. Over time, especially after his death, certain teachers made discoveries of their own concerning mind and body unification, discoveries that caused them to teach and practice in new ways. A case in point, Tohei Koichi Sensei, a top proponent of aikido, Zen, and breathing exercises as well as one of Nakamura Sensei's senior students, gave birth to a new group called Ki no Kenkyukai. He created his own style of Shin-shin-toitsu-do, modified by his experiences with other arts, and he created a new martial art called *Shin-shin-toitsu aikido*.

Like Tohei Sensei in aikido, other students mixed the principles of mind-body unification with their particular interests or jobs. This isn't surprising since Nakamura Sensei encouraged pupils to apply his teachings to their daily lives. For instance, in addition to being a practitioner of Shin-shin-toitsu-do, my teacher Hirata Yoshihiko Sensei was a musician. Even after retiring from teaching Shin-shin-toitsu-do, he made his living offering music lessons based on coordination of mind and body principles.

Nakamura Sensei attracted leaders from various fields including fine arts, sports, healing arts, and other disciplines. A number of these teachers integrated mind-body unification exercises and concepts into their particular subject. (They haven't always, unfortunately, acknowledged their debt to Shin-shin-toitsu-do.) This represents another direction taken by some of Nakamura Sensei's pupils after he passed away.

A multitude of books, audio tapes, and CDs of his ideas have been published; they're generally accepted by the average Japanese as the essence of his teachings. Many talented people devoted many hours, for many years, to preserving Shin-shin-toitsu-do, and in many ways they've succeeded. Nevertheless there isn't now, nor has there ever been, a single and universally practiced standard for this art.

Moreover, during Nakamura Sensei's life, and to a greater degree after he passed away, some folks deified him as a god-like being whose words cannot be altered and whose methods shouldn't be allowed to evolve. This quasi-religious approach to Shin-shin-toitsu-do would have dismayed their sensei, who stated that organized religions sometimes divide people, where he wanted to bring them together. Nakamura Sensei further emphasized that Shin-shin-toitsu-do seeks the source from which all spirituality emerges—before it's organized and altered by institutions. Hashimoto Tetsuichi Sensei, one of his close students, writes:

> First, Nakamura Tempu Sensei was really broadminded enough to accept all persons as his students, including Buddhists, Christians, non-religious people, agnostics, and atheists, if they sincerely wanted to learn and practice his Shin-shin-toitsu-do. This is the reason why the Tempu Society is a zaidan hojin (nonprofit educational organization) for promoting our mental and physical human condition. It is not a religious foundation of any sort,

and this organizational direction is based upon the generous intention of its original founder Tempu Sensei.

Secondly, Tempu Sensei used to call himself "a finger pointing at the truth" and not the truth itself. Therefore, he strictly instructed us not to worship him.

Thirdly, Tempu Sensei also used to encourage us by saying, "You can and must start from the point I have reached." Therefore, he would be most happy if his disciples, thankfully believing in his words, try to go beyond limitations of any kind, regionally, racially, culturally, etc. In other words, you do not have to enter the Himalayas as he did or become Japanese. You can make use of Shin-shin-toitsu-do in your own way, but you must not forget that you are encouraged to surpass the achievements of our teacher.[4]

Sawai Sensei also quotes Nakamura Sensei as saying:

Each of us was born with a unique mission and role in life, which we must personally discover. I don't desire to tell you what to do in your lives. I teach methods to help you find the strength and creativity to be able to do anything you decide you're meant to do. There's no need to copy me.[5]

According to Sawai Sensei, his teacher hoped Shin-shin-toitsu-do would be spread outside of Japan, which is also a long cherished dream of Mr. Sawai's. Yet Shin-shin-toitsu-do cannot be understood by Westerners who merely read books like this one. We need to actually practice mind and body unification to discover our connection to the universe as Nakamura Tempu Sensei did. And the upcoming chapters can aid us in doing just that.[6]

Chapter 2

MIND-BODY
RELATIONSHIPS

Each action we make is an act of self-expression.

This simple statement reveals a profound and innate connection between the mind and body that lies at the heart of Shin-shin-toitsu-do, a discipline based on the realization that the mind and body are connected. Mind and body aren't interrelated in merely a metaphorical or philosophical sense. Their fundamental connection is literal and real, yet we commonly don't take this into account.

For instance, the way we cut up food is a purely mechanical action for many, having little to do with the mind. Yet while the hands move knife and fork, precisely how our hands move relates to our mental state. Someone that's angry enough to burst a blood vessel may wield their knife differently from a depressed person, who may slice through food differently from a happy individual. The mind influences the hands; the hands express a particular psychological condition. Even something as mundane as how we eat reveals our feelings at that moment, because the mind and body are one.

Sadly, we often behave as if this isn't the case. As this book progresses, you'll see how this can hinder our ability to see our genuine nature and our capacity for manifesting our full potential.

Self-expression is inborn, even inevitable. By examining what our bodies express we gain insight into our character. This is essential, because we've all met people that think they're positive, helpful, or kind individuals, yet objective observers don't see this revealed in their actions. In short, such people are deluded, and their delusion must be seen for what it is before positive growth can take place.

Shin-shin-toitsu-do helps us see what's buried in our unconscious, which is constantly revealing itself through seemingly insignificant actions and postures. In this manner we see who and what we really are, allowing us to move from negative self-expression to positive self-expression. Realizing that human beings don't just express the soul via art and music is a significant first step in Shin-shin-toitsu-do; grasping what we actually express from moment to moment, and whether or not this works for us in life, is equally important.

Seeing that the mind expresses itself through the body isn't the end of the story. Even if we move toward consistently positive and constructive forms of self-expression, are we expressing ourselves effectively? When I began studying art, some teachers indicated my ideas were top-notch, but my craftsmanship was poor. I had, in other words, no problem expressing creative concepts when drawing and painting. I just didn't express them well.

In life and painting, self-expression isn't enough. Our expressions must be effective and skillfully rendered. Accomplished, efficient self-expression goes beyond mere activity and enters the realm of art. Just as writing can become calligraphy—if it's imaginatively and dexterously executed—so can all other behaviors become art. In Shin-shin-toitsu-do life itself becomes an artistic statement.

In this sense, Nakamura Tempu Sensei discovered the art of living, and we can do the same. Just as a ceramic artist or painter can mold clay or brushed images into their idea of beauty, we can shape our lives. Nevertheless, just as an artist needs particular qualities to proficiently create a painting or exquisite vase, we have the same needs.

Mind and Body Unification

No fine art occurs without inspiration. Too bad inspiration alone won't result in art or success.

Painters, for example, work with brush, paint, and paper. Yet not every brush works well with every variety of paint. To achieve talent in painting the artist must discover the characteristics of the tools at his or her disposal as well as the relationship between these tools. Art needs inspiration, an understanding of one's tools, and another ingredient—an efficient technique for using these tools.

Similarly, to express ourselves adeptly in various endeavors in life, with greatest effectiveness and least effort, we also need to grasp the relationship between the mind and body, our only innate tools with which to live. Chapter Two delves into this relationship. Succeeding chapters outline Nakamura Sensei's art of mind and body unification as a powerful technique for using our tools to live well.

Nakamura Sensei, after returning to Japan, created and shared with the public principles and exercises that were universal. He offered concepts connecting to any pursuit and all people regardless of age, gender, or ethnicity. Practices with obvious and repeatable results, along with principles and exercises that can survive objective examination, were of foremost importance to him. These principles and exercises were (and are) aimed at helping us comprehend the relationship between mind and body, while aiding us in unearthing the most useful way of using these tools.

In India he was constantly chided by his guru to discover the true value of human existence and to look deeply into life:

> In India, my teacher Kaliapa asked me, "What were you born into this world to do?" At first, I thought the question strange. I wondered, "How can we know that? Who came into the world with some purpose in mind?"
>
> But instead of saying this, I arrogantly answered, "I know the answer, but I cannot put it into words." Kaliapa, having none of this, suddenly shocked me and said, "You speak as if you're stupid, more stupid than I thought!"
>
> Then, I was ordered to think about these questions: "Where did you come from, and where are you going to?" and "Why were you born in this world?"
>
> I thought and thought for half a year. Gradually a dawn came to my soul.[7]

As the result of this contemplation and his subsequent spiritual realization during meditation in the Himalayas Nakamura Sensei later wrote of six essential qualities that most agree are needed for happiness and success. He promoted an understanding of the mind-body relationship, along with mind and body coordination principles, so people could manifest the following traits to live their very lives as art:

1. *Tai-ryoku*: "the power of the body," physical vigor, fitness, and stamina
2. *Tan-ryoku*: "the power of courage"
3. *Handan-ryoku*: "the power of decision," good judgement
4. *Danko-ryoku*: "the power of determination," willpower for firm and strong-minded action
5. *Sei-ryoku*: "the power of vitality," energy or life power for fortitude and resolve

6. *No-ryoku:* "the power of ability," the potential for comprehensive talents and skillful accomplishment

In considering these six points realize that none are purely mental or exclusively physical. The mind and body intersect in each quality.

Most of us understand the mind moves and runs each part of the body. The heart and internal organs are regulated unconsciously through our autonomic nervous system, but the mind still holds sway over the body. In some cases this is conscious, in other instances unconscious. Regardless, the mind commands the body, while the body mirrors our mental condition. Via the autonomic nervous system the mind and body are connected, and in the somatic nervous system (the conscious part of us, which controls activities like motor function) the mind-body link is equally pronounced. The more we understand these connections the easier it is to discover how to arrive at success in a given activity. Additionally, because of the bond between mind and body, the mind can positively or negatively affect the mind-body connection.

For example, positive mental imagery has long been used in yoga to benefit health. Western medicine is just catching on to the psychosomatic treatment of disease, which Nakamura Sensei advocated decades ago. Case in point, the American Cancer Society (ACS) now indicates:

> A review of 46 studies conducted from 1966 to 1998 suggested that guided imagery may be helpful in managing stress, anxiety, and depression, and lowering blood pressure, pain, and some of the side effects of chemotherapy. Another review in 2002 noted that imagery was possibly helpful for anxiety, as well as anticipatory nausea and vomiting from chemotherapy. (After a few doses of chemotherapy have caused nausea or vomiting, some people have nausea or vomiting just before the next dose is to be given. This is called conditioned or anticipatory nausea or vomiting). A 2006 review of clinical trials of imagery found that only three of the studies showed improvement in anxiety and comfort during chemotherapy. Two other studies showed no difference between those who used imagery and those who used other measures.[8]

The ACS goes on to state:

According to some studies, guided imagery may help reduce some of the side effects of standard cancer treatment. Some studies also suggest that imagery can directly affect the immune system.[9]

Although science provides evidence supporting these claims, it is possible—and actually vital—to objectively discover the truth of such statements ourselves. The mind-body experiments coming up give you a chance to do just that.

Realizing the mind-body link when this wasn't widely acknowledged in the West, Nakamura Sensei envisioned Shin-shin-toitsu-do as a process for individuals to determine for themselves how to harmonize their two life tools, while learning to regulate and fortify their autonomic nervous systems. In his book *Shin Jinsei no Tankyu* (*Searching for Truth in Life*) he wrote that a violin, however well made, cannot produce beautiful music if it lacks a first-rate violinist. Even with a skilled musician we still can't hear fine music without a high-quality instrument. Nakamura Sensei's analogy is true for human beings as well; the mind can be compared to the violinist and the body to the violin. Both mind and body must be kept in excellent condition, be equally developed, and work in harmony with each other.[10]

Using his training in medicine Nakamura Sensei researched the nervous system, as well as mind and body unification, to achieve his objective. The outcome was his Four Basic Principles to Unify Mind and Body, which will be detailed in the next chapter.

The Mind-Body Relationship

Let's delve more deeply into the ideas that the mind controls the body, and the body reflects the mind. We don't need to—and shouldn't—take these statements on faith.

What allows us to hear? A good number of people believe hearing is a function of the ears. Of course without ears we can't make out sounds, but do the ears really hear independently of the mind? Nearly everyone has experienced someone speaking when they're distracted, only to realize with a start that they have no idea what the speaker said over the last few moments. We don't have a problem with our ears, but we may have a problem with concentration.

The mind hears through the ears; the mind sees via the eyes. Whether or not we notice everything in our environment, and how we view what we see, if we really hear everything around us, and how we interpret what we hear reveals our mental structure. Maybe it's an aspect of our psychological state hidden in the subconscious, but it is still part of the mind that's influencing the body.

But don't take my word for this or anything else in *The Teachings of Tempu*. If you do, no self-knowledge will result. By watching ourselves and others we can personally determine if these statements are true. That stated, I've found people that carefully observe their lives discover their minds affect their bodies and actions in life. Contemporary medicine is starting to note the same, at least in conjunction with certain illnesses. In 2007, ABC News reported on scientific studies of this phenomenon:

> In one startling drug study in the 1980s, a young woman who had been virtually homebound by the energy-sapping effects of chronic fatigue syndrome had a miraculous recovery.
>
> But, it wasn't the drug that cured the patient – she was in the trial group that was taking sugar pills. It was the "placebo effect," — a well-documented phenomenon that has intrigued doctors for decades.
>
> When patients believe a drug will help them, they sometimes heal themselves.
>
> "She and her parents were so excited about her profound improvement," said Janet Dale, a staff scientist at Clinical Investigation at the National Institute of Allergy and Infectious Diseases. "And she sustained her health and continued to be well."
>
> It's human nature, explained the study scientists, who reported nearly 50 percent of the participants on placebos got better.
>
> But now, with advances in neuroscience, researchers at Columbia University and the University of Michigan have been able to see how the placebo effect works.
>
> When volunteers were convinced they were receiving pain medicine, their brains actually released natural relief, or opioids.[11]

If the mind motivates and manages the body then there should be a flip side to this fact. Just as we recognize hot only because of the presence of cold, every facet of our relative world includes a corresponding opposite. So if the mind moves the body, then the body follows the mind. Suppose you see a friend tapping their foot and drumming their fingertips on a table. And your friend isn't listening to a particularly catchy tune at the time. What would you conclude?

Quite a few of us would guess we're watching an anxious person. We arrive at this conclusion because it's clear that the hands and feet mirror the mind. Although we may realize that the body in some ways is a visible representation of the mind, we don't normally use this to see into our psychological makeup. And we don't always consider how our "body language" causes others to see us. Carmine Gallo, in an article for *Businessweek Online*, writes:

> Only a small percentage of communication involves actual words: 7%, to be exact. In fact, 55% of communication is visual (body language, eye contact) and 38% is vocal (pitch, speed, volume, tone of voice). The world's best business communicators have strong body language: a commanding presence that reflects confidence, competence, and charisma.[12]

The Teachings of Tempu is structured around the idea that when we grasp that the mind controls the body and the body reflects the mind, we also understand the most basic relationship between our "tools." In short, mind and body are interconnected. This knowledge makes it easier to see why coordination of mind and body is a sensible vehicle for utilizing these tools to maximum effect. What's more, because every action and expression comes from the mind it's crucial to genuinely know the mind and intelligently determine the way we want to use our minds. A nervous and negative mental state doesn't make for a healthy constitution, and psychosomatic illness is further proof that the body mirrors the mind.

Tedd Mitchell, M.D., medical director of Dallas' Cooper Clinic, has written about the connection between depression and heart disease. He cites an article in *The Journal of the American Medical Association* by Dr. Mary Whooley, a Professor of Medicine, Epidemiology, and Biostatistics at the University of California, San Francisco:

> Depression triggers biological systems that create a less healthy environment for the heart. Such physiological changes may heighten susceptibility to arrhythmias (abnormal heartbeats), increase the inflammatory markers associated with cardiovascular disease and thicken blood, which raise clotting risk.[13]

In another example, Ted A. Grossbart, a Harvard Medical School psychologist and author, indicates "30% to 60% of people who see a doctor for a skin problem have emotional issues, so they're not likely to get the results they hope for from the best conventional medical care." Grossbart recommends meditation and alternative mind-body therapies for acne, hives, and other skin problems, explaining that anger, depression, and anxiety can alter the immune system, which can cause or exacerbate several dermatological conditions like acne.[14]

Psychosomatic disease is well-known but what about psychosomatic wellness? A Swedish study discovered that individuals that looked at and discussed art were more upbeat, plus they had lower blood pressure—proof that psychosomatic changes needn't inevitably be negative.[15] Nonetheless, although nearly everyone has heard of psychosomatic illness, few consider preserving health or alleviating different maladies by changing their mental condition. Of those who've considered this idea, I wonder how many have done more than that. Perhaps our stumbling block in moving toward psychosomatic wellness is that while we understand the body reacts to the mind we don't know how to go further than this.

Experimenting with the Mind-Body Connection

Nakamura Sensei was in the same position, which resulted in his worldwide journey to discover "the next step." Owing to his background in medicine, he objectively evaluated health improvement techniques and mental training he learned in the USA, Europe, and India. Rather than accepting or rejecting new ideas based on faith or prejudice, he experimented with them using his tuberculosis and depression to measure effectiveness. He subsequently encouraged his students to also perform something akin to experiments to understand the mind-body relationship; I've done the same in *The Teachings of Tempu*. In fact, let's try an experiment to personally experience the relationship between the mind and body.

EXPERIMENT ONE: MOVE THE FINGERTIPS BY MOVING THE MIND
Entwine your fingers; with the two index fingers extended and separate as in **Fig. 1**. Sit or stand up straight, but remain relaxed, then focus your eyes softly on your fingertips. You'll try to move your index fingers together with the power of your concentration as in **Fig. 2**.

You can achieve this in more than one fashion. First, create a mental picture of your fingertips coming together. Close your eyes if this helps you visualize the fingertips moving toward each other.

Repeatedly imagine the fingers moving to contact each other. Keep these successive images firmly repeating in your mind and wait. Do your fingers remain in place or

Fig. 1. Interlace your fingers. Look gently at the index fingers.

Fig. 2. Make no conscious effort to move the fingers. Simply imagine the index fingers coming together and maintain this mental image. What happens?

do they move? If friends or family seriously try this experiment—more than once—do they get the same result?

The experiment can help us determine if the mind indeed holds sway over the body. Still, an experiment is only valid if it's observable, repeatable, and universal. This explains the necessity of trying this exercise several times, on different occasions, and ideally with more than one person conducting the experiment. And all of this has taken place in Shin-shin-toitsu-do for well over 80 years.

EXPERIMENT TWO: MOVE THE FINGERTIPS WITH A VISUALIZED IMAGE

Next, imagine your fingers are already touching and maintain that image. This isn't a series of mental pictures, like the fingertips gradually coming together, but rather a single static image of the fingertips touching each other.

For some this visualization produces better results. Nevertheless, the basic idea remains the same as in Experiment One.

EXPERIMENT THREE: MOVE THE FINGERTIPS WITH INTERNAL DIALOGUE

This experiment is similar to the last two, but this time "talk to yourself" in the sense of mentally commanding the fingers to touch. Use a silent mental order like, "Come together; come together . . ."

Each experiment represents a comparable thought process, but some individuals have more success with one tactic than another. The main point is to use the force of a concentrated mind to affect the body and to notice how your body reacts to whatever idea is in the mind. An unconscious reaction is fundamental to this exercise, and we're experimenting to discover if this is possible.

Avoid knowingly bringing the fingertips together. Instead simply direct your mind strongly toward one of the previous visualizations, continue concentrating, and notice what occurs. If concentration doesn't falter and the body is relaxed, many people find their index fingers stirring without any deliberate effort on their part. Conversely, because we're experimenting with the mind's effect on the body, if attention wanes and/or you think you can't get any physiological reaction by using concentration, your fingers may not respond. It can also take time for the fingertips to slowly touch, but this gets better with practice.

Some might observe that because of the arrangement of the hands the index fingers already are inclined to come together. This is true.

In spite of this sometimes distracted people can only get their fingers to touch through extended periods of concentration, and in certain cases not at all, which confirms that the mind affects the body. And this impact isn't inevitably helpful, that's why if we believe we can't cause the fingers to move with mental focus, the body will comply with this belief.

EXPERIMENT FOUR: MAKE THE FINGERTIPS IMMOVABLE WITH A VISUALIZED IMAGE

Let's try a different form of this exercise. Recognizing that the fingertips actually want to come together, keep them apart. Imagine you've inserted a stick or object between your index fingers. Holding this picture in your mind, wait. Allow several minutes to go by. When you genuinely maintain this mental image, do your fingertips touch by themselves?

Guessing at any of this is invalid. That's why actual experiments form the foundation of science. Nakamura Sensei, with his education in Western medicine, frequently asked students to perform such experiments. According to several of his senior students, he initially used the above exercise in the 1920s to show the mind's influence on the body. His writings stress that human beings understand better through real life experiences than by only reading about the experiences of others or through philosophizing.

We can also note the effect low energy, sadness, happiness, and other psychological states have on our capacity to achieve results in the above exercises. Moreover, since concentration causes the fingers to move, logically one can suppose these experiments are an opportunity to realize the nature of attention and how to arrive at it. At the Sennin Foundation Center for Japanese Cultural Arts we've found children enjoy the above exercises; their repeated practice, along with other Shin-shin-toitsu-do disciplines, produces enhanced concentration and better grades in school.

The Mind Influences Everything We Touch

If the mind controls the body then our psychological condition should also involuntarily affect anything the body contacts. If true, then our minds influence everything from the golf club we're holding to the car we commute in. In fact, when lots of us learned to drive we experienced a phenomenon sometimes known as "target fixation." Briefly, when a novice driver looks at something alongside the street his or her car veers toward the object of concentration.

Beginning motorcyclists experience a similar occurrence when training to swerve away from an object in the road. Their eyes lock onto whatever they're trying to avoid, and the motorcycle heads straight for it. Riding coaches emphasize to look where you want to go (as opposed to looking at what you don't want to hit). We usually concentrate on what we're looking at, and both examples illustrate how the mind causes unconscious reactions in the body and affects what the body contacts. The mind's creating subtle movement in hands, which then influence the car's steering wheel and the motorcycle's handlebar.

To demonstrate this phenomenon Nakamura Sensei asked students to experiment with a pendulum (or pendulum-like object). They were instructed to hold the top of the string and focus their eyes gently on the pendulum. They visualized the pendulum swinging circularly, while they tried to hold their hands motionless. Typically the pendulum followed their mental commands, even when they had no sensation of directly moving it. With training, and with improved concentration, his students made the pendulum swing in larger or smaller circles, sideways, and in other directions. This took place with little visible movement of the hand. We can try this as well, and not only does it show the influence the mind has on whatever it touches through the body, it likewise demonstrates the oftentimes subtle effect the mind has on the body.

One's mind affects the pendulum through surprisingly slight movements of the fingers and/or hand. Dissimilar to occult-like philosophies, Nakamura Sensei never indicated this was more than an experiment to illustrate the great influence the mind has on what we touch. Nothing supernatural occurs, but the exercise does show the mind sways not only us but anything we contact. This further indicates how positive or negative mental states strongly impact the swing of a sword, the trajectory of a baseball, or even the balance of a bicycle. Logically, athletes and martial artists benefit from Shin-shin-toitsu-do, and a number of successful Japanese atheletes studied this discipline's methods for developing an unflinchingly positive attitude.

An Objective Approach to Universal Truths

Through personal, impartial examination and experimentation we can notice different aspects of the universe as they actually are. Unearthing the principles which preside over living things and how the universe works is straightforward. A universal certainty should be—on some level—measurable. If we can't observe how a principle or idea works, we can't say anything about it with confidence. At the minimum we should observe its operation through deduction. Experimentation is a means of understanding the world. Not only should we see concrete outcomes from our experiments, we should get the same result more than once. Experimental results should be repeatable.

Still, even noticeable and repeatable results don't inevitably indicate universal truth. The experiment must be repeatable and observable universally. Subjects of varying ages, in different parts of the globe, of dissimilar genders, ethnicities, and religions should get similar results. Then we can feel a principle or theory is universal. And this is exactly what's gradually taking place in Shin-shin-toitsu-do.

It's true that after returning from India Nakamura Sensei didn't venture out of Japan, but don't assume only Japanese people studied with him. He taught non-Japanese living in Japan, and most achieved the same benefits from mind and body unification training as did Japanese students. In addition, since 1981 Americans and people from outside the USA have successfully learned Shin-shin-toitsu-do at my occasional seminars in various American cities and at the Sennin Foundation Center for Japanese Cultural Arts in California. Of equal importance, since *Japanese Yoga: The Way of Dynamic Meditation* was published in 2001 readers around the world have tried the exercises, experiments, and meditation described therein, and they've let me know they're experiencing results comparable to their Japanese counterparts. Thus far the results have been observable, repeatable, and universal.

That's obviously a good thing because Shin-shin-toitsu-do is concerned with principles relating to every facet of living. Nakamura Sensei's experiments, more of which will be detailed soon, help us directly discover principles that are intelligently valid. Throughout his life Nakamura Sensei continued experimenting with the exercises and forms of meditation in this book. Though he arrived at certain "conclusions," he didn't look at these conclusions as an end. As the result, training changed and was refined on a recurring basis when he was living. Just as science evolves, Nakamura Sensei constantly discovered new aspects of universal truths. We can do the same as long as we aren't attached to previous conclusions and as long as our minds reside in the present more than the past.

We've seen the relationship between our basic tools—mind and body—but now we need to discover an effective technique for using these tools—mind and body unification. That's coming up next.

Since the mind motivates the body Nakamura Sensei placed two principles for the mind at the start of his Four Basic Principles to Unify Mind and Body, which will be detailed in the next chapter. Of the four ideas, the first: "Maintain a positive mind" should be given top priority. Later we'll look into the conscious and subconscious aspects of the mind, and I'll explain Nakamura Sensei's Five Basic Principles for a Positive Mind as well as techniques of autosuggestion for eliminating negativity.

Understanding the roots of our negativity is crucial. Kaliapa, Nakamura Sensei's teacher, emphasized a related point almost 100 years ago. He once asked Nakamura Sensei, "If you complain about being feverish, does your fever go away?" It did not, and he resolved to cease complaining and live with a positive mind for however many years he had left.[16]

Without a positive outlook we seldom have the resolve or motivation to seriously explore—let alone follow through and understand—any practice. If we believe it's too hard to memorize four different principles, that we never do well anyway, or that we aren't bright enough to comprehend all of this, we may even fail to read this book to its end. Simply put, without a positive mind we give up before we begin. Bearing this in mind let's move to the next chapter, which deals with the two principles for the mind, and the following section that explains Nakamura Tempu Sensei's two principles for the body.

Chapter 3

PRINCIPLES
FOR THE MIND

1. Maintain a positive mind.

2. Train the mind to arrive at full concentration.

3. Use the body obeying the laws of nature.

4. Train the body progressively, systematically, and regularly.

Nakamura Tempu Sensei's teachings boil down to the four simple statements above. Yet simplicity doesn't inevitably indicate lack of depth. We can investigate the deeper meanings behind these principles without ever reaching an end, and that's not a bad thing. It means we can continue to grow and develop throughout our lives. The mind is essentially infinite, and Nakamura Sensei frequently referred to this immeasurable potential in his seminars:

> We see thousands of stars twinkling in the night sky with just the eyes alone. In reality, however, millions of stars can be observed with a high-powered telescope. Some stars are as big as the sun and many are even bigger. And some stars, like our sun, are accompanied by planets.
>
> Judging from these facts, we can imagine the largeness of the physical universe. If we travel through it with the speed of light at 186,320 miles a second, it will take five billion light years to reach the halfway point of the universe (according to Dr. Einstein).
>
> When we realize this, we feel the solemnity and magnificence of the universe, regarding it with reverence. This is important, but what's more important is the human mind is greater than the physical universe.

When we look at the moon, our mind is larger than the moon shining on us. When we observe the stars, our mind is bigger than them, because our mind encompasses them. Our mind can imagine something bigger than a planet or star. So, we can conclude the human mind is far greater than anything in this world.[17]

Realizing that the mind controls the body, Nakamura Sensei placed the principles for the mind at the start of his Four Basic Principles to Unify Mind and Body. These initial two principles are what we'll examine in this chapter. The last two points are covered in the following chapter.

The Four Basic Principles to Unify Mind and Body are universal in character and applicable to every aspect of life. They describe the most natural and efficient way for human beings to live, and yet many are unaware of these ideas. At the least, we often are not aware of their deeper significance, and these universal principles of mind-body harmony aren't exactly a hot topic in the 21st century. Unfortunately the same was true during Nakamura Sensei's lifetime:

When a human being is born he or she is surrounded by the truths of the universe, even if that person is unaware of them. Like a fish living in water may not reflect on the genuine nature of water, because the fish has never known anything but water, we may not see the true nature of the universe and life (because it's so omnipresent). Plus, the mind's tendency to attach itself to various thoughts and sensory impressions distracts us from the essence of life.

Everything in the universe functions according to natural laws, or universal principles, which we can call "the Way of the universe," or "the truths of the universe." We're able to live because of certain universal principles (like gravity), but we are often oblivious to them, living with minds filled with materialistic cravings, constant mental chatter, and our attachments to things we desire. A mind that's caught up in relative phenomena, attached to impermanent things, and even attached to thought itself, cannot easily see the Way of the universe that is absolute. Our attachments, which fill our minds, become like a blindfold preventing us from seeing the true nature of living.[18]

Based on the above, let's start by considering the way lots of people look at the world. Most of us have heard of, for example, the power of positive thinking. But what is this force and does it have a genuine effect on our lives? Before you mentally respond to my question, consider that it's impossible to answer it without personal experience. Assuming that positive thinking has power is as unsound in reasoning as the supposition that no such force is real.

We know this, but we may still lean toward assumption in our lives because assuming is easy. We often base our thinking on whatever we've previously thought, heard, or supposed in the past. We may additionally focus on what we wish to be true but which we haven't truly experienced ourselves. Similarly, we frequently have faith in what everyone else believes, once more without personal confirmation. We're also inclined to feel that by grasping the definition of a word or saying we've understood its genuine meaning. Many folks can use words like "concentration," "calmness," and "positive attitude" when writing or speaking, but how many can really concentrate, remain calm, and be positive?

Preconceived ideas and theoretical understanding are "secondhand knowledge." We typically don't have firsthand, direct understanding of countless important aspects of living, and we don't personally know if certain ideas were true, are true, or will be true in the future. Nakamura Sensei was unwilling to accept this. In his search for a tuberculosis cure he found that purely trusting in established ideas and supposed authorities didn't help him. Motivated by impending death, he was forced to personally try various treatments and philosophies, not all of which were valid or effective. In the end, Kaliapa emphasized he alone was responsible for his health, and that others couldn't help him see the value and reason for his existence.

Considering his tuberculosis it isn't hard to understand why Nakamura Sensei was motivated to search for firsthand knowledge, but we may not feel the same burning motivation. We, after all, aren't about to die. Unfortunately, this way of thinking is delusional. We *are* going to die.

We like to assume death is far in the future, but the future comes today. We've no idea how much time we have in life, and in this sense our situations are not so different from Nakamura Sensei's. As the result, Shin-shin-toitsu-do emphasizes not just assuming a certain idea is true or false but instead uncovering the truth ourselves. And the truth is discovered in our immediate perception of the moment. This is the only moment which legitimately exists.

Remembering these points when reading this chapter will make it easier to examine being positive and the characteristics of concentration. We can look at these topics right now, and *The Teachings of Tempu* can be a catalyst to determine firsthand the actual nature of reality.

Principle One: Maintain a Positive Mind

To use the mind positively is the first of the *Shin-shin-toitsu no Yondai Gensoku* ("Four Basic Principles to Unify Mind and Body"). In numerous ways the positive, energetic use of the mind is the most critical point in Shin-shin-toitsu-do. Without it we often fail to persevere in studying any subject (including this one), and psychosomatic sickness occurs more than is imagined. Just chronically worrying about the possibility of illness creates stress, which weakens the immune system leaving us susceptible to disease. Scientific studies have demonstrated a positive worldview, and the laughter that accompanies it, has a tangible effect on health:

> Researchers from the University of Maryland Medical Center studied the "humor response" of 300 people—half with heart disease and half without. They found that folks who had heart disease were less likely to laugh at potentially stressful situations (such as a waiter spilling water on them).
>
> Recent research also indicates that laughter may be linked to the healthy function of blood vessels. The more chuckles, the more the tissue in the blood vessels dilates, increasing blood flow and potentially reducing the risk of atherosclerosis (hardening of the arteries).[19]

A positive mindset is vital for mental and physical health. If nothing else, a more positive mind is more likely to take steps to remain healthy and fit:

> "Research shows people who feel good about themselves take better care of themselves," says Christy Greenleaf, assistant professor in the department of kinesiology, health promotion and recreation at the University of Texas.[20]

Being positive isn't being stubborn as this goes against the idea of "toitsu," which suggests harmony. A genuinely positive mind has confidence in a positive ending to most events. As the result, it's capable of being peaceful, flexible, and appropriate under any circumstances. Since it can manage all situations, a positive mind has no need to be distressed or to struggle. This condition is termed *fudoshin*, or an "immovable mind," in Japan. Fudoshin isn't inflexibility. It's mental stability.

Fudoshin is expressed via a stable posture, a calm demeanor, and a frequent smile. Smiling was one of Nakamura Sensei's favorite topics:

> Smile all the time. If people think you're a fool for smiling, let them think that. But they should never keep you from smiling. If your spouse nags you, let them do so and smile. She or he will often stop when they're met with calmness and a positive attitude. Many times the more we try to stop someone from nagging us, the more they want to do it.
>
> Smile even if the mountains tremble. We might live for over 100 years, but our life will never be repeated. No matter how long we live, if we're unconscious and unhappy, our lives are wasted. I have only one life, so I choose to live smiling all the way through.[21]

When the mind is positive coordination of mind and body is preserved, and we display our full potential. If we feel negatively about something we're about to do, the mind will reflexively withdraw from action that it doesn't "feel good about," which in turn causes separation of mind and body. This makes us incapable of reacting successfully in a crisis or when confronted with a difficult task. In Shin-shin-toitsu-do we train to throw 100 percent of ourselves into whatever we're engaged in, and this positive state is called "the projection of life energy (ki)" by some teachers of this spiritual path. We've all met unusually positive and vigorous individuals, people projecting a "big presence." The indefinable—but unmistakable—"big presence" a dynamic individual gives off can be thought of as life energy, and it's a central part of Shin-shin-toitsu-do.

Ki

In Japan the universal essence that permeates and gives life to nature is called ki.

An understanding of ki cannot be completely explained in a book, but it will be discussed throughout *The Teachings of Tempu*. For now, understand that ki equals the animating energy vitalizing all creations. Positive use of the mind sets it free, while negativity produces *ki ga nukeru*—"the withdrawal and loss of ki." Just as we've met people with a big presence, we have also met individuals who are depressed. We sometimes characterize them as "withdrawn." The characterization is accurate, but what exactly "withdraws" in depressed people?

People who are unusually shy are frequently described as "introverted." This is derived from the Latin: *intro*, "inward," and *vertere*, "to turn." It implies something "going in" or "pulling in." What is it?

In Japan in general, and Shin-shin-toitsu-do in particular, we'd say ki is withdrawing in depressed, introverted people, just as ki is given off by dynamic individuals possessing a big presence. The word "ki" expresses what's commonly felt, but which is beyond easy description. Ki has been described in various ways in various books. Even so, in *The Teachings of Tempu* it's best thought of as the central building block of nature. It's that omnipresent essence from which all things originate, exist as, and return to: the connective energy of the absolute universe. And the ki of the universe exists within us as much as outside of us. Just as the body's cells are ultimately indivisible from the body, we find only an artificial distinction between the universal ki and the ki of individuals. In short, everything in nature is interrelated with ki at the core of this relationship.

Nakamura Sensei discussed ki in several of his popular books, including *Tempu Meiso Roku*:

> What do we need to easily sustain life? There are five elements—air, food, water, earth, and sunshine—which are essential for keeping a person alive, but we need one more often forgotten thing to function as an efficient "life machine." That is ki, which manifests itself in this world through the mind and then through the body.
>
> Why does a stomach medicine not always cure indigestion? It fails if the ki in the stomach particularly, and in the human being generally, is too weak to use the catalyst of the medicine to produce a reaction leading to healing.
>
> How does a car engine run? With gasoline, of course, but gas isn't enough. It needs ignition through the electrical system. Ignition in a human being is mind. Ki is like gasoline. So, it's best to firmly believe that we're the power of the universe itself, to think of ourselves as crystals of ki power.
>
> What is the mind? It is the essence of human life, and it expresses the invisible workings of the ki of the universe.[22]

Since at least the 1980s, Japan has experienced something of a "ki explosion," with abundant books and classes about ki being offered. Yet not every approach to ki is the same, with some claiming to demonstrate the power of ki in ways debunked by professional magicians as tricks to con the public. That stated, Kouzo Kaku's book *The Mysterious Power of Ki: The Force Within* features Nakamura Sensei, indicating he was one of Japan's earliest and most prominent researchers into ki. His study of the correlation between the mind and ki is documented in this book.

Nakamura Sensei taught that positive or negative mental states have an important effect not merely on our bodies but also on the movement of ki. He indicated he was echoing yogic philosophy by explaining that "the active thinking of the mind creates one's life." When he encountered this worldview in India he was puzzled as to its deepest meaning. Over time, as he contemplated his illness and the meaning of life, he grasped that the way the mind works influences the way our human life force functions, a life force constantly received by living things from the universe. Ki, "life energy," isn't just received by the brain. It also flows through the nervous system, animating body and mind.

Nakamura Sensei experienced that the absolute ki of the universe is one and without duality, yet when it appears in our relative world, it displays relative characteristics. For this reason, depending on our mindset, ki can be life-giving or harmful, positive or negative, powerful or feeble. In a nutshell, the mind modifies the action of ki. A positive mind encourages a positive, constructive, and powerful projection of ki into whatever we're doing.

Nakamura Sensei pointed out that once negative ki is set in motion by pessimistic thoughts we draw negative circumstances to us. A positive mind correspondingly gives rise to positive ki, which becomes active in a person's life, stimulating good fortune. In layman's terms, how we think influences how others react to us. Since the mind controls the body it alters emotions, spoken words, body language, and the effectiveness of our efforts. All of this determines, or at least influences, the course of our lives.

Shin-shin-toitsu-do isn't a religion, but it does delve deeply into the mysteries of living. Nakamura Sensei explained that ki is present in the relative world in different forms, but each variety of ki is a different aspect of an individual, absolute, primordial energy he sometimes characterized as uchu rei, the "universal spirit." He indicated the energy of the universe, or ki, is first received by our brain and then carried to our nervous system, which gives power to the body. We can think of the life energy of the universe as primary ki, while electricity, magnetism, vapor, and other phenomena are secondary ki. While he sometimes called primary ki the universal spirit, Christians call it God, and Japanese Buddhists sometimes name it Hotoke. To Nakamura Sensei they were all the same thing.[23]

He regarded relative, dualistic aspects of life as well as electricity, magnetic power, and other environmental phenomena as *koten no ki*—"subsidiary or secondary ki." Such secondary ki are related parts of one universal and primary ki. While he was aware of ki from his exposure to Japanese meditation, healing, and martial arts, Nakamura Sensei first intensely experienced the reality of the universal ki in the Himalayas, where it's termed prana:

> During my meditation in India I felt invisible ki maintaining the existence of everything around me. Just one element lies at the bottom of everything in the universe, and that's ki, which is both spiritual and mysterious. I also found the functioning of the universal ki to be omnipotent and intelligent.
>
> I felt in meditation that all the objects around me were not made by humans, but the ki of nature. The green grass before me, the trees, the clear blue sky, the clouds floating above, and the waterfall—I could sense ki in all these things. The sun sets in the West and night comes. Night breaks and morning comes. Spring is gone and summer arrives; summer is gone, autumn follows, and then winter arises. The order of seasonal events, and of night and day, is controlled by nature. And I felt the movement of the ki of the universe in every movement in nature. More than this I sensed in the workings of ki something far beyond our intelligence, far beyond what we can conceive intellectually, but not beyond what we can feel in our soul. I sensed something with great depth, value, and intelligence.[24]

Although ki is invisible the effects of ki are not. Undoubtedly it's difficult to observe ki as something separate and distinct from the limitless different parts of nature, but ki can be observed via natural activities. Nakamura Sensei noted as much saying the physical universe we can see is born of a deeper "real existence," or ki. He felt we're mistaken in denying the existence of whatever we cannot perceive with the five senses. For Nakamura Sensei something existed even if it was unseen just like electrical waves exist even though they're invisible.[25]

We commonly consider the universe using a relative worldview—a dualistic way of perceiving life. Certainly relativity and duality exist. Everything is one, but it still hurts when we unintentionally close a door on our fingers. Obviously enough of a separation and division exist for the door to crush our fingers.

A nondualistic worldview doesn't deny the relative world but sees the absolute oneness of life underlying relative distinctions. Wooden doors, for instance, come from trees, and according to science humans and trees ultimately have a common evolutionary ancestor. In a similar vein, when we eat fruit from a tree, the tree becomes part of us. The various parts of nature are interdependent; in traditional Asian cosmology they are differing aspects of one universal ki.

In addition, the aforementioned wooden door came from a tree, which came from a seed. We, likewise, are born of our parents, who came from our grandparents. If we ask ourselves what came before our grandparents, and our great grandparents, and before that, and before that . . . we eventually reach a point where seemingly nothing existed. The same can be said for the door, which came from a tree, which came from a seed, and so on.

Using this line of thought everything can be reduced to a "zero point," where apparently nothing exists. Yet something cannot arise from nothing. This "something yet nothing, nothing yet something" is the ki of the universe. It's the origin of us and the door which squished our fingers. Both we and the door are facets of ki; both will eventually dissolve and return to the ki of the universe. Ki changes form, but it doesn't disappear.

In this case the door is ki; the trees it comes from are ki. Watching trees swaying in the woods, we know the wind is blowing them. We can't see the wind, but we deduce its existence by the bending trees just as we can observe ki in nature by inference. And when wind causes trees to tilt, it is ki blowing. We're also ki looking at the movement of ki in the universe, which is ki itself. All are diversified outward expressions of ki: the totality of the universe, which to Nakamura Sensei was much more than stars and planets. Ki isn't supernatural, hidden, or intangible. Instead, like the water surrounding Nakamura Sensei's aforementioned fish, it's all-encompassing.

So if ki is "everything," why use this term? The answer lies in a nondualistic awareness of life. There's no English word as all-inclusive and broad as ki. When we study nondualistic awareness this word helps, causing us to observe commonplace aspects of living differently than we're accustomed to. In researching ki and different states of consciousness, it's also useful to have direct experience relating to the topics being studied. The following experiment is valuable for arriving at firsthand understanding of ki, positive visualization, and coordination of mind and body.

EXPERIMENT FIVE: *ORENAI TE*
Nakamura Sensei's teachings about ki and mind-body unification somewhat paral-

lel those of the founders of various classical Japanese arts, including calligraphy, flower arrangement, and martial arts. He thought of the mind as an invisible portion of the body and the body as the visible part of the mind. Like Kaliapa, he compared the mind and body to a river, in which the mind was like the upper segment of the river, and the body was the lower portion. If we throw garbage into the upper section, it'll flow to the lower part. Similarly our thoughts influence our bodies and health.

Ki is the connective energy of the universe; it's also the link between mind and body. Unrefined ki equals the body; refined ki corresponds to the mind. Ki is seen in nature through its reflections, i.e., the actions of nature's integral parts, and so too is the movement of ki reflected on the body. Even so, this sort of discussion can devolve into vague philosophy, and the experiment I'm about to introduce should help prevent this.

Hashimoto Tetsuichi Sensei, one of Japan's top Shin-shin-toitsu-do teachers, indicates Nakamura Sensei created Experiment Five to allow students to research the connection between mind and body. This experiment also gives us a chance to unearth the innate power of mind-body coordination and grasp the reflected motion of ki. It is one of Nakamura Sensei's most famous exercises, and it's commonly known in Japan as orenai te. "Orenai" suggests something which can't be bent or collapsed, while "te" is hand or arm.

Several Japanese arts besides Shin-shin-toitsu-do value positive development of ki as well as unification of body and mind. Consequently, this exercise found its way into popular disciplines like the martial arts (aikido in particular) and healing arts. (In certain cases it's also been taught with mysterious connotations not found in Nakamura Sensei's no-nonsense presentation.)

You'll need another person to try orenai te with:

1. Extend your arm about shoulder height, level with the ground. Make a tight fist, and stiffen your arm to try to make it firm. Have your friend hold your wrist and the inner bend of your elbow with each hand. He or she should attempt to slowly bend your arm by pushing your wrist toward your shoulder, while the other hand moves downward against your elbow. Try to hold your arm straight, and focus your attention on where your partner is touching you. Unless your friend has much less physical strength than you, the power of two arms will beat the opposition of one arm as in Fig. 3.

2. Now try a different tactic. Relax your arm, open your fingers, and keep a natural bend in your elbow, but don't go limp. Then visualize a stream of

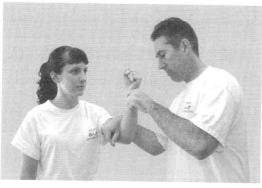

Fig. 3. Your partner tries to bend your arm with both hands—one touches your inner elbow and one holds your wrist. He slowly pushes your wrist toward your shoulder. Tense your arm and try to resist this action. How easily can you keep your arm from collapsing?

Fig. 4. Relax your arm, without going limp, and visualize ki flowing endlessly outward from the fingertips. Your attention is not on yourself. It is moving through a point infinitely far away. Can you more easily keep your arm from bending?

ki flowing through your arm, out of your fingertips, and continuing forever through anything in front of you. Imagining a beam of light being projected also works for some people.

3. Soon you'll be unable to follow this image as it will reach a point where the ki is too distant to picture. At that time do nothing and let the sensation of ki rushing outward continue on its own.

4. Have your partner slowly, so as to not disturb your concentration, bend your arm with the same amount of force as before. As long as your attention is unbroken and your body is relaxed, the arm will be unaffected by your partner's efforts as in **Fig. 4**.

This is a comparative exercise; you aren't competing with each other. Ask your friend to use equal effort each time for accurate comparison.

When we visualize ki flowing through the arm and outward, our minds move in the same direction our fingers are pointing (toward what we're facing). In other words, the mind and body are unified, and we see the power of mind and body coordination via this experiment. We furthermore see the dramatic effect a positive mental image has on the body. An arm which can't be easily collapsed is remarkable, but transferring the same power of mind and body unification into our jobs, hobbies, and lives is more impressive. The following chapters will help us do that, but we can learn more about coordination of mind and body through the next exercise.

EXPERIMENT SIX: ORENAI TE AND LIMPNESS

We've seen how tension inhibits outward movement of ki, but how does physical limpness relate to ki and attitude? Let's find out:

1. Try letting your body sag limply, while your friend attempts to crumple your arm. Even if you think of ki flowing through your arm this is rendered ineffective by a flaccid posture.
2. Now extend your arm again in a relaxed—but not limp—manner. Create the positive image of ki rushing through your arm, out of your fingertips, and continuing endlessly forward. Which approach gives you the greatest power with the least amount of effort?

Most soon realize a limp, drooping posture is as inefficient as one that's excessively tense. Life energy efficiently moves outward in a positive manner when we're relaxed and neither tense nor flaccid.

An arm or body that's sagging looks lifeless. In a way, it is. Ki withdraws as much when we're limp as when we're tense. Limpness is the outward expression of resignation and other negative mental states. Mind and body constantly influence each other, so a positive mind relates to positive physical expressions as much as the dynamic outward movement of ki.

EXPERIMENT SEVEN: ORENAI TE AND THE MOVEMENT OF KI

Let's experiment again with orenai te:

1. Picture an outward movement of ki, which continues to connect with the ki of the universe. Your arm will probably be as immovable as before.

2. While your partner continues to drive your wrist back to your shoulder,
   suddenly imagine strongly drawing ki back into the arm. What happens?
3. At the instant most people visualize pulling in ki the arm starts bending.
   Your friend just needs to continue his or her pressure.

In this example, your partner's muscular force is constant, regardless of what you're visualizing. In addition, we aren't contrasting a tense arm and a relaxed arm as in Experiment Five. The sole distinction between the two states being tested lies in the mind and ki. When we think of sucking ki in we withdraw psychologically from life just as when we fall into depression or think negatively. We see in this experiment how withdrawing ki weakens us. As a result, Nakamura Sensei placed the greatest emphasis on the first of his principles: "Maintain a positive mind."

This positive movement of ki isn't inevitably dependent upon visualization; in fact, such an image in the end becomes a problem. Obviously we cannot function during the day while constantly holding onto a particular mental picture. The mind needs to be free to concentrate on any activity. It's consequently vital to discover how to let the visualization grow fainter as ki moves too far away to envisage, while maintaining the stream of ki and mind-body coordination.

The trick is to notice how you feel when doing orenai te. Once you're sure of the psychophysical sensation that's mind and body unification, let the image of ki fade as it moves away from you. Just do nothing and the arm will remain unbent. As this mental image is released only pure attention remains. This state doesn't divide the ki of the experimenter from the ki of the universe.

EXPERIMENT EIGHT: ORENAI TE AND A POSITIVE MIND

Everything we've experimented with thus far is important for personally understanding mind and body unification. But despite my comments about transcending the visualization of ki, it still may not be clear how to bring the power of ki into our lives. You may be thinking, "Sure, these exercises are interesting and the power generated is impressive, but how can I achieve the same competency and strength in school or business?" That's a legitimate question.

While you might win the occasional free beer by challenging people to bend your arm, someone interviewing you for a job is unlikely to care about such things. Moreover, we can't walk around constantly imagining ki flowing out of our fingers, toes, or eyes. So how can we take the strength realized in orenai te into other endeavors, and how can we do this without conscious effort? Let's try another experiment to find out:

1. Before you extend your arm say aloud, "I cannot." Then raise the arm. See how much strength it takes for your partner to bend your arm.
2. Before lifting your arm, say out loud, "I can!" Lift the arm and ask your partner to attempt to bend it again using the same force as before.

Most people find the second approach vastly more powerful. They get the same result as when they visualize ki streaming through their arm and out of their fingertips. In short, optimism and the outward radiation of ki are intimately entwined.

Although we can't continuously think of ki flowing outward in daily life, we can notice if our attitude is positive, which also releases ki. The words we use, audibly and silently in our minds, indicate if we're positive or not. Words have power, something Nakamura Sensei noticed long ago:

Words we use have the strongest power of suggestion of all the elements our subconscious is exposed to in life. Life is philosophized by words and made scientific by words. Thus words can decide the course of our lives.

Some people say in summer, "Very hot, isn't it? I can't stand it." This greeting is negative. Why not say, "Very hot. It makes me cheerful."

The words we use have bad or good influences not only on ourselves but also on people who hear them. Make a habit to use only positive expressions. Once we've made this habit we don't need any effort to speak positively. It happens naturally through the actions of the subconscious.

I always say to people, "You look fine, today." I never say, "You look pale, is there anything wrong with you?" Some folks may say this to us, but we needn't be affected by these negative greetings. Say to such people, "Is your sight OK? Green peas are pale, but they taste good."[26]

In addition to noting your attitude and how it's reflected in your spoken expressions, notice if your posture is tense or slumped over. As in the above experiments, limpness or tension inhibits ki and mind-body coordination. And this can shape how people relate to us.

Ever had someone shake your hand so hard they almost crushed it? Most of us have, and it doesn't create a good first impression nor does it transmit ki well. How about the limp noodle handshake? Kind of creepy, right? We generally have the best impression of a person who shakes our hand in a relaxed, but still firm, manner. This handshake is neither tense nor wilted, and it's the same physical condition displayed when we execute orenai te correctly.

Again, we can't always think ki is flowing outward, but we can notice if our posture is tense or collapsing in on itself. Thinking of an outward movement of ki requires conscious visualization, at least for beginners, and this would keep the mind from being able to fully focus on any other tasks. On the other hand, noticing a change in posture—falling limp or growing tense—does not require visualization. It amounts to noting a change in how the body feels.

In time, realizing a balance between tension and collapse becomes a habit, and this kind of balanced carriage facilitates the dynamic release of ki. The same can be said for positive words and a positive attitude, which unconsciously maintain the outward flow of ki. We don't need to consciously visualize ki streaming outward; we just need to notice what kind of verbal expressions we use in life. Orenai te is simple; so are the lessons we learn from it.

It isn't meant for developing supernatural power, for astonishing friends, or for serving as a marketing trick for ki. Despite what some writers claim, orenai te isn't inexplicable, it isn't literally "unbendable," and it doesn't transcend the physical laws of nature. No occult-like force is used; actually a change takes place in the way the muscles work when orenai te is correctly executed. This makes the arm unusually hard to bend. By concentrating the mind in the direction we're facing—the identical direction the fingers are pointing—we utilize the unified power of the mind and body. Employing the mind and body as a unit is more effective than concentrating solely on muscular strength. Plus, integrating mind and body heightens muscular power.

The experiments outlined also offer opportunities to consider the influence of concentration. It's easy to lose concentration or confidence if a huge person tries to collapse your arm, particularly during a public class. When concentration is defeated, or when confidence is lost, the arm bends. But with continued training, we increase our capacity to positively concentrate, even in action or under pressure. The next principle looks into what concentration is and how to achieve it.

Principle Two: Use the Mind with Full Concentration

If the mind and body are in accord we feel in harmony with ourselves, and we're using our full—as opposed to partial—power. Considering each moment in a positive manner encourages the mind to concentrate on the actions the body is performing. Along these lines, the ability to deeply concentrate on anything the body's engaging in, regardless of how much pressure we're experiencing, makes it possible to sustain coordination of mind and body. The distinction between a distracted mind and a concentrated mind is like the difference between a flashlight and a laser beam. Nakamura Sensei highlighted this point in the second of his Four Basic Principles to Unify Mind and Body.

This is because the strength of ki, and the capacity to use ki, is connected to a positive attitude and concentration. Furthermore, if the positive use of the mind releases ki, concentrated utilization of the mind directs and focuses ki. It's critical to consider what sort of training leads to concentration. It's also essential to note that concentration equals keeping the mind in the present moment, unless we intentionally decide to ponder the future or past. Accordingly concentration can, and should be, cultivated in the midst of daily existence. This was one of Nakamura Sensei's favorite topics, and he taught that in order to concentrate we should first clear and calm the mind, focusing it on what we're doing at that moment. Most people, however, only do this when they're about to undertake some important task. As the result, they rarely develop excellent concentration that they can easily maintain throughout the day.

Our bodies only exist in the present, and if we want to coordinate the mind and body we need the mind in the present as well. Concentration is keeping the mind in the moment—whether or not we're doing something of particular importance. If we want deep concentration when we do something important, we must train ourselves to keep the mind clear and focused all the time.[27]

The Influence of Concentration

Concentration can be observed through its influence on our bodies. Keeping this in mind, let's try more experiments to learn how a focused mind can be tested through the body. My instructor Hashimoto Sensei and other senior students of Nakamura Sensei point out that he began teaching the next test of concentration and mental strength in the early 1930s. According to Mr. Hashimoto, this test of mind and body coordination was used to help explain the Four Basic Principles to Unify Mind and Body in Nakamura Sensei's introductory lectures, and this is also the case with the other experiments in this book.

It's true, however, that since his death these exercises were added to other forms of mind-body training, especially aikido. This isn't unexpected; he encouraged his pupils to use what he taught in every part of their lives. Since numerous Japanese arts value coordination of mind and body instructors of other disciplines came to his classes. In the case of top aikido teachers, Shin-shin-toitsu-do was particularly well received, owing to the friendship between Nakamura Sensei and Ueshiba Morihei Sensei, creator of aikido. Starting in the 1950s, Tohei Koichi Sensei, among the most advanced students of Ueshiba Sensei and Nakamura Sensei, introduced Shin-shin-toitsu-do exercises and teachings, notably orenai te and Nakamura Sensei's autosuggestion, to Japanese aikido students and people outside of Japan.

Nakamura Sensei compared the mind to a camera lens. If the lens is unfocused no truthful depiction of reality is possible. Using the mind with complete attention is akin to working with a focused camera lens. Bearing this in mind, it's easy to see the significance of optimism and concentration. But not everyone knows how to personally test their concentration. The following exercises let you do just that.

EXPERIMENT NINE: THE O-RING TEST AND THE POWER OF CONCENTRATION

Once again, we'll compare two different ways of using the mind and body. While comparing both methods maintain the same conditions each time:

1. Make a ring of the thumb and index finger, so your fingertips touch in an O shape, as in **Fig. 5**.
2. Have a friend place each of their index fingers into the ring as in **Fig. 6**. One finger hooks around your index finger and the other one hooks around your thumb. Your friend—using the strength of both hands—will try to gradually pull your fingers apart. Attempt to keep them together by using the muscular power of your fingers.
3. The limited strength of the fingers seldom matches the might of two hands and arms. Consequently, the ring is broken as in **Fig. 7**. Note how much muscle was needed to drag the fingers apart and how rapidly they separated.
4. Next, picture your fingers as a solid ring of iron. Since this ring cannot be opened there's no need to exceptionally tense your fingers, which actually weakens your harmony of mind and body. Nonetheless, push the fingertips together enough that you feel a solid connection, which facilitates the visualization of a solid ring.

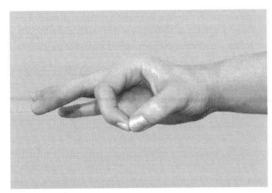

Fig. 5. Make a ring of your thumb and index finger. The fingertips should touch.

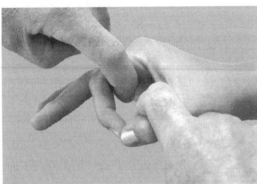

Fig. 6. Your partner will insert his index fingers into this ring. Next, he will attempt to slowly and gradually pull your fingers apart.

Fig. 7. Tense your fingers as much as possible. Your partner will try to pull them apart. Next, press the fingertips together firmly, but without great tension. Imagine your fingers form an indestructible ring. Ask your partner to apply the same amount of force as before. Is the ring as easily broken?

5. Concentrate intensely on one thought: your fingers are an unyielding ring. Ask your partner to pull them apart once more. Have him or her use the identical amount of power as before. What's the outcome? If you practice a bit you'll probably arrive at an unbroken ring that looks like **Fig. 6.**

Lots of people discover a distinction between using the limited might of the body versus the limitless potential of concentration in combination with physical power. Have your friend avoid abrupt applications of strength to avoid shattering your concentration. In every mind and body unification exercise make a legitimate, objective evaluation, and remember that persons with meager concentration or fragile self-confidence may need to practice awhile to get an unbreakable ring. This repeated training is a technique for discovering attentiveness.

EXPERIMENT TEN: THE O-RING TEST AND THE MOVEMENT OF KI
You can also try this variation:

1. Make an O-shaped ring and tense your fingers as before. See how much strength it takes for your partner to slowly pull the fingers apart.
2. Instead of envisioning an iron ring, imagine ki flowing through the arm and into the fingers. Further imagine this ki flowing around and around within the thumb and index finger ring.
3. Can you experience a difference in the strength of the ring when contrasting using muscular strength versus ki?

Either visualization will produce a seemingly unbreakable ring, but the point of Experiment Ten is to discover that concentration and ki movement are interrelated. In brief, concentration is an unbroken flow of ki. When the mind attaches itself to a distracting thought or a physical object, ki stops at that point. This keeps the mind from concentrating on anything else. For example, if while your partner tests you, you get stuck on the thought that you'd be embarrassed if your ring opens, then it's hard to concentrate on ki flowing around the ring itself.

EXPERIMENT ELEVEN: THE O-RING TEST AND ONGOING CONCENTRATION
We need more than concentration in life. We need sustained concentration. The

next exercise deals with maintaining concentration, and it offers us a chance to develop continuous concentration via repetition:

1. Once you successfully create an unbreakable ring of ki have your friend sustain his or her pressure for some time.
2. What happens if you're sidetracked during this period? Can you preserve concentration (and the ring which is a manifestation of concentration) for more than a few seconds?

EXPERIMENT TWELVE: THE O-RING TEST AND DISTRACTION

Just as weightlifters progressively add weight to an apparatus to develop more strength, we can do something similar in these exercises of mind and body unity:

1. For a more tricky test of concentration, ask your partner to talk while applying pressure as in **Fig. 6**, tap your shoulder and swiftly resume the test, or in some other manner try to distract you during the experiment.
2. If your mind becomes sidetracked by where you've been tapped or the words being uttered, what's the effect on the ring? If you notice these sensations but continue focusing on an unbreakable iron ring or a ring of energy, what's the result?

EXPERIMENT THIRTEEN: THE O-RING TEST AND RECOVERED CONCENTRATION

Even if we can concentrate for extended periods, we may still lose concentration from time to time. What then? Can we regain concentration?

Using Experiment Thirteen we can examine recovering lost attention:

1. Make an O with your fingers again. Concentrate to make the ring unbreakable. Ask your partner to apply pressure to verify your concentration.
2. While your friend continues trying to pull your fingers apart, let the thumb and index fingers separate by an inch or so, but keep the same mental image of an iron ring or of ki moving in a circle.
3. As long as you don't lose this image or get upset by the fingertips separating, you can bring your fingers back together despite your partner's resistance.

Even if we meet with momentary failure or a lapse in concentration, we can recover as long as we remain positive. But once we decide concentration is completely destroyed, it is.

These experiments let you visually and tangibly check the effectiveness of concentration as well as study its relationship to mind and body unification. Experiments Ten through Thirteen help you determine the nature of concentration and its associated topics, such as keeping the mind in the moment and learning how to deal with distractions. At the same time, they offer a means to evaluate your strength of attention. We can realize more through a few moments of direct, mindful experience than we can through hours of reading and/or guesswork.

Shin-shin-toitsu-do is unique in that it's a spiritual discipline influenced by science and common sense. Carl von Weizsacker, a prominent German physicist and colleague of the famed quantum physicist Werner Heisenberg, insisted that matter can be empirically known in two ways: It may be phenomenally given or it can be inferred. In other words, we may see a dark spot on a piece of fruit, and this is phenomenally given. We can also infer that if it's an apple the mark may indicate a worm in the fruit. We make this inference based on what we see and on our knowledge of fruit and worms. From a perceivable phenomenon we can infer what remains unseen, and this principle is used in the experiments in this book. Shin-shin-toitsu-do represents something of a merger of science and spirituality.

A Natural Center in the Lower Abdomen

If we use the mind attentively mental strength improves, and if the mind is concentrated in the moment it is easier to harmonize mind and body. Even so, in terms of mind-body coordination, what can we concentrate on which will consistently assist us in discovering this condition of coordination?

In Japan people traditionally focused mental strength in the shita hara, or "lower abdomen," to realize their complete potential. Japan has viewed the shita hara as the fundamental center of humankind in a way comparable to the Western view of the heart or brain. However, the importance of the lower abdomen isn't totally unfamiliar to Western people: when Westerners are distressed they mention "butterflies in the stomach." A Japanese expression indicates an angry person's "hara is rising up," while *hara ga nai hito* describes a cowardly individual, "a person with no hara." Americans speak of such people as being "gutless."

We'll more fully investigate later how this spot connects to mind and body unification. Simply stated, the weight of the upper body reaches its maximum point of density below the navel, and this region equals the proper center of gravity and balance for one's body. If we concentrate the mind at a point on the front surface of the lower abdomen, roughly four finger widths below the bellybutton, we're coordinating the mind and body in the same spot. The body exists exclusively in the present, so calming the mind at this point below the navel equals bringing the mind into the moment as well. This unifies mind and body, and we can focus the mind at this lower abdominal point before we try anything important. Repeated centering of the mind at the shita hara makes mind and body coordination a habit we carry with us, readying us to unleash our greatest power when and where we need to.

Focusing ki, or physical-mental power, in the shita hara has a lengthy history in Asia. Shin-shin-toitsu-do uses concentration on this spot for not only unifying the mind and body, but also for achieving psychophysical stability, balance, and the return of lost calmness. Calming the mind in the lower abdomen helps in sports, art, public speaking, job interviews, and any activity which benefits from composure. If we put all of our attention at a point below the navel, no part of our mind focuses on fear or failure, resulting in tranquility. Of course we can't keep the mind consciously centered below the navel while speaking, driving, or engaging in other actions. That understood, we acquire negative habits through repetition, usually without realizing we're creating habits. We acquire positive habits the same way, and each time we center the mind in the lower abdomen, we not only calm the mind, but the feeling of mind-body coordination is also imbedded in the subconscious. Influencing the subconscious can result in habits, both good and bad.

The soundness of this statement can only be evaluated through practice. Try focusing the mind at this balancing point for the mind and body on a daily basis; determine what the shita hara is through direct experimentation. Here's how:

1. First learn to deeply concentrate the mind on a single thought: the shita hara.
2. Then learn to sustain this concentration for a few moments. This will take some practice.
3. At this point, notice the feeling of calmness and stability that is produced by concentrating below the navel.

4. Learn to sustain this feeling even when you no longer think of the shita hara.

5. Once you can do the fourth point there's no need to constantly think about the shita hara. Just note when you feel upset or unsettled, and focus ki at the shita hara to recover the previously identified feeling of composure. You can do the same before performing an important task to guarantee mind and body unification.

6. Finally, notice if repeatedly centering yourself in the lower abdomen results in a greater sense of peacefulness in daily life (even when you aren't consciously concentrating on the shita hara).

There's more about the shita hara and living a happier, healthier life in upcoming chapters. I'll cover how it connects to posture and coordinated body movement, and I'll explain how this natural center in the lower abdomen relates to some Shin-shin-toitsu-do exercises, too. But for now, let's make sure we understand the important distinction between concentration and fixation.

Concentration vs. Attachment

Concentration, attachment, and obsession aren't equivalent states. Nakamura Sensei distinguished between concentration and attachment in his book *Searching for Truth in Life*. He wrote that what many people think of as concentration is merely the mind becoming fixated on something. This is actually attachment or obsession, rather than natural concentration.

How can we tell the difference between being attached to something and concentrating deeply? When we're attached to something or obsessed with something like money, the mind constantly moves toward money as something separate from itself to strive for. In other words, the mind moves toward the object of concentration . . . and this can be anything the mind's attached to.

However, when we deeply concentrate on an item, the mind isn't drawn to the object of concentration; it draws the object into itself to become one with it. Concentration doesn't involve chasing after things, constantly trying to obtain things, or having the mind always moving toward the thought of something. All these states of mind are actually attachment.[28]

How attachments weaken us—mentally and physically—will be explored throughout this book, but as we close this chapter it should be now evident that the mind influ-ences and controls the body. A positive, concentrated mind has a healthy, positive effect on the body. All the same, unless the body is natural and relaxed, it fails to rapidly and capably respond to even the most focused mind. Mind and body harmony is undermined by ineffective use of the body. The crucial role of the body in Shin-shin-toitsu-do and life is coming up next.

Chapter 4

PRINCIPLES
FOR THE BODY

FOUR BASIC PRINCIPLES TO UNIFY MIND AND BODY

1. Maintain a positive mind.

2. Train the mind to arrive at full concentration.

3. Use the body obeying the laws of nature.

4. Train the body progressively, systematically, and regularly.

We're linked to nature from birth to death. This is readily apparent, but many of us don't reflect on its significance and how it relates to our lives. And being connected to nature is no assurance that we'll function as part of nature. Thus the third of the Four Basic Principles to Unify Mind and Body encourages us to discover how to live naturally. In this way we realize our profound bond with nature: the infinite source of life.

Nature (the universe) is eternally changing, evolving, and renewing, which is our true essence as well. This essence, or ki, is one with nature and nature's power. Nakamura Tempu Sensei traveled around the world just to experience this oneness firsthand. Yet in the end, sitting motionless by an immense waterfall in the Himalayan Mountains, he discovered he'd always been one with the universe. The answers he sought in the USA, Great Britain, France, Germany, and India always surrounded him—and were within him—from the start of his journey.

He expressed what he realized in ways both simple and direct. Nakamura Sensei insisted that if we focus exclusively on our mental life and ignore physical existence, we cannot discover a genuinely natural way of living. While it's true the mind controls the body, it is a mistake to think this means the body should be ignored. It's even worse to disassociate ourselves from the body, or to attempt to repress anything having to do with the body, as some people tend to do.

Having both a sound body and mind is the core principle of mind-body unification. As the result, we should train the mind and body equally. Many training methods are one-sided, choosing to concentrate on developing only the mind or only the body. Yet nothing can be accomplished in life with just one or the other.[29]

In this chapter we'll look into postures and ways of using the body which are optimum for sustaining mind and body unification. At the same time, we'll delve into naturalness and examine daily habits for maintaining physical health. We often view topics like meditation and philosophy as cerebral, yet Shin-shin-toitsu-do philosophy embodies mind and body unification in all of its aspects. It's a philosophy with a physical expression.

Physically weak or ill people can't meditate or accomplish much else without difficulty. That's why physical training was always part of Nakamura Sensei's pragmatic teachings. Based on his background in Western medicine, he realized that positive physical training is necessary because it strengthens resistance to unhealthy stimuli around us. The more advanced civilization becomes the more we notice harmful stimuli in our surroundings. When we think of the new diseases which have come into being over time, we might believe we're doomed to a sickly existence. But this is to forget that humans are able to adapt to a wide variety of circumstances, which accounts for our continued existence and ongoing evolution.

If a stimulus is given repeatedly to part of the body that part reacts, changing its quality and form to adapt to the stimulus. Look at a runner's strongly muscled legs to see how his or her legs adapted to the ongoing stimulus of running. In the same way, we can adjust to a wide variety of seemingly negative circumstances as long as we maintain a positive mind and as long as we train our bodies to adapt in a progressive, systematic, and regular manner.

Nakamura Sensei's training for the body involves physical exercise, training to keep the body flexible, deep breathing, methods to strengthen the skin (allowing it to more easily adapt to extremes of heat and cold), natural diet, and various other techniques. All these methods strengthen the body so it can more easily and rapidly adjust to changes within its environment. A body which more freely and quickly adapts is a body that's more capable of survival.[30]

Jogging, swimming, and other physical exercises are excellent, but not if they're performed in a tense and unnatural way. Unnaturalness leads to excessiveness and injuries, because it forces the body to perform in ways it was not designed for, so we should first consider how to use the body naturally.

Principle Three: Use the Body Obeying the Laws of Nature

Nakamura Sensei realized plants and animals seldom behave unnaturally, acting opposite to their true makeup. People are also natural entities, but at the same time we're conscious beings. We consequently have free will and must choose to not only be part of nature but to also follow the laws of nature. Scores of natural laws affect our bodies, and it's too difficult to examine them all in this chapter. So I've focused on just a few everyday activities to illustrate Nakamura Sensei's philosophy of naturalness. Case in point, animals eat when hungry and nap when sleepy. This was Nakamura Sensei's recommendation for people as well.

It's common sense. Unfortunately, common sense isn't so common.

Eating

Human beings regularly eat without cause because they're bored, jumpy, or gluttonous. Some people won't eat when they're starving due to self-consciousness about their looks. Others munch unconsciously and without appreciation for the vegetation and/or animals that are sacrificed so they can live.

One facet of obeying nature is eating primarily when we're truly hungry. If we observe ourselves in the here and now, in a condition free of preconceptions, we perceive our genuine reactions toward eating. This means we notice if we were full a couple minutes ago and if we really need another bite of cheesecake. This alone can contribute to maintaining a weight that's natural for us, resulting in better health. Keeping the mind in the moment also allows us to deeply experience reality.

Although we might imagine eating is purely physical, the mind eats through the body and it decides when, what, and how much to eat. Nakamura Sensei also noted our mental state is connected with his third principle. He wrote that because the mind controls the body, physical training should be carried out with a positive attitude. Without such an attitude we frequently fail to train ourselves regularly, often giving up when we encounter even slight difficulties. According to Nakamura Sensei, the feeling which most effectively promotes a positive mental state is gratitude.[31]

Being thankful to nature for food and not wasting it makes sense. All the same, people fail to heed this advice. If this recommendation is seen as just theory it has slight impact, and perhaps this is why so many eat unconsciously.

When humanity's union with nature is seen as fact—directly and for ourselves— love for all creations becomes real. Then eating gratefully is normal. With thankfulness

99

comes an authentically positive outlook toward eating. This is even truer if we eat when we're really hungry; that's when most meals taste pretty good. Because the mind controls the body, grateful and positive feelings even helpfully influence digestion, just as eating when upset can lead to an upset stomach.

Genuine Awareness of Nature and Sleeping

Keeping the mind in the present not only supports mind and body unification, it allows us to feel the truths of reality and nature firsthand. The upcoming forms of meditation are based on this state of mind, a condition in which humanity's oneness with the universe is personally and acutely felt as true. This mental state is essential if the laws of nature are to be perceived as actuality instead of mere theory.

As we meditate, we can search for the line between the meditator and the universe engulfing him or her. Can this division actually be discovered?

In a relative sense we can theorize about differences between us and everything else in the natural world, but in the deepest sense we're biologically and spiritually linked to all creations. Physical laws apply to us as much as other parts of nature. In this context (and others) the interconnection of everything is scientifically viable. If so, why do many people feel disengaged from one another, from other living things, indeed from nature itself?

Nakamura Sensei realized we're commonly attached to relative, impermanent aspects of life, and these attachments prevent us from feeling the deeper reality of interdependence which pervades nature. Relative attachments also prevent us from grasping the nondualistic essence of life as well as how to live naturally.

Harmony with nature is vital, but it must be real. Like oneness with nature, deep sleep cannot be forced or faked. Actually, when it comes to sleeping the more we struggle to sleep, the more we keep ourselves awake. Nakamura Sensei indicated that sleep is vital for health, but lots of people have trouble sleeping. This is frequently from worry, but it can also stem from a particularly sedentary standard of living. Folks who get little exercise and oversleep every day may in time be incapable of sleeping. More physical exertion during the daytime and sleeping less can occasionally reinstate standard sleep patterns.

We need to pay attention to and respect our bodies, not forcing ourselves to sleep when we aren't really sleepy and not staying up when sleep is required. Nakamura Sensei advised to sleep when we actually feel the need to sleep. He also mentioned that obsessive, compulsive, and anxious people are often stuck on some fixation, and this can tie into their sleeplessness.

Life takes care of itself, and worrying about sleep makes sleep unattainable. When we let ourselves be natural and simply *do nothing*, sleep occurs effortlessly. In subsequent chapters on meditation, we'll look more at the principle of mui, "doing nothing," and its link to naturalness and relaxation.

If the mind rests peacefully in the moment, in an innocent, naturalistic state liberated from predetermined ideas, is it possible to see what does and doesn't work for your body? Anything less is seeing ourselves and nature through the eyes and theories of others, who don't actually know us. Instead of personally unearthing what's natural for us, we often imitate what others claim is natural or memorize someone's instructions about natural living. But can we have confidence in what's copied or memorized versus what we've seen for ourselves? Without this self-assurance and self-reliance, relaxation isn't easy. And relaxing equals harmony with nature.

Functional Relaxation

Relaxation is critical in every activity, and while teachers and coaches know this they're occasionally at a loss as to how to teach it. Yet without relaxing, it's tricky to get mental stability and physical power in any endeavor. Even if we memorize Nakamura Sensei's books, this has slight significance if we're incapacitated by stress-related ailments like headaches. Ultimately, Shin-shin-toitsu-do must help us make our lives free from constraints, including physical and mental illnesses, which can stem from stress-related problems. Relaxation is a secret to a long and productive existence, much like the lengthy life Nakamura Sensei enjoyed. Living to over 90 years old, when few lived so long (or so well), is testimony to him using his body in a natural, relaxed way.

Countless people feel assaulted by stress every day. Shin-shin-toitsu-do helps us learn functional relaxation that can be carried into daily interactions. In fact, if we can't remain unruffled even during great stress, it's unlikely that we'll arrive at freedom of expression in life. Since the body mirrors the mind, if we freeze psychologically in a disturbing situation we freeze bodily as well, making us incapable of executing successful action. We may understand this, but few pull off relaxation in action, leading some to conclude relaxation is unnatural and difficult.

Students of Shin-shin-toitsu-do find this difficulty arises from misguided viewpoints and habits. For instance, keeping our shoulders slightly elevated produces tension and stiff shoulders. We're frequently unaware of these bad habits, but once we train to relax and let our shoulders fall into their proper place, it's easier to arrive at calmness in action.

Another stumbling block on the road to relaxation is the fact that numerous people, knowingly or unconsciously, think relaxation is comfortable but powerless. Some believe relaxation doesn't let them manifest much physical power, and others conclude when they're relaxed they're not working hard. These are mistaken ideas. Physically—and mentally to boot—we move and react quickly only when relaxed. Tension immobilizes us. Reacting to stress by locking up our muscles makes them less capable of producing power. Tension and anxiety only hamper clear thought while they fatigue the body.

Shouldn't we try hard to do our best? Sure, but this needn't be interpreted as tension. Maybe it's more important to *try correctly*, meaning to unify mind and body, than to "try hard."

Once unfounded beliefs become part of the subconscious they negatively alter conscious actions. As a result, in a nerve-racking situation we're powerless to relax even if we'd like to. A basic principle of Shin-shin-toitsu-do holds that as we deliberately learn to relax under pressure in exercises like orenai te, we develop the knack for relaxing under stress as a subconscious condition. Orenai te lets us learn to handle stress; it shows how functional relaxation is actually powerful. These realizations can have an undeniable influence on how we respond to life.

Three Ways of Using the Body and Mind

We can psychologically react to life in three general ways:

- Conflict (fighting)
- Resignation (giving up)
- Acceptance (nonattachment)

The first two polar opposites are negative dysfunctional conditions which create suffering. No one wants to exist in perpetual conflict with others, although many are; nobody enjoys feeling beaten down by life either. The third option, being nondualistic in nature, isn't the opposite of any other condition; it represents a positive functional state of mind.

Each of these three psychological states has a corresponding physical expression, which Nakamura Sensei noted by indicating the body reflects the mind. These three physiological conditions and postures are:

- Tension and stiffness
- Limpness, collapse, and dysfunctional relaxation
- A balanced posture that's neither tense nor limp

In trying the orenai te exercise in the last chapter, we experimented with the following:

- Tension/fighting vs. positive relaxation/outward flow of ki (Experiment Five)
- Limpness/resignation vs. positive relaxation/outward flow of ki (Experiments Five and Eight)

In these experiments we were actually testing the difference between these three states of mind and ways of using the body. Experimentation is needed in that people tend to think in dualistic or antagonistic terms, whereas Nakamura Sensei pointed toward a psychophysical state beyond duality. It's a very different way of living that's difficult to communicate solely using words, and these experiments let us feel an alternative way of functioning that's unfamiliar to many. This is important because most of us don't look at human existence in this way. For example, ask the average person to name the opposite of tension. They'll typically reply "relaxation." Yet in reality the opposite of tension is collapse, which in *The Teachings of Tempu* I've termed negative or dysfunctional relaxation. Relaxation is actually not in opposition to anything. It's purely natural: not tense but not limp, not fighting but not giving up.

Still, human beings tend to vacillate between extremes: resignation/fighting and limpness/tension. Shin-shin-toitsu-do offers an alternative to these extremes: the natural use of the body we characterize as positive functional relaxation. Since we're usually unfamiliar with this posture/mental state, Nakamura Sensei taught a special means of using the body to discover a positive and practical form of relaxation that's easily sustained in daily actions. This unique way of using the body and stabilizing the nervous system is based on Kaliapa's teachings. It's called kumbhaka, and I'll introduce it soon.

For now, remember positive relaxation indicates a vibrant posture in which the mind and body are in accord. When mind and body work as a single entity we're in our most natural and relaxed condition, but we're also brimming with strength as we saw in preceding experiments. Negative relaxation equals relaxing while devoid of mind-body unity. It's a dead posture, one of physical and mental collapse which equals surrendering vitality. Positive relaxation is packed with energy but free from needless tension. In Shin-shin-toitsu-do and in life a dynamic state balanced between tension and limpness is desirable.

Let the Body Settle into Its Natural Posture

One way to obtain the energetic state of positive relaxation is to respect gravity. Everything, including the body, falls downward. In other words, the mass of objects settles down. This simple observation can generate important changes in how we function.

Since things settle or fall downward, to relax and go with nature, we should let body mass settle downward naturally. Every object, including one's body, has a center of gravity. A stable and consequently "calm" object's center of gravity settles to a comparatively low position; an unstable object possesses a higher center of gravity. By assuming an erect, aligned position, which doesn't droop or slouch, upper body weight drops to a spot beneath the navel. This point equals our center of gravity and center of balance: our shita hara.

Japanese traditionally believed that to produce our fullest power we must concentrate power in the abdominal area (hara). Nakamura Sensei espoused the same concept. Yet this is a fairly non-specific statement, and general statements are often only generally accurate. More explicitly, we must center the mind's power in the lower abdomen, which is called shita hara or *tanden* in Japan. Still more specifically, we should focus energy at a point, or natural center, below the bellybutton. This spot is sometimes explained to be three *sun* beneath the navel. (Sun is an antiquated Japanese measurement; three sun is roughly 3.6 inches.) In current times, for bigger Westerners and larger modern Japanese, around four finger widths underneath the bellybutton is a fine place to focus the mind and thus ki.

The precise place differs according to individual size. Accordingly, instead of saying the right center of concentration is unerringly four inches beneath the navel it's more useful to measure using your fingers. A slighter person has smaller fingers, and a bigger individual's fingers are wider as a rule. Although a measurement of four inches might be correct for typical adults, it's excessively low on a child and may not be low enough for unusually tall men. Using varying size fingers circumvents this difficulty; most of us have fingers in proportion with our bodies.

Assume an upright, relaxed posture and the center of gravity settles at a point on the front exterior of the lower abdomen, which relates to our center of balance. By sinking awareness to this spot, we interconnect the mind and body achieving positive relaxation. Harmony of mind and body then results in an extremely stable posture and dynamic condition.

This posture and mind-set is powerful to the point of being apparently immovable. Nakamura Sensei would regularly sit in the lotus position as he relaxed and unified his mind and body. He would ask a volunteer to stand behind him, squat, and then try to lift him off the floor. Even though he was of slender build, unless he deliberately lost coordination of mind and body, he was nearly impossible to lift; and he could teach the average person to duplicate this immovable mind/immovable body feat. On the other hand, although this posture produces great stability of mind and body we're still capable of fast response and graceful movement.

By frequently experimenting with the differences between collapse, relaxation, and tension, we implant these distinctions in the subconscious producing functional and positive relaxation. In this manner we achieve a relaxed but energetic condition in which we're prepared to coolly meet any crisis or hectic circumstances. To try this out stay away from a posture that's flaccid and looks small, bent, or withdrawn. Also steer clear of exaggeratedly erect, stiff positions. Not sure why? Look at people who use their bodies with effectiveness, dexterity, and mobility. We rarely see top athletes adopt rigid, uptight stances because speedy movement from such postures isn't easy.

Does this also ring true for non-athletic activities? To find out, experiment with a posture that's fully erect and relaxed—but not inflexible—a position embodying the large presence mentioned earlier. This is the posture of mind and body coordination; it's more comfortable, more relaxed, more powerful, and far healthier than some other ways of using the mind/body.

When we utilize Shin-shin-toitsu-do to learn to relax under stress we discover moving meditation that contains true and immovable calmness. And in the end, serenity is strength.

Kumbhaka Posture and Breathing

Let's recap what we've covered thus far with Principle Three: Use the Body Obeying the Laws of Nature:

1. We accomplish little with the mind alone so training the body to be healthy and efficient enough to effectively respond to mental commands is important.

2. When the mind is in the present we sense what's natural in terms of sleeping, eating, and posture.
3. A posture embodying positive, functional relaxation is vital for mind and body coordination and health.
4. We arrive at this posture that's "not tense/not limp" by dropping the shoulders and body weight down toward a natural center in the lower abdomen.
5. Focusing our ki and mental power at this point is also useful.

Points four and five connect to a dynamic posture which Nakamura Sensei emphasized results in calmness, mind and body unification, and the "stabilizing of the nervous system." Though it's possible to center the mind at the shita hara to become calm, if the nervous system is strained during heavy stress this isn't always easy. So, Nakamura Sensei presented his adaptation of a special technique for regulating the nervous system and focusing ki in the shita hara that he learned in India. It's called kumbhaka in Sanskrit (*kunbahaka* in Japanese), and you'll recall it was one of the first exercises Nakamura Sensei practiced in Gorkhe.

To recap, Kaliapa taught that kumbhaka was important for maintaining a positive condition in the mind and body. He indicated it was akin to a "spiritual body," which could endure hardships in the Himalayas. Since he only gave hints about how to do kumbhaka he tried to help students discover it themselves via meditation in an icy stream. With his lower body submerged, Nakamura Sensei attempted to find a posture which would enable him to endure the cold. The idea was that once he could stay still in the freezing water for some time he'd have intuitively hit upon kumbhaka. He eventually manifested this immovable mind and body.

In Nakamura Sensei's straightforward method kumbhaka refers to two techniques for mind-body unity:

1. A posture of self-harmony that settles upper body weight beneath the navel, coordinates mind and body, and regulates the autonomic nervous system
2. A breathing technique to center ki at the shita hara even in moments of severe stress

Let's start with the kumbhaka posture. Posture and attitude connect to the nervous system, which Nakamura Sensei explained in his books, writing that our nervous system is highly sophisticated in terms of processing, reflecting, and reacting to various facets of its immediate environment. Stimuli from this environment are transmitted to the brain through the nervous system where they affect various senses and feelings. Those leading a life filled with negative feelings and tension tend to have a nervous system that's over-reactive. For such people even a small stimulus—if it is perceived as being negative—is carried to their brain and exaggerated. This, in turn, creates more tension and negativity.[32]

Perhaps by repeatedly activating the "fight or flight response" in the nervous system the body becomes accustomed to utilizing this reaction. It seems logical that a person who's habitually tense will respond to numerous situations with tension, leading to pointless activation of the sympathetic nervous system, which encourages anxiety and unneeded adrenalin production. Although science must further research this phenomenon, Nakamura Sensei's observations make intuitive sense. He wrote that constant and needless activation of the sympathetic nervous system causes mental stability to be lost, and the overwrought nervous system has a damaging impact on the body's health as well as most aspects of life. Adjusting and calming the reactions of our nervous system is most easily accomplished by "stabilizing the *shinkei so* (plexuses) existing in some of the major parts of the body."[33]

A plexus is a nerve center where multiple nerves join and signals are sent to (and received from) different body parts. If a plexus is disrupted this leads to serious problems in the nervous system, so perhaps we can enhance nervous system functionality by improving the performance of various plexuses throughout the body. Unfortunately scientific studies haven't been done to determine how kumbhaka "stabilizes" nerve centers. As a result, we need to experiment with these ideas and personally determine their worth.

To accomplish this, we can start by noting how we feel when we use kumbhaka posture and/or breathing. Do we feel calmer? Can we remain unruffled under pressure, especially during moments of sudden stress (like a car loudly backfiring)? Does our nervous system report stimuli as they really are, without exaggerating them? All of these examples indicate stability of the mind and nervous system, which is what kumbhaka was designed to promote.

Furthermore, some people's autonomic nervous systems may be dulled, in that they react to stimuli as if the stimuli are muffled. They display under-reaction, sluggish reaction, or no response. Using a correct, natural posture and a harmonized mind and body it's possible to preserve the autonomic nervous system in a balanced, ordered state. To arrive at kumbhaka posture is crucial in Shin-shin-toitsu-do, and Nakamura Sensei condensed its fundamentals to just three principles:

1. Relax and drop the shoulders.
2. Focus ki at a point in the lower abdomen.
3. Close the anus.

Although these points are simple to read, a true understanding of precisely what Nakamura Sensei meant by them is another issue. Not all of his students concur on their explanation of the above principles. The subsequent details are based on what I've absorbed from working with direct pupils of Nakamura Sensei. It reflects my present understanding of kumbhaka posture.

Relax and Drop the Shoulders

Dropping the shoulders is imperative for relaxation. Due to gravity, unless the shoulders stay in their natural position, relaxation is challenging. Let the shoulders settle with gravity into their most comfortable location. It isn't difficult.

Just lift and drop your shoulders three times. On the third time, leave them alone. Don't hold them up, but don't deliberately press them down.

Dropping the shoulders is simple but sustaining this state is another matter. People elevate the shoulders abnormally when leaning on something, when carrying a suitcase, when shaken by a backfiring truck, and in countless other situations. The unsettling of the shoulders doesn't have to be large to generate unease, tense shoulders, and headaches. Just slightly lifting them produces tension; this throws the nervous system out of equilibrium. Nakamura Sensei noticed that relaxing and dropping the shoulders prevents the diaphragm, where nerve plexus are centered and dense, from "going up and losing energy." When people are shocked, angry, or sad, their diaphragms are often unsettled. This upsets natural abdominal breathing causing us to breathe from the upper chest and shoulders, which also tend to be unsettled. Such unnatural breathing has a harmful effect on the body and nervous system. Just dropping the shoulders makes us feel calmer and more settled.[34]

When the diaphragm and shoulders rise up abdominal movement correlating to natural breathing alters, with the solar plexus and nervous system being negatively affected. In *Searching for Truth in Life* Nakamura Sensei wrote that nerves are highly concentrated in the solar plexus, the pit of the stomach just below the sternum (breastbone). This spot is a *kyusho*, a vital point in the human body. If it's struck hard in Japanese martial arts it has a damaging effect, which is why martial artists attack this point in their opponents even as they strive to protect their own solar plexus. He also wrote:

> Ki is life energy; it exists in every cell in the body. It flows through the body's nerves. As the solar plexus is a large collection of nerves, we can say a great amount of energy exists in the solar plexus. This method (kumbhaka) enables us to balance, regulate, and preserve the energy in this region, which has a vitalizing effect on the whole body.[35]

The solar plexus is a thick bundle of nerve cells and supporting tissue, located behind the stomach in the area of the celiac artery, just below the diaphragm. Abounding in ganglia and interrelated neurons it's the largest autonomic nerve center in the abdominal cavity. Experiment with keeping the shoulders down and relaxed; you can see if this promotes breathing from the diaphragm and what this does to the solar plexus and nervous system. If you master this state you'll soon note that the shoulders are more relaxed, and that they stop heaving up and down even when breathing deeply. Instead, breathing will produce more movement in the abdominal area than the chest and shoulders, movement that in turn affects the solar plexus. And all of this should result in deeper levels of calmness and in a nervous system that is "stable."

Note as well that our shoulders don't raise themselves. What do we feel when they rise up? What psychological states lead to this moment? One's body mirrors the mind, so raising the shoulders not only produces tension; it's a sign of anxiety. What beliefs, attitudes, and habits produce this anxiety? Answering these questions is crucial.

Dropping the shoulders is easy. Sometimes keeping them down isn't. Why do they go back up? In other words, once we relax why does tension return? What's its starting point?

By remaining in the present, without predetermined ideas or beliefs, we can observe ourselves clearly so we needn't guess at questions like these. We can see into our genuine nature by watching ourselves in relationship to others and the universe.

Focus Ki at a Point in the Lower Abdomen

Relax the upper body and weight settles to a point under the navel, which leads to Nakamura Sensei's second rule for kumbhaka. Precisely how to put ki into the lower abdomen is what must be understood. As noted, this can be accomplished by releasing tension, allowing body weight to fall to the shita hara by working with gravity, and focusing concentration, and therefore ki, about four finger widths underneath the navel. Concentrating the mind at that abdominal point makes certain the body's center of gravity is in the lower trunk because the mind moves the body.

With this technique we focus psychophysical energy in the shita hara. Once the mind grows still at this spot the body relaxes and upper body weight responds to relaxation. In short, body weight settles into the shita hara. A posture that's remarkably stable, yet capable of rapid reaction, is formed. It's a steady structure, bottom-heavy instead of top-heavy. This is one of the keys to Nakamura Sensei's remarkable ability to make his body very difficult for another person to lift or move when he sat in the lotus position. He could produce the same effect in other postures and while lying down, making it hard for students to lift his shoulders and upper body off the floor. (I'll explain how you can do this as well in a few more paragraphs.)

Once we get the sensation of unifying the mind and body by centering ourselves in the shita hara, we needn't persist in focusing the mind here. At this juncture, to bring the power of mind-body harmony into daily dealings act naturally and go about your business. If we become on edge, or in some way drop this condition of relaxed harmony, we just have to to re-center ourselves in the shita hara.

Close the Anus

To coin a term, relaxation can be misconstrued as "collapsation," which is unproductive for mind-body unification and regulating our nervous system. To generate postural balance Nakamura Sensei indicated the body's muscles—especially the sphincter muscles—shouldn't collapse or fall flaccid. Why he presented this recommendation has roots in India, where he encountered the concept, and certain Japanese techniques, which are to some extent comparable. The fundamental idea is that the constricting power of the anus is associated with human life power.

Certain works on Indian yoga depict an anal *bandha*, or "lock." (Bandha typically involve contraction of specific muscles.) The importance of naturally closing the anus is also associated with Zen meditation. Zen teachers sometimes recount the following story which emphasizes this point.

In ancient times a ferryboat was wrecked by a storm, and most people on board drowned. A coroner came and examined the bodies. He found a man, who looked like a monk, that didn't appear to be dead yet.

He said to his subordinate, "He doesn't seem dead."

The assistant answered, "He's not breathing. He's dead."

The coroner retorted, "He's capable of being revived. Examine his anus. I think you'll find it's closed and not flaccid."

His anus was examined and found "closed." They took care of the drowned monk and revived him. The coroner asked him, "Who are you?"

"I'm just a monk practicing Zen. My teacher is a priest named Hakuin. When I started this trip, he advised me not let my anus fall limp, particularly if I encountered some moment of great stress. I thought it was strange advice, but when we were hit by the storm I followed my teacher's guidance."[36]

This tale illustrates not only the advice of the famed Zen teacher Hakuin, but also the nature of *kappo*, an ancient Japanese art of resuscitation. It can revive an individual whose breathing has ceased due to drowning or strangulation. However, while kappo healers could bring around people who'd been insensible in the water for a number of minutes, recovery wasn't always feasible. To decide if they should try kappo some experts inserted a finger into the victim's anus. If no muscular resistance or response was present, the situation was deemed impossible as the nervous system no longer reacted to stimulus. Conversely, if resistance was present, or if the muscles weren't lifeless, then kappo was attempted often with successful results. Like Zen and yoga, some Japanese healing arts see a connection between the contracting vigor of the anus and life power.

Proper harmonization of mind and body requires an equally proper posture. This posture is one in which all body parts, internally and externally, are tied together. We want a posture in which our muscles work as a unit. As noted earlier, it's a position that's not tense but not floppy or disjointed. This lack of slackness extends to internal and external parts of the body, in this case, the anus.

What Does the Kumbhaka Posture Feel Like?

Although kumbhaka can be described via the three points above, it's difficult to verbally communicate physical sensations and psychological states. To remedy this I have students try this exercise:

- Lie down on your back with the arms and legs straight.
- Lift the buttocks a couple inches off the ground.

- Gently lower the buttocks back down. Touch the floor lightly and without allowing the lower back to sag.
- Wiggle the arms and legs to make sure they're relaxed, but maintain the firm feeling just generated in the lower back, lower abdomen, and buttocks/anus.

This exercise results in positive relaxation. You're not tense, but you're not limp. Of equal importance the lower abdomen feels moderately firm as does the lower back. These areas aren't tense, but they also aren't flaccid. We can note the same for the anus. However, this condition can't be found if the buttocks drop limply and heavily to the floor.

The sensation produced relates to kumbhaka posture. Because the middle portion of the body (abdomen, lower back, buttocks/anus) is gently firmed the entire body works as a unit. Successful athletes always use their bodies this way, and these days they often refer to it as "engaging the core," although how closely this parallels kumbhaka probably depends on individual interpretation. Conversely, if the middle part of the body is loose and limp we can't easily coordinate the actions of the upper body and the legs/feet. Then we function in a disjointed manner like a marionette. This is negative relaxation.

Still, if we keep excessive tension in our midsection we're uncomfortable, easily tired, and unable to move fluidly and quickly. The above exercise gives us the feeling of connecting the entire body in a potent way that's neither tense nor slack. Want to find out how potent? Try the following test of your kumbhaka posture with a friend:

- Lie down on your back with the arms and legs straight. Lift the buttocks, and then drop them heavily to the floor.
- Ask your partner to kneel behind you, near your head, and slowly lift your shoulders straight up with both hands. Note how easily they come off the floor.
- Next, lie back again with the arms and legs straight. Lift the buttocks, and then gently lower them to the floor. Touch the floor lightly and without allowing the lower back to sag. Maintain the slightly firm feeling in the center of your body.
- Have your partner slowly lift your shoulders again, and notice if it is more difficult for him to do so.

If done correctly he or she will have surprising difficulty because the whole body must be moved as one piece. This is yet another test of mind and body unification devised by Nakamura Sensei in the 1920s, and the power of this unified posture is impressive. It's an important part of what allowed him to produce the nearly "unliftable" posture alluded to earlier. But remember, if you just plop your butt down limply your shoulders can be lifted.

We can maintain this feeling in various positions—besides on our backs—in everyday life. Because this natural approach to kumbhaka equals sitting, standing, walking, and lying down with a light, uncollapsed posture which looks big, we can maintain it without much deliberate effort. Make sure your kumbhaka posture is comfortable. It's difficult to produce a habit through repeated practice when the trained activity doesn't feel comfortable. We don't frequently practice what we don't enjoy.

We can maintain this relaxed, but not limp, sensation in the shita hara and anus in positions besides reclining using slightly different techniques:

- Sit cross-legged and slumped (**Fig. 8**). Observe the loose feeling in the shita hara, buttocks, and anus.
- Next, with complete awareness, little by little straighten your lower back, so you re-establish your natural forward lumbar curve (**Fig. 9**).
- As you correct your posture note how the muscles slightly firm up in the abdomen, lower back, and sphincter. The sensation is more subtle than in the preceding exercise; you may need to attempt this drill several times to find the feeling described.

Be careful not to over arch the lower back. This is more tension than kumbhaka, which involves an expansive posture that feels buoyant. When sitting in a chair, for example, sit down lightly. You'll hit upon positive relaxation as before. In contrast, notice what happens to the look of your posture and the sensation in your muscles when you plunk down heavily. Be buoyant in every position as if you're floating as the axis of the universe, and you can sustain kumbhaka in daily living.

Simplifying the Posture of Kumbhaka

Nakamura Sensei's books primarily explained kumbhaka posture using the three points above; the same was true of his classes for the public. However he taught some

Fig. 8. Slump into a collapsed posture. Notice the flaccid feeling in the lower abdomen and around the anus.

Fig. 9. Slowly roll the pelvis forward and restore the natural forward curvature of the lumbar vertebrae. Continue this action until you feel the lower abdomen and the area around the anus become more firm. This results in a posture based on kumbhaka.

advanced students a way of realizing these three points in life without deliberately focus-ing on them. It ties into the preceding postural advice, and I'll explain one aspect of this simplified kumbhaka posture now:

- Stand with your feet side by side, about shoulder width apart.
- Lift your heels at least two inches off the floor, keep your eyes parallel to the ground, and find the posture you can easily balance with (**Fig. 10**).
- Without lowering your heels note that balance is most effectively main-tained when your weight is centered toward your big toes. What happens to your balance if you let your weight roll to the outside edges of your feet, toward your little toes?
- Without lowering your heels note that you can also balance most easily when your posture is erect but relaxed. What happens to your balance if you make your spine ramrod straight or if you slump?
- Without lowering your heels note that balance is effortlessly maintained when your shoulders are down and relaxed. What happens to your balance if you lift and tense your shoulders?
- Without lowering your heels note that a balanced posture isn't tense nor is it limp. The lower abdomen and buttocks become gently firm while the anus closes. Simultaneously upper body weight moves forward and down toward the shita hara.
- Finally, lower your body straight down while keeping your weight toward the big toes (**Fig. 11**). To do this, don't rock back on your heels flat-footed or lock your knees. Place the heels lightly on the ground with a slight bend in the knees. In short, don't alter the correct and balanced posture you dis-covered while the heels were raised.

By standing lightly and keeping the big toes pressed firmly against the ground, we more easily and unconsciously maintain kumbhaka posture in daily actions. Look at your shoes to see if your weight is typically toward your big toes. If the outside edge of your shoes wears out first you're rolling your feet toward the little toes as you walk and stand. This upsets balance and makes coordinated movement in life difficult. And a chronically unbalanced posture is chronically tense.

Arriving at kumbhaka posture, by keeping the weight and power focused toward the big toes, is a technique championed by Yamada Chikaaki Sensei, who until his death

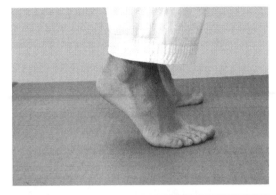

Fig. 10. Lift your heels. Keep them elevated until you find a stable posture. Note that this occurs when your weight is concentrated on the underside of your big toes.

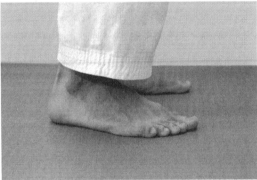

Fig. 11. Lower your body straight down and lightly touch your heels to the ground. Do not alter the stable posture you discovered while balancing on the balls of the feet. There should still be a sensation of power in the big toes.

in 2006 was one of the oldest living students of Nakamura Sensei and one of the most senior Shin-shin-toitsu-do teachers in Japan. (Some photos of Nakamura Sensei in this book are courtesy of the late Yamada Sensei.)

It can take time to intuitively find the optimal way of balancing with the heels elevated. Try staying in this position for a minute or so, gradually refining your balance. Then touch down lightly to preserve both balance and the three points for kumbhaka posture. (Focusing your mind at the shita hara, the natural center in the lower abdomen, also helps you balance with your heels raised.)

In everyday life, see if you're resting on your heels or if your big toes are pressed firmly against the ground. You can regain correct posture anytime by raising your heels so your big toes press strongly against the floor and then touching the heels down lightly. Repeated practice creates a positive habit equaling positive relaxation.

Kumbhaka, Breathing, and Recovering Composure

What if calmness and relaxation is lost and attempts to still the mind at the shita hara fail to generate composure? To handle this situation Nakamura Sensei taught kumbhaka breathing.

What's your breathing like when you're asleep or stress-free? How about when you're frightened or mad? In Asia full and slow breathing is linked to serenity and meditation. Hurried, shallow respiration is thought to indicate psychological and physical tension. Yet this phenomenon isn't exclusive to India or Japan. If you examine your breathing and mood I think you'll see the mind-breath link is a worldwide experience.

Kumbhaka breathing involves deep, unhurried respiration—including the deliberate retention of breath after inhalation and exhalation—which utilizes our complete lung capacity. Oxygenated blood has a soothing effect on the body. Sadly, few people employ their lungs wholly and effectively, so their health suffers. Nakamura Sensei was well aware of this, writing that breathing exercises, or pranayama, are an important part of Indian yoga. His advice was to perform deep breathing a few times whenever exhaustion is experienced. Make sure the posture of kumbhaka is maintained, especially between exhalation and inhalation, and fatigue lessens.[37]

What follows is an adaptation of Nakamura Sensei's kumbhaka breathing; it's simple enough that the average person can easily use it to recover lost calmness. (It's also what I'm teaching to the general public. Other teachers have sometimes varying interpretations of kumbhaka.) We can apply it in most situations, but it's critical to personify the three postural principles.[38]

Although we can execute kumbhaka breathing using the mouth, it's frequently simpler and more discreet to breathe through the nose:

- Exhale and then breathe in slowly, fully, and peacefully as if you're filling your entire body with oxygen. As you breathe in, mentally direct the air to your shita hara. Make sure your shoulders don't come up.
- Then hold your breath for a few seconds. Have the feeling of sinking all of the air in the direction of your lower abdomen and center your ki in the shita hara. This is a critical moment in kumbhaka breathing.
- Now breathe out gradually, peacefully, and completely. The exhalation is longer and stronger than the inhalation. Pause and hold your breath for a moment at the end of your exhalation, another important moment in this breathing method.

Just a few repetitions of this breathing cycle helps restore composure. Because you're mentally aiming air in the direction of the shita hara you'll efficiently breathe from the diaphragm, breathing fully and abdominally. This is healthier, deeper, and more calming than breathing from the chest. When you imagine retaining your inhalation in the lower abdomen the descending force of the diaphragm creates a sensation of peaceful power in the shita hara. This visceral feeling makes it easier to concentrate the mind (and thus ki) beneath the bellybutton. Therefore, you can more successfully quiet your mind in the shita hara. Holding a lungful of air, so a descending movement of the diaphragm is created, is the most vital moment in kumbhaka breathing.

Holding the breath right after exhaling is similarly important. At the end of breathing in or out power is concentrated under the navel, and the anus is closed. Nonetheless, this should occur naturally and with no great strain. Avoid vigorously thrusting the shita hara in and out as you breathe or too forcefully tightening the shita hara and anus. Based on discussions with direct pupils of Nakamura Sensei, photographs, and films, it's clear to me that Nakamura Sensei's breathing was natural and relaxed.

It is the improved oxygen intake, with descending pressure of the diaphragm to the shita hara during breath retention, which makes this an uncomplicated method to relax and still the mind at the shita hara even in the midst of immense stress. Teachers of Indian yoga also point out that ancient yogis realized when something startling happens people have an innate inclination to momentarily hold their breath, which allows for rapid response and quick decisions. Nakamura Sensei noted we naturally stop breathing when threading a needle or when exerting great effort to move a heavy object. We do this whenever we need the full power of either the mind or body. For this reason, Kaliapa and Nakamura Sensei taught appropriate and brief breath retention aids in mind and body unification.

While kumbhaka breathing is used before trying something difficult or when we lose our cool, the posture of kumbhaka is maintained throughout every exercise in Shin-shin-toitsu-do. Actually we can maintain it during daily activity, and the right posture is helpful for eliminating back pain, stiff necks, and physical awkwardness. It aids in a long, comfortable life.

Kumbhaka in Indian Yoga

Typically in Indian yoga kumbhaka refers exclusively to the moment in pranayama breathing when the breath is suspended. This moment can occur after inhalation, after exhalation, or at both times. In some instances in Indian yoga kumbhaka is accompanied by various bandhas, "locks," which entail muscular contraction. Commonly performed in conjunction with deep breathing, the most common bandhas in pranayama involve:

1. "Lifting" or flexing of the muscles near the perineum (*mula bandha*)
2. Closing the throat by dropping the chin to the chest (*jalandhara bandha*)
3. Flexing of the abdominal muscles (*uddiyana bandha*)

In some cases *ashwini bandha*, contracting the anus, is substituted for mula bandha although the former seems more common. Two out of three of these "locks" have something in common with Nakamura Sensei's kumbhaka breathing. Nevertheless, Nakamura Sensei's method represents either a unique version of pranayama breathing taught by Kaliapa, or it's Nakamura Sensei's alteration of what he learned in India. Perhaps kumbhaka breathing is a combination of the two, and since no official version of yoga exists in India scores of singular, lesser known interpretations of pranayama exist. Although the precise origins and evolution of Nakamura Sensei's kumbhaka breathing are a bit cloudy, using "kumbhaka" to express a posture appears to be his adaptation of this word. In India kumbhaka usually describes the retention of breath during breathing exercises.

The Power of Mind and Body Unification

The first three of the Four Basic Principles to Unify Mind and Body equal mind and body coordination in action. When these three principles are integrated and embodied an outward projection of ki is released, abdominal centering occurs, and we attain functional relaxation as the shoulders and body weight settle into their natural place. This produces a remarkable strength that's essentially our full human potential, a power rarely realized. The extraordinary power of mind and body unification can be manifested at work, in school, during sports . . . any time in life.

Let's try another experiment to personally perceive this power in action. The following exercise like several others in this book was first taught by Nakamura Sensei in the 1920s.

EXPERIMENT FOURTEEN : MIND AND BODY UNIFICATION IN MOTION
As before, you'll need a partner to try this with.

- Ask your friend to lean forward, bracing himself so he'll be difficult to push backward. Stand a few feet away with your arms naturally extended. Refer to **Fig. 12** to get the idea of these positions.
- Focus your attention on your friend's body, walk forward, and try to push your partner backward using all your muscular strength. Unless you're considerably larger than your friend, given the braced posture this is difficult to accomplish (**Fig. 13**).
- Next, look gently at a point far off in the distance behind your partner. Think of sending ki through your arms, out of your fingers, and through the point you're concentrating on. Begin walking toward your partner.
- Then, when your hands contact your friend's body don't tense up and don't concentrate on their body. Keep your mind focused on the predetermined point with the feeling that ki from your hands is passing through your partner and moving through this spot (**Fig. 14**).
- Finally, continue walking toward this point, just as you would if your friend wasn't in your path. Don't stop physically or mentally at the point of contact; move your shita hara and hands ahead as a unit. Correctly done, this allows you to walk forward easily, effortlessly pushing your partner across the room as in **Fig. 15**.

Unlike the prior exercises Experiment Fourteen requires unification of mind and body in motion, which is more complicated. It's also more important in that we typically move in daily life. Here are a few tips for getting the desired result from Experiment Fourteen:

1. In Experiment Five you produced an arm which was difficult to bend. This type of arm (orenai te) must be maintained as you walk toward your partner. Leave your arms extended, or let them bend a bit, but once you touch the other person's body they must not collapse back toward you.
2. The shita hara and the hands move together. When you touch your partner if you only push with your arms you have limited power. If you let your arms collapse and only move your shita hara toward your partner nothing is accomplished. Move the lower abdomen, hands, and arms forward together while maintaining the space between your hands and body. In a nutshell, using your shita hara as the basis push with your entire body.

Fig. 12. Your partner braces himself to resist your push. Extend both arms and stand a few feet from him.

Fig. 13. Walk forward. Focus your mind on your partner's shoulder. Tense your body and try to push him backward several steps. Can you do it easily?

Fig. 14. Walk forward again. Focus your mind through a distant point behind your partner. Keep your mind there as you push your partner. Use a soft touch, relax, and do not alter your natural posture.

Fig. 15. Continue to concentrate off into the distance, without focusing on your partner, and you can effortlessly push him several steps across the room. You are displaying the power of mind and body unification in action.

3. Maintain the kumbhaka posture as you walk and then push. This allows the body to work as a unit.

4. A positive attitude is important. Before you walk feel that you'll definitely reach your point of visual focus. Succeed before you begin.

5. Concentration is important. Concentration is accomplished when the mind isn't attached to distracting thoughts and sensations. Don't worry about the person standing before you, especially when you touch them. If you stop your mind on them your body will stop too. If you try not to think about this person, you *are* thinking about them. Focus your ki in the direction you want to go in and then *do nothing*, walking forward as if they aren't in the way.

6. Struggling and fighting with your partner is being mentally fixated on them. This doesn't work. Neither does giving up. Walk as you would at any other time. Don't fight with your partner; don't give in to them either.

7. Along the same lines, don't tense your body as you push. Don't go limp. We want a mindset that isn't in conflict but isn't giving up; we want a body that isn't tense but isn't floppy.

8. Don't lean forward, hunch your back, or lift your shoulders as you push. Stand erect, keep your head and eyes level with the ground, and walk naturally.

This exercise embodies a positive, concentrated mind. It's a mind which perceives obstacles in life and yet isn't attached to these obstacles. Moreover, Experiment Fourteen illustrates the effectiveness of using the mind and body as a unit. So powerful is this coordination of mind and body that several *sumo* wrestlers have used these principles to become champions. One way of winning in sumo is by pushing the opponent out of the ring, and wrestlers trained in the above exercise have displayed a clear advantage over their massive adversaries. It's an advantage we can also learn to display in countless facets of life. To accomplish that, we must consider the most rational and efficient way of training our minds and bodies to accomplish this goal. That leads us to the last of the Four Basic Principles to Unify Mind and Body.

Principle Four: Train the Body Progressively, Systematically, and Regularly

Shin-shin-toitsu-do practice contains multiple types of physical training, most of which aren't outlined in *The Teachings of Tempu*. Some methods for training the body were detailed in my book *Japanese Yoga: The Way of Dynamic Meditation*, but they're beyond the scope of *The Teachings of Tempu*. With that noted, in such movements it's crucial to exercise naturally. We can say the same for any variety of physical training. If we don't exercise naturally, we're certain to sustain injury, making ongoing practice hard. Nakamura Sensei's fourth rule gives us an opportunity to consider what is—and is not—natural in terms of training our bodies.

The body must be developed gradually to circumvent pulled muscles and other problems. It's regrettable that some folks began a program of physical education to protect themselves from sickness as well as injuries, and in the process they hurt themselves. To sidestep injury exercise progressively. As doctors and sports medicine experts will verify an ideal means of "warming up" for any physical activity is to softly carry out the actions of this activity. Students should move gently at the start of an exercise and with every repetition steadily add force. As an example, Nakamura Sensei was fond of jogging; if you feel the same way jog lightly as you start your run and add speed as you warm up.

We not only progress by degrees from week to week. We develop from moment to moment within a particular exercise. How slowly a person builds up to greater effort is decided by age and body condition. It's possible for older people—who are serious and genuine—to practice the majority of Shin-shin-toitsu-do, but they should increase the intensity of their training gradually. We can apply the same idea to weight training, aerobic exercise, and other methods of physical development.

It's also indispensable to exercise the mind and body in an organized, habitual way. Physical parts of Shin-shin-toitsu-do which are engaged in infrequently aren't just less valuable; they can be possibly risky if carried too far. This is obviously the case for any type of exercise. Placing abrupt stress on a body that may have fallen out of shape isn't smart. Consequently it's better to exercise a reasonable amount on a regular basis than to train a lot occasionally.

Keep in mind as well that both mind and body seldom stay the same for long. All of nature exists in a state of incessant transformation. The benefits of Shin-shin-toitsu-do lie in sustained practice. If we stop practicing, regardless of how long we've studied (or how gifted we are) our wellbeing and skill degrade. Shin-shin-toitsu-do is useful only as long as we're somehow participating in it. The same is true for running, swimming, martial arts, and most exercise.

At times Shin-shin-toitsu-do students wonder if the time they devote to their practice is worth what they get out of it. This seems sensible, but it actually shows a failure to grasp Shin-shin-toitsu-do. Essentially, the time we put into practicing a meditative discipline *is* what we get out of it. It's the *process of involvement* that's really valuable not some far away objective or by-product of involvement.

Life exists solely at this moment. The past and the future dwell only in our thoughts. In Shin-shin-toitsu-do we learn to rest calmly in the here and now. In a timeless perception of the moment we understand a state transcending fear of the future, regret about the past, and duality itself.

Thus, the practice is the objective. Time and thoughts of future development needn't be involved. To practice Shin-shin-toitsu-do with real awareness is to concurrently perceive the special benefits of Shin-shin-toitsu-do training.

It's possible, regardless of age, to take part in Shin-shin-toitsu-do and meditation in some manner, if we truly desire to do so. *The Teachings of Tempu* focuses mainly on the worldview of Nakamura Sensei, principles of mind and body unification, and meditation. Nonetheless, Shin-shin-toitsu-do includes forms of physical training, and we might imagine these must be curtailed for elderly practitioners. Nothing could be further from the truth. My teachers are senior citizens, but they're in excellent health. Actually, with gradual, ongoing, and logical Shin-shin-toitsu-do exercise it's possible to keep improving even as we grow old, because the art doesn't need great physical might, and it equals an endless, moving meditation. And in the rare cases where we sustain a chronic, debilitating injury or health problem it's possible to customize training programs. Elderly practitioners can also continue learning and growing via teaching and writing about Shin-shin-toitsu-do. The key to regular and lifelong practice is attitude more than physical condition.

Plus, ongoing physical exercise has been scientifically documented as affecting the brain and attitude. According to writer Jorge Cruise:

Researchers at the Salk Institute for Biological Studies in San Diego have linked physical exercise to neurogenesis, the scientific term for new brain cell growth.

"There is growing evidence that regular and consistent, moderate physical exercise can improve cognitive performance in young, healthy individuals and the aging population," says Fred H. Gage, lead researcher of the study and Adler professor at the Salk Institute. "Our own research revealed that physical exercise increases the birth and survival of new brain cells in the mouse hippocampus, a brain area important for learning and memory."[39]

Such evidence reinforces Nakamura Sensei's assertion that the mind and body are one. It also could suggest that consistent exercise may help in everything from the prevention of Alzheimer's to avoiding locking your keys in your car.

Natural Methods to Train the Body in Daily Life

Besides kumbhaka posture and breathing, Nakamura Sensei taught a variety of methods to train the body in the midst of daily activities and offered broad advice to keep the body healthy, which will be covered in an upcoming chapter. To train our bodies regularly we needn't solely depend on Shin-shin-toitsu-do exercises that are troublesome to learn from a book. Nakamura Sensei mentioned we can use simple everyday actions and forms of exercise to stay healthy. This is important because getting exercise is essential for maintaining a proper metabolism. But moderation in exercise should be considered, too. Over exercising, just like overeating or overdoing anything, isn't ideal for the body.

We can get ongoing exercise in the course of our everyday lives if we rely on ourselves instead of technology. We can walk instead of drive, take the stairs instead of the elevator, exercise as a form of recreation instead of watching TV. However, exercise in the midst of ordinary living may not be enough to sustain the health of the average person. Therefore, Nakamura Sensei's advice was to take a brisk walk each day. Some forms of exercise aren't easily available at all times or to all people, and some exercises are too severe for the elderly and infirm, but usually walking can be easily accomplished. It's free, and it evenly exercises the body as a whole.[40]

The Four Basic Principles to Unify Mind and Body, which consist of significant sub-points such as the outward movement of ki, centering in the lower abdomen, positive relaxation, and letting body mass gravitate, can be utilized by people of any age, culture, or sex. The first principle refers to a mental state to be maintained, and the second principle indicates the best way to use the mind in this state. Similarly, the third principle refers to the state we should keep the body in, while the fourth principle indicates how to use or train the body (to remain healthy).

These four principles, along with related concepts and methods like kumbhaka posture and breathing, come under three broad categories frequently mentioned by

Hashimoto Tetsuichi Sensei, a top student of Nakamura Tempu Sensei. He teaches that continuing, organized training in Shin-shin-toitsu-do in the end consists of just these three straightforward and wide-ranging fundamentals:

1. Practice to reveal the essence of a positive mind.
2. Restructuring the subconscious mind
3. Maintaining a balanced and stable state in the nervous system.

Subsequent chapters of *The Teachings of Tempu* cover techniques which also correlate to these three central pillars of Shin-shin-toitsu-do listed above. It's an elegantly simple and unusually profound art of health maintenance and spiritual transformation.

Chapter 5

PRINCIPLES FOR REALIZING A POSITIVE ATTITUDE & CONCENTRATION

FIVE PRINCIPLES FOR A POSITIVE MIND

1. Examine the mind.

2. Analyze suggestions received from your environment.

3. Examine your attitude toward others.

4. Discover the present, and let worrying about the future or the past fall away.

5. Experience and follow reiseishin.

Throughout *The Teachings of Tempu* I've repeated Nakamura Tempu Sensei's emphasis on a positive mind, since positive thinking is central to his teachings:

To summarize, the essential principle of my realization is this:

This world is intrinsically a beautiful place, in harmony with itself, where people should be cheerful and happy. It is not a realm where people must suffer or live in agony.

The essential attitude we must take in Shin-shin-toitsu-do is this:

We must maintain a positive mind under any circumstances while living nobly and with confidence.[41]

These two simple ideas are incredibly insightful, containing within their words life-altering truths. The 21st century Zen teacher Brad Warner notes something similar with a writing style accessible to numerous Americans today:

> . . . This world is better than paradise, better than any Utopia you can imagine. I say that in the face of war and starvation and suicide bombings and Orange Terror alerts. This world is better than Utopia because—and follow this point carefully—you can never live in Utopia. Utopia is always somewhere else. That's the very definition of Utopia.
>
> Maybe you can go to a paradisiacal island, far away from your boss and your bills and anything else you want, but pretty soon you'll be complaining that you've got sand up your ass, or the snack machine ate your dollar, or hermit crabs stole your thongs. You'll always find something wrong with wherever you are because it will never quite match your idea of what "should" be.
>
> You can't go to paradise. Not now and not after you make your first million. Not after you die. And not if you eat all your peas and are really, really good. Not ever. What you call "you" can never enter the gates of heaven, no matter how convictedly [sic] you believe. Heaven and paradise aren't in your future because you have no future. There is no future for you. There is no future for anyone. There is no future at all. Future is an idea.
>
> You can't live in paradise—but you are living right here. Make this your paradise or make this your hell. The choice is entirely yours. Really.[42]

Warner's books reflect his punk rock background, but he writes of the same essential truth as Nakamura Sensei, aspects of which are contained in this chapter. Namely, the past and future are artificial constructs of the mind. They're unreal, and a truly positive mind exists now or not at all. As we'll see, it's this mind which can discover "this world is intrinsically a beautiful place." We'll also observe how we can change our reality via our attitude, something also noted by Zen teachers like Mr. Warner.

Positive thinking has been heralded by motivational speakers, athletic coaches, and doctors for some time now. Andy Barton, a British psychologist who successfully works with athletes in various sports, indicated in *Two Wheels Only* magazine:

The key to overcoming mental blocks is to focus on the positive, not the negative aspects of a situation. The brain can't actually make a representation of a negative, it can only make a positive one. For example if you tell a golfer not to think about hitting their tee shot into the woods, the brain will instantly image hitting a ball into the woods.

So you need to give your brain a positive scenario to focus on. Rather than thinking about what will happen if you miss the corner, crash or do something bad, focus on the good aspects. Think 'if I brake later I will go around the corner faster' rather than "if I brake later I could run into gravel.' The brain can only focus on one thought at a time. If you are thinking a positive then you can't think about a negative.[43]

Nakamura Sensei was one of the earliest proponents of the "attitude affects reality" philosophy. More than this, his rational step-by-step methodology was unique, and it remains uniquely effective even roughly 40 years after his death. His pragmatic approach is summarized above in the Five Principles for a Positive Mind, which he taught for decades to top Japanese athletes, captains of industry, famed writers and artists, and even a past Emperor (Hirohito). Here are just some of his more well-known students:

- Hara Takashi, Prime Minister of Japan
- Togo Heihachiro, Fleet Admiral of the Japanese Navy during the Russo-Japanese War (a.k.a. "the Nelson of the East")
- Sugiura Jugo, famed educator and President of Tokyo University
- Ishikawa Sodo, esteemed Zen Buddhist priest and head of Sojiji Temple
- Yokota Sennosuke, well-known politician and Justice Minister of Japan
- Prince Higashikuni Naruhiko, Prime Minister of Japan
- Ozaki Yukio, recipient of the Order of the Rising Sun and member of the House of Representatives of the Japanese Diet (a.k.a. "the father of the Japanese Constitution")
- Count Goto Shinpei, Home Minister and Foreign Minister of Japan
- Asano Soichiro, a famous Japanese businessman and entrepreneur

Of course, these principles have worked for ordinary people like me as well. Later I'll introduce methods for implanting positive ideas in the subconscious mind, which are performed just before falling asleep and upon waking up. The Five Principles for a Positive Mind, however, are used in the midst of our daily lives.

Principle One: Examine the Mind.

A positive outlook is most effortlessly arrived at through conscious and cogent examination of what's necessary to manifest positive thoughts in the first place. We can start by reflecting on the real and current state of the mind. Is your mind actually positive?

We've all met people who see themselves as being positive, yet aren't viewed by others in that way. Accordingly, we have to be sure to honestly examine our minds, but how do we examine something with no form, color, or weight? One's mind, being invisible, is elusive. It's therefore easier to observe the character of the mind through verbal expressions, actions, and postures. For instance, if we dramatically state, "It's so hot this week I feel like I'm going to die! I hope I don't get heatstroke!" then our feelings and language are negative. But if we just say it is 98-degrees Fahrenheit, this is a statement of fact. This statement isn't necessarily negative, and how we state this fact determines whether or not we're using negative verbal expressions. Such self-examination is introspection, and it's a vital first step in Shin-shin-toitsu-do. Maintaining an attentive state, in which self-awareness becomes doable, allows us to determine the roots of pessimism. This gives us a chance to become positive so our expressions and conduct are also positive making friends and family feel at ease, happy, and encouraged.

Our words indicate our mental state. They simultaneously affect the mind. If we say something we first have to think it. Repeated thought patterns alter the subconscious, where they're reinforced.

We might conclude from this that being positive means to constantly smile and say everything's wonderful. Smiling certainly benefits mental and physical health, but being positive doesn't rule out criticism and commenting on negative actions. It doesn't indicate we have to invariably say "yes" instead of "no." Nakamura Sensei was known for his encouraging speech but also for being a blunt and an outspoken critic of social ills, many of which are driven by excessive materialism. In a 1960s seminar he conducted for top CEOs and business leaders in Japan, he scolded:

> I don't think anyone has met someone who came into this world a second
> time—even if he or she was a great saint, a wise philosopher, an ordinary

person, a good person, an evil person, beautiful or not. All humans live only one life. This is why we must search for the best way of living.

If most of you were in your twenties or youths with many more years to come, I'd not give this kind of introduction to my talk. All of you look pretty old to me. The older we are the more deeply we have to think about our lives.

However, you might think, "My life isn't going to last much longer. Therefore it's useless thinking about life." If you feel this way, your way of living is clearly unconscious. It is definitely not aware or thoughtful. As the result, your life goes on in its usual haphazard way: sometimes good, sometimes bad, and all by accident. The result is you've wasted your life, without ever discovering the meaning and value of your existence. Despite this fact, I'm guessing this isn't what you really desire.

Please try to determine with me the first and most important thing we need to know about life. It's a bit strange to say this perhaps, but you know what you don't really need to know, and you don't know what you really have to know. When you face a big problem—a problem dealing with one of the profound uncertainties in life—your knowledge turns out to be of no use. You inevitably end up being scared as you don't know what you should know about life. You look very noble, confident, and calm when there's no serious life problem. But I'll bet many of you have even been confused or panicked by some small incident in your private or public affairs, haven't you? It's because you know what you don't really need to know, and you don't know what you really have to know.

You might be insulted by my words, but I'll not retract them because you really are obsessed with so many useless things. When I talk face to face with one of you, I'm often surprised by your great amount of knowledge about rubbish.[44]

Clearly Nakamura Sensei had no problem directing criticism toward attitudes and actions he felt were destructive. Thus saying no to poverty, bigotry, bloodshed, smog, and other collective problems isn't negative. It's smart.

Such remarks are statements of fact, and they should be stated with great conviction and vigor if we're to be positive. We can say, "Violence toward people, animals, and the environment is destructive to everyone, and humanity has the capability to eradicate it." This is a positive expression.

On the other hand, we might say, "Violence toward people, animals, and the environment is destructive to everyone, and humanity is doomed because of it." This is different from the first statement and clearly negative.

Being positive is to project ki completely into anything we're doing, to take action dynamically with the full force of the mind and body, throwing our whole being into the instant. It doesn't prohibit criticism. It actually refers to making each act—whatever that may be—with the total strength of one's mind and body. It's to live fully at every moment.

Principle Two: Analyze Suggestions Received from Your Environment.

It's not only imperative to consider if the mind is positive or negative, but we should also mull over the characteristics of our environment. Our surroundings are influenced by the language and actions of other individuals and by the look of our environment. A home or workplace that's organized and clean creates a different atmosphere from surroundings which are chaotic and filthy. And these are but a few of the nearly infinite assortment of factors that influence our attitudes daily. These factors equal "suggestions" we collect from our environment and circumstances. Which of these day by day suggestions are positive and which are negative is an important consideration.

By making this determination we can reorganize our surroundings so our subconscious minds are inclined toward positivity. Positive elements persuade the subconscious, which then sways our conscious feelings and actions. At the same time, by being cognizant of the influences in our environment—especially those we cannot control—we can be unmoved by the downbeat expressions, actions, or gestures of others. In this way we keep our minds free from pessimism.

Shin-shin-toitsu-do students stay away from negative statements, such as: "I'm not good enough to do it," not only because it weakens them, but because it creates a gloomy atmosphere for people around them. This brings us to the third of the Five Principles for a Positive Mind.

Principle Three: Examine Your Attitude Toward Others.

To manifest a positive mind, we must reflect on the effect our words and actions have on people near us. If we speak to them in a dispiriting way it can obviously depress them. Life is interrelated, so if we depress others this poisons our own surroundings.

Our friends, family, and coworkers after all comprise our daily environment.

When our actions encourage negativity among these people their depression can make us less optimistic and energetic. Before long we craft a "vicious cycle" via our negative conduct. This is a commonly unrealized source of conflict within families and even the world as a whole.

In Japan harmony has traditionally been greatly valued; Nakamura Sensei wasn't unique in emphasizing this idea, and harmony is important in Western culture as well. Lacking this quality a family, business, or country cannot function successfully. Harmony can—at least partly—be cultivated by using optimistic, heartening terms when addressing others.

Principle Four: Discover the Present, and Let Worrying About the Future or the Past Fall Away.

Residing in the here and now is also crucial for a positive psychological state. In old Japan, warriors frequently reflected on this idea. Descended from Japan's traditional warrior class, Nakamura Sensei occasionally indicated that for a samurai facing death was a daily concern. Japanese compare the samurai's life to the cherry blossom, which flowers for a short time, displays vibrant color and splendor, only to be strewn by the wind after a brief existence. Samurai were bound by a harsh system of behavior and accountability. Their foremost obligations and ethics centered on giving their lives in the service of their nation, clan, and feudal master. Associated with their responsibilities was the recognition that they could be forced to lay down their lives—with no hesitation—at any time.

For that reason, some warriors determined to live every moment as if it were their last. In doing so, according to historical writings, they lived wholeheartedly in the present, without hesitancy or regret. The samurai's objective wasn't to only survive but to live a complete and vibrant life.

For a samurai to preserve a positive outlook in the face of potential death, he learned not to be anxious about what went before or (especially) the future. This advice is also critical for modern people in both East and West. In essence, if the mind stays in the moment it's not possible to worry. Upon careful contemplation it becomes obvious that people worry only about an incident that previously transpired or which could occur in the future. This is true even if the event just happened or may take place in the next second. The present contains no time or space for anxiety.

Our past cannot be altered, and worrying about it isn't productive in terms of time or effort. By losing sleep over the future we drain ourselves, making us less capable of efficiently responding when the future actually arrives. Additionally, by worrying about a misfortune which may or may not happen we endure the incident two times: once when imagining it, and once more if and when we really experience it.

What's more, a mind locked in the past tends to recreate its past—not a good thing, especially if our past wasn't so great. Sports psychologist Andy Barton has explained to motorcyclists why this matters:

> Past experiences can also hamper performance. If someone crashed before, or even has watched a crash on TV, then this can form a phobia. This can also be overcome by thinking positive. The brain is protecting the body from what it sees as a threat, and you need to re-educate it. Change the language you use to think about your performance and always concentrate on positives rather than negatives.[45]

Barton has effectively worked with top soccer players, rugby players, swimmers, boxers, cricketers, cyclists, and PGA European Tour golfers to enhance their performance. His present-day advice about the mind creating phobias of past events and the need for positive thought echoes Nakamura Sensei's ideas.

In *Searching for Truth in Life* Nakamura Sensei emphasized the significance of keeping the mind in the present. He told a tale of a foolish person, who raises up his torch walking along a road at night, trying to see what lies over 100 meters ahead. While he's worrying about what might be off in the distance he'll stumble over what's beneath his feet right now. If he watches his step with the torch, noticing his present situation, he can walk easily. He also quoted an old Japanese saying, "Keep your mind on the immediate present, and do not worry about what has already gone and what has not yet come."[46]

By holding the mind in the moment, except for when we intentionally want to think about the past or tomorrow, we face life without trepidation. At that moment no thoughts of previous disappointments or upcoming troubles are in the psyche. This results in a genuinely positive psychological condition: fudoshin—the "immovable mind."

REALITY IS NOW

If the mind resides in the past or the future we're not experiencing reality. We are instead dealing with memories, preconceived notions, and deep-seated viewpoints. Our past no longer exists apart from recollections, which are extremely subjective. The future is unformed; any ideas we have about it are guesses based on prior experiences. So even when thinking about the future, in a way we're focusing on the past; this is often the case when the mind is attached to prior events. That's why Nakamura Sensei encouraged people to let go of attachments.

We frequently rely too much on the words of authority figures, ancient texts, and just about everything but tangible existence that's right in front of us. Actually, lots of us think deeply about almost anything except *what is*. "What is" means the real nature of life at this moment, and the meditation Kaliapa taught Nakamura Sensei aimed at directly encountering reality.

Note that Kaliapa gave Nakamura Sensei questions to contemplate which tied into what life genuinely amounted to. Kaliapa didn't simply tell him what he thought life was all about. Via yogic meditation, Nakamura Sensei was given tools to personally discover bona fide reality and the value of existence. No scriptures or spiritual master told him what to think, which encouraged him to find answers in the universe before him and within himself. He eventually experienced reality in the present moment, a moment in which time stopped; it's uncertain if this would have occurred if his mind was on someone else's thoughts about reality. Instead, alone in an ancient forest along the India-Nepal border, he abandoned the past, future, and prior beliefs to see life as it really was in the instant. To do so he had to let go of his arrogance and rigid ideas, none of which had helped him to deal with tuberculosis. It was only when he did this that Kaliapa agreed to teach him, saying "You're thinking, 'I've studied medicine in America, I'm from a civilized country, and I've read a lot of books on philosophy.' You're filled with pride. If you're not empty, whatever I say will not genuinely enter your mind. Please come to my room with a mind like a newborn baby's."[47]

When Nakamura Sensei acknowledged that *he did not know*, he let go of predetermined conclusions and ceased making assumptions based solely on his past, which allowed him to give his complete attention to reality as it is in the moment. We can do the same, but we'll need to go into the undiscovered. Because if something is already known, it's tied to the past; whereas genuine reality is a direct, undiluted experiencing of the now.

The unknown isn't far away. It's not realized in the long run. It is enclosed within what's right before our eyes. The core of reality is born at this instant; it's never existed before. Reality is continuously created and destroyed. In this eternal change is something unborn and unending . . . something which cannot be encountered using the known or the past. But leaping into the unknown can be scary. We've conned ourselves into believing we know what's going to happen tomorrow and even that tomorrow will arrive. Yet a bit of reflection reveals we have no idea what will definitely happen from moment to moment. Our fears come from the fact that we can't control what happens in the next instant since this moment is unknown. We can, nonetheless, control how we react to these moments as they come into existence. This confidence inspiring realization, along with a positive mind, lets us live fully in the moment, allowing us to successfully navigate uncharted waters.

In the instant, devoid of the known—with no past and no future—is a space in which perception of time ceases. In this space the undiscovered and ever-changing present exists. This present contains every possibility, the totality of life, absolute reality.

Reality is now.

Principle Five: Experience and Follow Reiseishin.

It's only in the present that we encounter the real nature of the universe. In doing so, we experience our oneness with the universe. Religious figures, philosophers, meditation practitioners, and people from various walks of life, from all over the world, for centuries have periodically indicated that they've experienced a profound connection to something greater than themselves. In India the word yoga means essentially "union," which some yoga teachers suggest is a joining with God or the Divine. In Japan proponents of Zen meditation also speak of oneness with the universe, while followers of the martial art aikido claim to experience *aiki*: "union with the ki of the universe." Christian mystics in the West have written of a similar state, and occasionally people with no interest in meditation or religion, during moments of peak intensity, hit upon something comparable. In almost every case this feeling is described as "spiritual."

Nakamura Sensei said his experiences meditating in India were likewise spiritual, in that he tapped into a part of himself linked to the spirit connecting all creations, a universal mind. He felt his universal mind perceived a direct link to the universe, and because this tie was fundamentally spiritual he called it reiseishin ("spiritual mind") or *reisei ishiki* ("spiritual consciousness"). He indicated human beings are multidimensional, with characteristics relating them to material objects, plants, and animals. Yet most importantly Nakamura Sensei discovered humanity alone possesses reiseishin, giving us the responsibility to care for the welfare the world.

MATERIAL OBJECTS AND PLANTS: FORM AND REACTION

The universal ki is one and absolute, however when it manifests in our relative world it takes on diverse characteristics. Though these characteristics are as infinite as the number of phenomena which exist, for the purposes of this book we'll create certain divisions, understanding that these divisions overlap somewhat and are artificial.

Non-living matter, such as rock, exhibits the material characteristics of ki. In this example, ki displays itself as form and solid structure.

In the plant realm we also see shape and structure but with a difference: the ki of innate reaction. A plant has structure, like an object, but it also curves in the direction of light without human intervention, displaying an impulse for growth and a preservation instinct. Stones don't have this characteristic, and this illustrates how inborn reaction separates material ki from the ki of vegetation.

ANIMALS: EMOTIONAL RESPONSE

In animals we observe both structure and instinct. Except ki in the animal kingdom has another aspect—emotion. Despite the fact that a few folks insist plants may have "feelings," most people concede emotion is more developed and noticeable among animals. In short, emotion is unique to the animal kingdom.

Finally, human ki shows outward form like any object and innate reaction through the autonomic nervous system. Most individuals, for instance, instinctively pull their hands away from something excessively hot. Like a plant bending toward light, this doesn't need to be taught.

We also display emotion as do dogs and cats. But early on we exhibit reason. Even though some bright animals show partial reasoning ability, the average person still considers this to be a human characteristic. Our civilization has greatly nurtured this attribute, touting it as the high point of the human race. We often accept this as fact, but is it really true?

HUMAN BEINGS: EMOTION, REASON, AND SPIRITUAL CONSCIOUSNESS

Certainly sophisticated reasoning facility is more evident in humans. Nevertheless in the unusual documented cases of children who've been reared by wild animals or grown up in an atmosphere largely void of human contact, they've revealed a lack of logic, working on a near animalistic level. So although the faculty for advanced logic appears inborn, it must be cultivated. Bottom line: refined analytical thought is in numerous ways an acquired attribute.

In addition, in civilization we notice a continuous fight between sentiment and logic. One is innate while the other is largely developed. It's possible to imagine scenarios in which both emotion and reason are equally compelling. At these times lots of us don't know how to proceed. What do we do when our feelings and our reason are at odds?

In India Nakamura Sensei was given several questions to contemplate, including "What is a human being?" Though all ki in an absolute sense is the same, Kaliapa wanted to know how human ki varied from that of stones, vegetation, and beasts.

Every creation is linked to the universe. We can't truly disconnect ourselves from everything else around us. Even to say we live as a singular entity needs comparison with something other than ourselves; our uniqueness is in contrast with other creations. Physically, spiritually, and biologically, we don't exist except in relationship to everything else.

All creations are united with the universe, but only people's minds can grasp this truth. Thus a human being is an entity which can realize this oneness and act from that realization. But few grasp this, preferring to live and make decisions solely through reason or emotion. Nakamura Sensei pointed to something constantly present, more innate than sentiment or logic, that's waiting to be perceived.

He called it reiseishin. Reiseishin is a mind which isn't just connected to the universe; it can identify its own oneness. This understanding shouldn't be confused with logic. Our reasoning intellect can't conjure up infinity or time without end. And when we discuss the universe and reiseishin that's what we're contemplating.

Plus, I'm not sure we can divide the mind which perceives the universe from the universe itself. If we cannot, then my reiseishin is your reiseishin, given that everyone's "spiritual mind" is connected to the same universe. Even if we understand that reiseishin is the spiritual aspect of our mind that's one with the universe, this isn't equivalent to experiencing our harmony with the universe as authentic truth. Fortunately Shin-shin-toitsu-do offers simple meditation techniques to determine the genuine character of reiseishin, which connects to what it means to be truly human. You'll be exposed to these methods in upcoming chapters.

Emotions make life worth living and retaining our facility for logic is smart but too many think these are our only options in life. This creates problems, and emotional baggage from long-ago alters our reactions to the present. Previous conclusions and fixed viewpoints based on analysis and calculation, which may or may not have been correct, also color our observation of reality. For quite a few people these rigid conclusions and attitudes prevent them from considering existence as it actually is in the moment.

More than this, lots of us fail to recognize that what's viewed as reasonable and correct now may not be seen as logical in the future or even in other contemporary cultures. Over 40 years ago at a seminar in Tokyo, Nakamura Sensei addressed this important and little considered point:

Please think about this. In the old days it was not always considered bad to kill someone to protect yourself. Prior to the 16th century, our country wasn't as perfectly governed by law. It was only you who could protect yourself. So when you were driven into a tight corner it wouldn't be a crime to kill your opponent. And the bushi ("warrior") class was allowed to kill anyone who was not a bushi. Merchants could be killed by a bushi if they did something impolite or offended him.

And even further back than the era of bushi you could be proud of the number of people you'd murdered. To kill other people used to be a way to preserve your own life and also something many people would boast of.

But gradually, as times advanced and human reasoning ability progressed, it became a crime to kill. However, whereas we insist now that murder is evil, we still hypocritically go on killing legions of people in wars. Many years from now I believe we'll spend a great deal of time discussing how to avoid war. It would be much wiser.

Long ago, when Confucius was living in China, men and women were forbidden to sit together if they were older than seven years of age. Did Chinese people in those days become sexually aware at the age of seven? Probably not. And nowadays some people say we're born sexually aware. It's a joke.

If he were living now, Confucius would be angry to see modern men and women socializing together. But now nobody thinks it's wrong for men and women to be seated side by side.

In this country there used to be an "adultery law" until 1945, which unfairly punished only a woman when she had an adulterous affair. Husbands, however, didn't have to worry about similar laws directed toward them. Now we fortunately have no such discriminatory law, so if you're a woman you can get a divorce if you don't like your husband. You needn't serve him like a slave. Law stipulates it. This shows how life changes according to the advancement of reason.

In 500 years we might end up swapping our spouse with someone else's once every year. Who knows? We cannot imagine what will come in the future of humankind. So, we must keep in mind that what our reasoning tells us is right and valid today might not be so tomorrow.[48]

What's reasonable isn't as clear and fixed as we might think. Emotional responses can be irrational, and our logic can be imperfect. It's hard to have deep confidence in either one, chiefly because they're habitually in conflict with one another, and they're in flux. Yet reiseishin resides in the immediate present, in an instant outside of time. It perceives the world as it really is. Since reiseishin is linked to the universe, it's the universe sensing itself. Just as the universe and its functioning is right and natural, so too are the dictates of our reiseishin, or spiritual nature, which is connected to the totality of existence. Thus reiseishin is something we can have complete confidence in, and with that assurance we can sustain a truly positive mind-set.

Nakamura Sensei explained this point in *Seidai na Jinsei* (*A Magnificent Life*) when he compared reiseishin to one's conscience that's linked to the universe. We should listen to this conscience and do what it tells us to do. Since our reiseishin is the part of ourselves which is more innate than either reason or emotion, and since it's linked to the universe itself, when we follow it we have confidence that we're following the Way of the universe. In a word, we feel positive that we are doing what's fundamentally right.[49]

This is not a matter of arrogantly assuming that our opinions are inevitably "right," rather it stems from a state in which the individual self is transcended. It is not, strictly speaking, a matter of self-confidence as the confidence alluded to stems from something much greater than the limited, impermanent being many think of as their "self." The discovery of a genuine self will be detailed later in *The Teachings of Tempu*, but all of this is impossible to fully explain in writing, which is why meditation is vital for the discovery of authentic confidence emerging from reiseishin.

If perceiving and following our reiseishin equals a confident and positive attitude, then we should consider how to perceive this spiritual consciousness. Each upcoming form of meditation aims at clearing away anxiety and attachments, allowing us to perceive our reiseishin. Reiseishin is always present, always something we can trust, but it's repeatedly obscured by the disturbance in our minds. If we compare reiseishin to a pure blue sky, one's unsettled mind is like the clouds covering it. Through meditation these clouds disperse leaving an unobstructed view of that which was always present.

Nakamura Sensei time after time spoke of our attachments to the relative world and how they upset the mind, making it difficult to perceive reiseishin. He indicated that when we consider the absolute reality of the universe, what we perceive through our senses isn't real. This is somewhat confusing, and by "real" he meant permanent, unchanging, and absolute. Thus whatever we perceive solely using our five senses is "unreal."

A tree, for instance, is connected to the soil surrounding it, but we think of the tree as having an independent existence. Yet the tree exists only because of soil and water, and if the tree eventually falls over it decomposes and merges with the soil around it. Likewise this tree can be cut down and made into paper, which we also think of as having independent reality. Part of the tree might become a pencil that we use to write on this paper. Earth and water, the tree, a piece of paper, and our pencil are all things we view as separate from each other. They aren't. And we sometimes act as if they have permanent reality. They don't.

They change form and even become one another. Everything we perceive through our senses is in the same boat: relative, changing, impermanent. Nonetheless, Nakamura Sensei indicated there's something which gives rise to the shifting phenomena of the relative world. This "something" which he called by various names (the ki of the universe, *kamisama*, *uchu rei*, the universal spirit) is real and timeless. Our actual, timeless, and genuine self can perceive it via reiseishin. But scores of us don't grasp this because mistaken ideas about the true character of reality misinform our viewpoints. Frequently our opinions about life function successfully only within the realm of shifting and impermanent phenomena. While it's important to be able to work with these fluctuating aspects of life, it's equally important to see beyond them. Yet few do and by clinging to impermanent and constantly changing things we're at odds with ourselves and life. Intellectually and psychologically we're trying to hang onto aspects of life we can't hang onto. This constant mental turmoil prevents us from perceiving reiseishin, which includes the relative facets of life but which is in the end tied to something eternal and absolute.

When we let go of our attachments to material things, the body, and even thought itself, we discover an absolute consciousness beyond relative thinking and impermanent phenomena that is reiseishin. In discussing human consciousness Nakamura Sensei explained the different traits which make up humanity (form, reaction, emotion, reason, reiseishin) according to who he was presently teaching, but the explanation was similar to what I've written above. At one seminar he gave a more abbreviated account of these ideas that's helpful for realizing the positive attitude associated with spiritual consciousness:

You might feel there is only one consciousness, but there are three kinds of consciousness, if we observe the mind more closely. The three are:

1. Nikusei ishiki or "physical consciousness"
2. Shinsei ishiki or "reasoning or analytical consciousness"
3. Reisei ishiki or "spiritual consciousness"

Nikusei ishiki works to keep physical life in existence. Reasoning brings about shinsei ishiki. Reisei ishiki will come from our spirit, or ki, which is the essence of a human being.

Great inspiration, spontaneous revelations, or what some call "the sixth sense" comes from reisei ishiki. You were born with this reisei ishiki, which comes from the ki of the universe. All of you have ki, or reikon, which is another word for "spirit." If I use the word "reikon," you might feel it is religious or Buddhist in nature, and that's why I tend to avoid this term. Scientifically it is a kind of energy. It's an invisible energy. You might think you don't have it, but each of you has ki as long as you're alive. If ki leaves you, you'll be dead.[50]

He explained physical consciousness and analytical consciousness in his usual straightforward manner. He indicated that physical consciousness resides in humans but also in any creature with a body, such as animals, insects, reptiles, and even microscopic creatures like amoeba. *Shinsei ishiki*, or "refined reasoning consciousness," and spiritual consciousness genuinely exist only in human beings, which he called "the lords of all creation." Some people insist their dog or cat is cleverer than humans are, but this is an exaggerated sentimentality which comes from their love of their pets. Neither a cat nor a dog has any high level of reasoning or spiritual consciousness. We've never heard of a dog kept tied up outside going on a hunger strike when it sees a cat being cuddled by his family inside their house. This is because the dog doesn't utilize reasoning to any great degree to accomplish its goals.

Humans have sophisticated reasoning capacity, so they often complain. If parents love a younger sibling more, elder ones complain, because they possess reason. Animals live primarily with physical consciousness, being principally concerned with physical existence. More simply, they don't think rationally. Whatever circumstances they face, they cannot effectively think of the conditions surrounding it, because they lack advanced reasoning skill.

Suppose a dog is tied to a tree trunk. It cries and tries to get away, because it wants to escape from the physical discomfort imposed on it. It acts according to its physical consciousness, or *nikusei ishiki.*

The canine doesn't think of why it's chained, but a person in the same situation would think about countless things and the causes behind them. "Why am I chained up? If I become sick while chained like this, what would I do?" Humans have a different type of consciousness. Of course Nakamura Sensei mentioned that animals have sharp senses and feelings, too. But they cannot think as we do nor can they use advanced reasoning.[51]

Lest there be any misunderstanding, Nakamura Sensei was fond of animals; he had pets, and he encouraged kind treatment of all living things. His above teachings are not intended to put down the consciousness of animals but rather to show how it's different from humanity. Plants, animals, and people each have unique attributes that are natural for them. But plants and animals always live as plants and animals should. Humans, on the other hand, aren't always so natural, frequently living on a semi-animalistic level and failing to realize their uniquely spiritual nature.

In this lecture delivered toward the end of his life, Nakamura Sensei explored rationality as well as its advantages and disadvantages:

> . . . We must not live by only using the principles of rationality. To do so is to undergo a lot of trouble. Numerous people don't realize this. I experienced it countless times when I tried to solve life problems by depending solely on my reasoning ability.
>
> But I'm not telling you to forego rationality, because advanced reasoning has brought about progress in civilization, the benefits of which we enjoy today. Rational thinking is valuable, but we cannot live well by depending only on it.
>
> We must decide what to do in life according to the judgment of our reiseishin or reisei ishiki ("spiritual consciousness"). This consciousness is not changeable and dependent on era, context, and culture. It never gives us a wrong solution to problems in life. Reason progresses with the development of knowledge, so the more knowledge we gain, the more different ideas come up. Today's conclusions reached with our present reasoning could be changed by tomorrow's reason. They're relative, whereas spiritual consciousness taps into our genuine self that's linked to genuine and timeless absolute existence, which is without distinctions and without duality.

Thus, as civilization advances more information is obtained and our reason develops further. Although reasoning makes our lives better in some ways it also makes our lives more and more complicated. Hundreds of years ago there were no labor disputes. Since the middle of the 19th century, labor disputes began with the advancement of reason due to more widespread education. Then, people began to correctly reason that even laborers should have rights and each person should have privacy. These are positive developments, but now many people can't be content with the present conditions in their lives.

People in older times weren't so clever as to think this way. They were satisfied with some food to eat, some place to shelter them, and someone for companionship. They didn't know any more than this, so no further demands or desires arose in their minds. Thus there was less in the way of needless psychological suffering coming from myriad unsatisfied desires.[52]

TWO KINDS OF ATTACHMENT

Our attachments to various desires constantly destabilize the mind, making it tough to perceive our ultimate and original nature, our reiseishin. Suffering starts when desires aren't satisfied, and we obviously can't always get everything we want. Nakamura Sensei identified two kinds of affliction plaguing humanity: materialistic suffering and mental suffering. Most people experience both kinds, but we don't always recognize them as such.

Materialistic suffering wears out the mind as our attachments to virtually anything coming along lead to one new desire after another. If we're attached to desires stemming from physical existence, instincts, and sexuality Nakamura Sensei called this materialistic suffering. He once gave two examples of this sort of suffering.

Suppose a woman wants a two-carat diamond. The woman next door proudly wears a two-carat diamond, and she's yearning for one, too. But she cannot afford one because of the small income of her husband. She thinks, "All I really want is just a two-carat diamond. What if I shoplifted one? No, then I could be arrested." She begins thinking of diamonds even when sleeping. This is an example of materialistic suffering.

Here's Nakamura Sensei's other example: A man is thinking, "I'm bored by my dull wife. The woman next door is pretty and charming. I wish I could go out at least once with her. But what would people say if they knew?" This is also materialistic suffering or sexual suffering.[53]

When humankind realized materialism couldn't satisfy inward desires or solve mental troubles, we looked for psychological salvation. This in turn gave birth to philosophy, psychology, and religion. Some philosophers try to solve mental misery using pure rationality, which clashes with humanity's animal nature and instinctive desires. Consequently they cannot resolve the conflict between reasoning and feelings. This is mental suffering. Nakamura Sensei commented that various forms of mental suffering lead to neurosis, and not every type of psychological distress can be resolved with reason:

> You're always trying to solve problems in life solely with reasoning, whether they belong to the category of mental suffering or physical suffering. You're also unaware that solutions based on rational thinking change. The result is that thinking itself is confused by the irrational impulses of physical desires and instincts. And this sometimes leads to disorders in your internal organs or circulatory system. You cannot keep living like this.[54]

REISEISHIN AND INSPIRATION

Not only do we have a spiritual nature, or reiseishin, we can learn from and receive spiritual inspiration from the universe, giving us insight into the paths to choose in our lives. These often spontaneous revelations stem from our spiritual consciousness that's one with the universe. This consciousness utilizes emotion and reason but transcends both. Nakamura Sensei regularly quoted Francis Bacon, an English philosopher, statesman, and writer, who's remembered for leading the scientific revolution with his "observation and experimentation theory." In Nakamura Sensei's favorite quote, Bacon (1561-1626) refers to spiritual consciousness as our "spiritual light," because it illuminates the correct path at every moment in our lives. Nakamura Sensei felt this aptly described reiseishin.

He also indicated that the immediate inspiration arising from reiseishin cannot be described in words. If we can't even fully describe the taste of a particular food to someone who's never eaten it, how could Nakamura Sensei explain the instant inspiration of reiseishin to those who haven't experienced it? Therefore, he emphasized each person must find reiseishin by calming the mind and releasing their attachments through meditation.

He also noticed some of his students were sensing what was intrinsically right for them in life, but they weren't listening to it, or they didn't understand what was taking place. He once mentioned an Osaka-based businessman who claimed his reiseishin never revealed any direction he should take in life. Nakamura Sensei reminded this person that he'd spontaneously decided to start a new business. His decision was personal, immediate, and not based on the counsel of others. And the business, then just two months old, was surprisingly thriving. Nakamura Sensei asked him where his inspiration came from to launch this business and why it was doing well. Hadn't he experienced something direct and unpremeditated which was inherently right for him? His student concluded he had, and he realized his decision to start his new enterprise came from a source that wasn't wholly dependent on either reason or emotion.

Countless people remain unaware of the inspired lessons offered to them by the universe through their spiritual consciousness (despite the fact that we all have the ability to learn from the universe). Nakamura Sensei spoke of relaxing and releasing the mind from conscious effort to set free a subconscious creativity linked to the creative force of the universe itself. It's the regularly ignored and forgotten link between humanity and the universe which gives us the deepest inspiration in life. This allows us to learn from the universe on profound levels that include—but ultimately transcend—reason and instinct. It is this unseen spiritual connection to the universe which Nakamura Sensei described as the origin of the numerous spontaneous revelations he experienced throughout his life. We can also sense this same connection and spiritual consciousness, and the upcoming forms of meditation are designed to lead us to this state.

CONFIDENT DECISIONS EQUAL A POSITIVE MIND

We can't feel positive if we second-guess our every decision. If we follow our reiseishin self-confidence is realized as confidence in the universe, which our spiritual nature is linked to. Noting that several scientific and artistic discoveries were only realized when the discoverer stopped struggling to solve their mental block, Nakamura Sensei quoted an old Japanese proverb: *Taijin wa akago no gotoshi.* ("A great person is innocent like a baby.") In other words, if we release attachments to calculated desires the mind becomes calm, clear, and more capable of resolving problems.

My teachers advised me to meditate when I didn't know what to do in life. During meditation I experienced moments where my best course of action became immediately clear; yet this wasn't a process of analysis. When I followed this unexpected eye-opener I always benefited.

Even a good night's sleep can help us suddenly see more clearly what's needed in our families or businesses. During sleep, and particularly during meditation, we stop arguing with ourselves (and others); we let go of attachments to emotions and analytical thoughts. Hitting upon spiritual illumination, we receive inspiration from existence itself. Through releasing our attachments to relative, impermanent parts of life we discover the absolute, unchanging portion of ourselves during meditation, and we uncover our reiseishin. Following this spiritual nature, which controls emotion and reason, we can act with deep confidence resulting in a vitally positive outlook.

WISDOM TRANSCENDS KNOWLEDGE

You can employ Nakamura Sensei's five principles above as a tool in life, but it's just a device. Even if we remember these five points, this doesn't ensure we understand them. The amassing of information isn't wisdom.

Humanity has stored generation upon generation of data, the zenith of which is the immense and handy assortment of technology we see in contemporary culture. Even with this large accumulation of knowledge and technology we still put up with starvation and warfare. The distinction between antiquity and the present, between more educated and less educated societies, is often the difference between clubbing our neighbors and shooting them.

We remain in conflict. Misery hasn't stopped. But we stick with the view that if we just stockpile a bit more information we'll be fine. On the other hand, perhaps a fresh intellectual theory will work or a new political regime. Yet all of this has been attempted many times, by many people, in many cultures, for many years.

Knowledge builds on what went before and has its uses. Wisdom is outside time. Despite how this word is often defined, wisdom is really the immediate awareness of actuality as it is, separate from any handed-down beliefs or memorized theories. In this direct consideration of *what is* lies the possibility of evolution . . . a spiritual evolution that's not just a revamp of earlier periods in life, a revolution of humankind which embodies the perpetually new. (This is, in numerous ways, the ultimate point of Nakamura Sensei's teachings, and it will be more fully explored in the final chapter of this book.)

Acquiring data is useful, but it's also one of the troubles facing human beings. Gathering hi-tech and scientific facts is constructive as long as it's seen for what it is: something valuable but not a means of solving every issue faced by humankind. Knowledge is a compilation of previous occurrences. The wisdom of realization exists at this instant, just as the person and the universe subsist now. Clarity of perception rests in the instant-to-instant seeing of life which transcends time (though our watches continue to trace artificial, chronological time). Nakamura Sensei's understanding of reality wasn't based on the past. It first took place during meditation, and it wasn't a function of memory. Both memory and past material are used for amassing of knowledge. And if we build up knowledge of ourselves, i.e., "I'm this kind of person; I can't be that kind of person," we fall short of perceiving our real ever-changing character.

If we don't become positive people it's because we've trapped ourselves. We see only cumulative memories, and we feel and see through compiled impressions about ourselves. Genuine learning, growth, and change become unworkable when trapped by the past. Meditation involves letting go of both past and future to experience a timeless present that's capable of positive change. Kaliapa echoed Raja yoga teachings when he taught a graduated progression from concentration (*dharana*) to meditation (*dhyana*). Before we take up meditation, however, let's look at Nakamura Sensei's easily understood analysis of concentration in daily life.

FOUR PRINCIPLES FOR INVESTIGATING CONCENTRATION
1. Concentrate on matters you believe you are familiar with.
2. Concentrate on matters you wish to accomplish in a hurry.
3. Concentrate on matters you believe are uninteresting.
4. Concentrate on matters you believe are of no value.

Meditation has time and again been utilized to unchain the power of concentration. Nonetheless, it's not only possible to produce significant concentration by engaging in daily actions; it is imperative to do so. Nakamura Sensei taught that the average person loses concentration at the above four moments. If we understand when we typically lose attentiveness, we can learn to sustain concentration. An intelligent second step is to make a point of focusing the mind when we usually stop paying attention.

Principle One: Concentrate on Matters You Believe You Are Familiar With.

When do you drop concentration and hence drop your awareness of the present? For most people, it's when they're doing something particularly familiar such as putting on their pants. Can you recall which leg first went into your pants this morning?

Be mindful of breaches in alertness, and you'll start grasping lucid perception and unsullied concentration. This continuous wakefulness allows the student of Shin-shin-toitsu-do to have fewer lapses in attention.

In addition, experimental psychology indicates the more energetically and attentively we use our minds the less mentally and physically tired we become. With this in mind, it seems reasonable to implement the samurai's viewpoint of concentrating on each deed as if it were the first time and as if it might be our last.

Principle Two: Concentrate On Matters You Wish To Accomplish In A Hurry.

Quite a few people become so fixated on the conclusion of an action that they don't focus the mind on the process occurring that second. In meditation, novices are typically so concerned with one day acquiring tranquility or better health that they don't pay attention to the meditative process that should be taking place here and now. They fall short of concentrating on the act they're presently engaged in.

Thus, when you're rushing to finish matters you're apt to lose concentration. This doesn't mean it's impossible to act swiftly and concentrate, but be sure to concentrate even when in a hurry.

You don't need to strain to concentrate. Concentration is when the mind is in the present moment. That's all. It's simple and invaluable.

But we can make it complicated. Focusing on this moment, on the experience we're having, makes concentration easy and comfortable. However, being fixated on the outcome of what we're doing, on the future, makes concentration difficult. There is no concentration in the future. There's no future at all. All we have is this moment, and that's the only place concentration can occur.

Principle Three: Concentrate On Matters You Believe Are Uninteresting.

Numerous individuals also turn off their awareness when they take part in actions they think are boring. For instance, learning anything well requires repetition. Music, painting, and other activities are only mastered through ongoing practice. Unfortunately, beginners struggle with the never-ending repetition needed for proficiency in a given task, finding it dull. This boredom guarantees the skill being repeated is often repeated incorrectly, which means we need still more repetition.

In these situations, understand that at the true core of any complex action are trained and refined talents that must be constantly drilled. Repetition allows these actions to be maintained as automatic responses. What if you fully gave your attention to such repetition? Would it still be mind-numbing?

Most assume the answer is yes, but if we actually concentrate and attempt to improve tiny aspects of multifaceted skills we may find this process isn't boring. That's why what's tiresome for one individual can be interesting for another.

Being fully engaged in what we're doing streams positive ki into the action being performed, giving us more energy and greater motivation. It also allows us to see interesting aspects of the activity that are hidden from individuals that are bored and not paying attention.

Additionally, whether or not we focus can be determined by whether or not we have a positive mindset. How many people struggle to concentrate when they go to a movie they've been dying to see? Not many, because they really want to pay attention at times like this. But what about previews? Maybe then concentration is a tad tough, right?

This is indicative of several important points:

- Most folks are already capable of concentrating. If this weren't the case, you couldn't successfully read an interesting magazine or watch a favorite TV show—and you wouldn't want to.
- Concentration is tied to attitude. Negative feelings about a particular activity often result in flimsy concentration.
- By positively paying attention we can find interest in the process of improving skill in a particular activity.
- Even if nothing of interest can be found in an activity, it's still possible to employ it as an exercise to advance mental focus.

Principle Four: Concentrate On Matters You Believe Are Of No Value.

Focusing on actions which we feel are worthless also relates to increasing concentration. What we believe to be valueless is relative. No fixed standard of worth exists. What if things you think are worthless only appear this way when you don't pay attention to them due to predetermined biases? By actually paying attention to certain actions it's possible to discover value where we thought none existed.

For instance, aside from Shin-shin-toitsu-do I also teach a traditional Japanese martial art. Beginners in this art must learn a specific way of kneeling down on the practice mat to sit and how to correctly stand from this kneeling position. They know this stems from ancient samurai customs, they know it can't be done properly the first few times they try it, and they often decide sitting and standing this way is mere tradition and meaningless. I once thought the same. I was wrong.

I was required to practice sitting and standing in this manner over and over, and since I wasn't interested in dropping out of the martial art, I eventually noticed what I was actually doing. I discovered that the way of moving demanded correct postural alignment. Such alignment promotes balance, and it becomes a habit that's carried into various throws and pins, which won't work without balance. Plus, Japanese martial arts require strong, flexible legs and feet. This way of moving from sitting to standing (and vice versa) promotes just such physical development. Once I paid attention, I realized the training would benefit the "more interesting parts" of what I was studying. It had value.

In addition, it's particularly essential for beginners in Shin-shin-toitsu-do to understand this discipline isn't based on immediate gratification, and the true worth of practice sometimes becomes clear only after loads of repetition. Of course it isn't necessary to look for matters of slight value to concentrate on, but keeping the mind focused on every action, even when it seems of scant value, can result in more powerful concentration.

Concentration, Habits, and Daily Life

In all of these situations if we don't concentrate we unwittingly develop a pattern. It's the pattern of not being capable of concentrating even when we'd like to. Every recurring mental or physical action, whether constructive or destructive in nature, builds up in the subconscious to form habits.

Again, rather than just memorizing the above four points, try experimenting with them. For example, for one day observe what your response is to actions you believe are worthless. Where does this response come from, and what does it signify in terms of attentiveness? Think of Nakamura Sensei's list as four diverse occasions to personally determine the real nature of a concentrated mind.

Shin-shin-toitsu-do meditation and mind-body coordination exercises give us substantial evidence of our capability to use the mind in a positive and concentrated way. As we grow confident in our ability to be positive and concentrate, this realization significantly alters our lives. Using Nakamura Tempu Sensei's principles for a positive attitude and concentration we throw 100 percent of ourselves into each instant, projecting ki into every part of life. In this way, we become fully alive and truly living instead of merely existing.

Chapter 6

METHODS TO TRANSFORM
THE SUBCONSCIOUS

You've thus far learned about Nakamura Tempu Sensei's no-nonsense programs for cultivating potent positivity and concentration. These simple methodologies are important for psychophysical health. They don't, however, fully address the relationship between the conscious mind, the subconscious, and habit.

How can a positive outlook and mental focus become habits? The answer lies in the techniques of autosuggestion outlined above and explained below.

Jiko Anji: Nakamura Sensei's Methods of Autosuggestion

Most folks understand the difference between the conscious and subconscious portions of the mind, but this wasn't always true. Even these days, with psychology being commonly practiced, the typical individual might know a bit about the conscious and subconscious and still be incapable of sensibly using this information. Autosuggestion is the process of altering the content of the subconscious, which then influences the conscious mind and its reactions to life. The subconscious can be changed consciously by oneself or by suggestions implanted by a hypnotist. Nakamura Sensei favored the former approach.

Historically speaking, Émile Coué (1857–1926) was one of the first people to advance a psychological method known as autosuggestion or self-suggestion. A French psychologist and pharmacist, he introduced a technique of autosuggestion that he claimed resulted in psychological wellbeing, healing, and personal development. He advocated using his well-known autosuggestion/affirmation: "Every day, in every way, I'm getting better and better." Coué encouraged his patients to say this 20 times or more each evening before falling asleep. It was also performed at the start of the day. The so-called "Coué mantra" is commonly called Couéism or the Coué Method today.

Nakamura Sensei was one of Japan's first scholars of Western psychology. He learned the rudiments of changing the subconscious mind while traveling in France in the early 1900s, and what he studied seems related to the Coué Method. His experiences in India gave him further hints about how altering the subconscious also alters unconscious daily routines. Over time he created five readily understood methods of autosuggestion (jiko anji). He used straightforward terminology to help his readers understand autosuggestion, noting that when we think, thoughts take place in surface consciousness, which characterizes the mind while awake. We can call this surface awareness the conscious mind. The conscious component of the mind is influenced by, and reacts to, elements in the subconscious, which lies beneath the covering of the conscious mind. The subconscious mind rises to the surface and "replaces" the conscious mind during sleep, only to submerge and act behind the scene upon waking.

Our subconscious is a storeroom of the mind. If the elements stored in the subconscious (which affect our thinking unconsciously) are negative, it is difficult for the conscious mind to think positively. And this is true even if we consciously try to be positive.

Factors in the subconscious minds of countless people are harmful, and this surreptitiously influences their conscious minds. As the result, they tend to think negatively, and they're easily angered, complain often, and are fearful of even minor incidents. Thus, Nakamura Sensei wrote that we should first eliminate pessimistic elements in the subconscious if we want to live a positive life. We have to "sweep clean the mind's storehouse."[55]

As the conscious mind responds to stimuli, elements stored in the subconscious crop up and mingle with our conscious mind to shape words and deeds. In certain cases our reactions may be emotionally focused and in other situations the rational parts of ourselves move to the forefront, but in each instance we're influenced by the subconscious. In brief, when we observe or listen to something, previous associations with it frequently establish the thoughts we have about it. Those associations are housed in our subconscious.

One's subconscious constantly affects the conscious mind, and Nakamura Sensei identified a current of suggestions and influences running from the subconscious into everyday consciousness. He taught that a suggestion is defined in psychology as something entering the mind and having an impact on it. Suggestions are received by the conscious mind and recorded in the subconscious mind. When we see, hear, or say something repeatedly, these suggestions have a relatively large impact on the subconscious. Likewise, an especially dramatic, traumatic, or intense event has a significant impact on the subconscious. Less intense suggestions, or those which take place rarely, make less of an impression on the subconscious. Nevertheless, whatever is stored in the subconscious tends to unconsciously influence conscious actions and reactions.

There are numerous sources for psychological suggestions such as verbal expression, the written word, and behaviors . . . basically any phenomena we perceive. As we study Shin-shin-toitsu-do we should become aware of the kinds of suggestions habitually reoccurring in our everyday environment. Such awareness is needed because both positive and negative suggestions exist. A positive suggestion influences the subconscious to be cheerful, energetic, and brave, while negative suggestions are the opposite.[56]

Anything we believe or experience in our waking and conscious state may become another factor stored in the subconscious. The subconscious and conscious communicate with each other in two ways:

- Elements in the subconscious stream into and alter the conscious mind
- Elements in the conscious mind stream into and alter the subconscious

The correlation between these dual facets of the mind is interdependent, moving back and forth in both directions. If material housed in the subconscious is mainly pessimistic it's hard to consciously respond in a positive manner. Negative deeds and turns of phrase made in our waking hours shifts into the subconscious to be retained as additional negative components. As the result, a negative loop is produced, with damaging suggestions moving from the subconscious to the conscious and back again.

If a pessimistic cycle can be cultivated so can an optimistic one. The issue is how an individual, who's grown up to be exceedingly downbeat, can sever the circle of harmful suggestions from the subconscious to the conscious and vice versa. Even if this person decides to be optimistic, owing to subconscious influences his or her efforts may be fruitless. In short, it's tricky for a pessimistic individual to transform his or her habit of negativity, and although it's true we're encircled by suggestions coming from our surroundings and other human beings, not every suggestion is encouraging. Actually, if our fundamental direction is pessimistic we have a powerful penchant for disheartening people around us. They will, as a result, demoralize us, too. And one more harmful loop of information is fashioned.

Jiko anji are techniques of altering the subconscious that we can apply to shape ourselves. (Jiko equals "self;" anji means "suggestion.") They're ways of placing constructive material into the subconscious which have a stronger impact than run of the mill suggestions obtained from the realm of waking consciousness.

Method One: Associated Positive Images

Renso Anji is a simple form of autosuggestion, and in his book *Searching for Truth in Life* Nakamura Sensei explained it well, writing that renso means "associated images," or to think of things one after another. Renso Anji is autosuggestion where we think of positive ideas successively once we slip into bed to sleep. From the time we lie down until we're asleep, we avoid thinking of anything negative or anything that makes us angry, sad, or fearful. The moments before sleep have a profound impact on the subconscious. Besides, we need to rest the mind and revitalize ourselves before morning; creating depressing mental images makes it more difficult to have a good night's sleep.

Renso Anji is easy and effective because surface consciousness blurs and the subconscious arises, becoming more dominant and active, before we fall asleep. Once asleep the conscious mind rests, with the subconscious coming to the forefront. For this reason, numerous people believe dreams reflect the workings of the subconscious.

When we're falling asleep we have a natural tendency to more easily accept suggestions into the subconscious. Such suggestions no longer have to filter through many levels of waking consciousness to reach the depths of the subconscious. Right before sleep they move effortlessly and directly from the conscious mind into the subconscious as the two are in transition. This is why the moment before falling asleep is the ideal time to positively influence the subconscious. If we think of encouraging matters, one after another, these elements enter our subconscious. Then the content of the subconscious gradually becomes more upbeat. Renso Anji doesn't require much effort, and over time people find themselves changed.[57]

Anyone can use this method to create a more cheerful waking state. Once you close your eyes move from one positive image to the next as you fall asleep. Try reviewing parts of your life you appreciate; focusing on gratitude produces a positive attitude. The attitude cultivated by using associated optimistic images aids in better sleep as well:

> Why not have happy dreams instead of negative dreams? Although they're more highly educated and cultured than in the past, scores of people in modern times hold on to negative feelings like anger, fear, and sorrow. As the result, they weaken the mind's power. Regardless of how much expensive gourmet food they eat at dinner they still often can't get enough rest each night. For such people the situation won't change until they change the nature of their minds. In particular, they must change what they think about before falling asleep. Only then will they sleep well.
>
> Deep sleep is immensely important. Sleeping lets us receive a vast amount of ki, or "life energy," from the universe. Philosophically put, it's the time when the universe and the individual are closely united.[58]

Sawai Atsuhiro Sensei, my teacher, had a profound experience with Renso Anji. At 18 he entered one of Kyoto's top universities. Like lots of college students Sawai Sensei was filled with dreams, but he fell ill. Despite the efforts of doctors, he couldn't cure his sickness, which affected his stomach and digestion. Depressed, he stopped attending classes. Thinking he might die, Sawai Sensei read about Buddhism and Christianity to discover what happens after death. He also thought continuously about the purpose of life, reaching a nihilistic conclusion. In short, he felt there's no purpose in life as we're born without knowing where we came from, where we're going, and why we're here. He felt utterly lost.

Mr. Sawai's aunt suggested attending Nakamura Sensei's lectures. He listened to a talk which mentioned Renso Anji, and without formal training in Shin-shin-toitsu-do he began using this autosuggestion nightly. In a short period his mysterious illness (which was probably psychosomatic) disappeared, and he remembers feeling "revived" in every portion of his life. He started studying Shin-shin-toitsu-do not long after. He eventually became a personal assistant to Nakamura Sensei, learning directly from him for many years until Nakamura Sensei passed away.

Method Two: Commanding Suggestion

Meirei Anji is an autosuggestion which takes place at a precise instant: the moment before we're asleep. As we glide into slumber our waking consciousness submerges, letting the subconscious come to the forefront. At this time we can most efficiently make suggestions to the subconscious mind without moving through layers of normal consciousness. Whatever we experience as we're about to fall asleep infiltrates the subconscious profoundly and directly. Understanding this, Nakamura Sensei said to keep a little mirror next to your bed. When you're about to drift off, hold the mirror and gaze intently at your face for several seconds. Then with an audible voice make a suggestion to your subconscious and go directly to sleep. You can craft the phrasing yourself, but Nakamura Sensei offered hints for using Meirei Anji:

> We verbalize a positive suggestion, using a single simple sentence, that's directed toward our face in the mirror (or more exactly, between the eyebrows). Speaking out loud to our reflected image is a stronger way of commanding ourselves to become what we need to be.
>
> Examples of positive suggestions for Meirei Anji are: "You will be positive!" and "You will not be nervous!" and "You will become cheerful!" We needn't say these suggestions loudly. Whispering intently is fine if we clearly hear the sentence.
>
> We don't need to speak loudly in bed to perform Meirei Anji, but we should be very serious when we make a suggestion to the subconscious. In addition, use only one sentence and say it aloud only once. Many suggestions confuse the subconscious and countless repetitions aren't needed. But intensity is necessary and the quality of the suggestion is more important than the quantity.
>
> It may be some days before you feel the effects of Meirei Anji, so be patient and continue practicing nightly. We acquire bad habits over months and even years. It's unrealistic to expect these habits to be instantly changed by Meirei Anji, but with repeated use the powerful effects of this form of autosuggestion can be clearly felt.[59]

Meirei Anji ("commanding suggestion") is potent because the command stems from both you and the likeness of you. Thus the effect on your subconscious is thought to be two times stronger than a suggestion lacking the mirror. Utilizing the word "you," instead of "I," is significant. Using the mirror you produce the feeling of directly ordering yourself to carry out something, and saying "you" is more efficient in this context. Autosuggestion changes routines, but the suggestion has to be properly worded. If you say to the mirror, "You'll never drink alcohol again," this may not be as powerful as, "You don't need to drink alcohol," or "You don't like alcohol." You may in fact drink again after employing autosuggestion; these techniques influence the subconscious through repetition over time. They won't inevitably let you stop drinking suddenly, and if your suggestion implies this will happen you may lose confidence every time you go against the suggestion. But if you just propose to your subconscious mind that you don't require, like, or desire something, over time you experience a lack of longing. Each individual should discover the precise words which work best for them and their personal pattern.

Nakamura Sensei offered further ideas for crafting commanding suggestions:

Actually, a French psychologist discovered this mirror method in the early 20th century, and based on my experiences in India I modified it for easy use. He suggested we do it as often as possible throughout the day. But my advice, based on personal experience, is to do it before falling asleep because it's psychologically the most effective time.

For example, students who are bad at mathematics can use a sentence like "You will become fond of mathematics." This is more effective than "You will be good at mathematics." If we come to like a subject we study it harder and naturally become good at it.

Children that chronically wet the bed can say, "You will wake up when you want to urinate." People wanting to stop stammering shouldn't say, "Your stuttering will be gone," but rather, "You will not care about stuttering!" In stuttering the person's psychological state and ability to speak are closely connected. If we stop worrying about stuttering, we often stop stuttering.

The same can be said for countless other problems in life. We create (or at least sustain) problems by constantly worrying about them. Along the same lines, individuals who are ill shouldn't state, "You will recover from the illness," but instead, "You will not be worried about your illness."

The sentence we use for autosuggestion should be an imperative order not a prayer or a request. For example, "Your confidence will be strong" is an imperative or command, but "I want my confidence to become strong" or "Please make my confidence strong" are requests.[60]

Don't do anything other than fall asleep after making the suggestion to your subconscious. If you watch TV or read after the commanding suggestion then what you see or read could easily be what enters your subconscious. Examples of this are common. Quite a few of us have dreamt about something we viewed on TV before falling asleep. This makes sense since dreams relate to the subconscious, which is active during sleep, and the moments before sleep strongly influence the subconscious. Advocates of sleep learning similarly try to manipulate the subconscious during sleep, in a style a bit analogous to Meirei Anji. That mentioned, it isn't easy to sleep well while listening to audible suggestions on a CD. And studies haven't conclusively proven the subconscious responds to subliminal suggestions it can't hear.

Method Three: Concluding Suggestion

Nakamura Sensei also taught Dantei Anji, which occurs right after opening the eyes, just as the subconscious mind is submerging and waking conscious is becoming stronger. To perform Dantei Anji ("Concluding Suggestion") use your mirror and repeat aloud the suggestion used the night before. If you like, you can alter "You must be positive" to "You have become positive." Although a mirror isn't absolutely needed for this concluding suggestion, some Shin-shin-toitsu-do teachers think it's more effective, while others feel our sleepy face isn't the most encouraging image to wake up to. (If you make the suggestion without a mirror, substitute "I" for "you.") Despite the fact that varying interpretations of these methods exist, the essential principles behind them are easy to grasp. It's these principles which are most important for effectively changing the subconscious.

Method Four: Repeating Suggestion

Hanpuku Anji is the technique of repeating (hanpuku) the same suggestion used in Meirei Anji and Dantei Anji throughout the day. No mirror is required, but you can use one if you want. Your suggestion can be verbalized or simply repeated in the mind. (If you use a mirror and make the suggestion audible this may have a stronger impact, but this isn't always practical during the course of the workday. In this case, simply repeat the suggestion mentally whenever it occurs to you.) The main point is to repeat it over and over during the day. Again, use the word "I" instead of "you" if you're not using a mirror.

Method Five: Affirmations

Nakamura Sensei, having been influenced by early psychological theorists and New Thought philosophers, advocated positive affirmations. He was, likewise, affected by yoga teachings, and numerous famous yoga experts like Swami Sivananda and Paramahansa Yogananda used affirmations for cultivating positive thinking. Yoga practitioners as a whole have long promoted an optimistic attitude, and Nakamura Sensei's similar emphasis, while pragmatic and easy to follow, wasn't divorced from this tradition.

Consequently he crafted a number of affirmations, or shoku, which could be read aloud, either alone or in groups. By verbally repeating these affirmations, as opposed to just silently reading or thinking them, we coordinate mind *and body*, resulting in a greater impact on the subconscious. Including all his affirmations is beyond the scope of this book, but this is perhaps the most important and wide-ranging one:

> I vow that for this one day I will let go of anger, fear, and grief. Honest, kind, and cheerful, with strength, courage, and enthusiasm, I will take charge of my own life. I will live as a respectable person with a mind filled with peace and love.[61]

Created as a motto for his students, this maxim was intended to be spoken aloud daily, and we can experiment with it as well. Affirmations are recited in a determined, clear, and powerful voice. Meek, half-hearted tones produce mediocre results.

Sawai Sensei suggests memorizing affirmations as the added effort of memorization has added impact on the subconscious. He further teaches that people needn't depend on the affirmations created by Nakamura Sensei. We can create personal affirmations by picking topics relating to our lives and Shin-shin-toitsu-do. The phraseology should be decisive, positive, and not too long or wordy. A few themes Nakamura Sensei addressed in his *Shokushu (Collection of Affirmations)* are:

- Absorbing Life Energy from the Universe
- Strength
- Mental Attitude

+ Awareness of Human Nature
+ Verbal Expressions
+ Imagination
+ An Immovable Mind

This concludes the Five Methods of Autosuggestion. Of the different types of autosuggestion outlined I feel the commanding suggestion, given prior to falling asleep, is most essential. And we should distinguish between getting ready for bed and actually falling asleep. Meirei Anji should be our last action of the night, if it's to be effective.

Habits vs. Direct Perception

Autosuggestion deals with changing unconscious behaviors and creating new habits. And habits are carried over from our past. However, for the mind and body to be coordinated the mind must function here and now. Legitimate learning and growth similarly occurs right now. If we approach fresh situations with a mind that calculates and responds based solely on past viewpoints, prejudices, and predetermined psychological routines, we don't experience the present as it is. We perceive the moment through the eyes of our past, which skews our opinions, keeping us trapped in our own ancient history. This makes the unearthing of anything really new impossible.

We might therefore think we'd be better off dropping habits in general, rather than altering the subconscious through autosuggestion. We could then possibly sense reality in its factual, unconditioned form and observe the genuine character of life. After all, it's only when we drop what we believe we know, that we perceive ourselves and existence as they are in reality. Right?

Yes and no.

Although purging habits seems logical from a meditative viewpoint, we must nevertheless mull over the nature of memory and routine in everyday living. We obviously can't forget math and writing skills. We must keep some habits to even type and use a computer. All the same, the instant—which is outside of time—can only be experienced by a mind that's not trapped by its history.

The association between habit and perceiving life as it is, with a mind unconditioned by what's gone before, and which is liberated and lucid, is complex. Nonetheless, we can't wholly disregard this matter, and themes related to it are in upcoming chapters. In the next section of this book I'll introduce Anjo Daza Ho meditation, and we'll have a chance to look directly at ourselves and the nature of being. We'll also have an opportunity to observe habitual routines and an unconditioned mentality that's not tethered to its past or to time. Let's briefly examine this subject now.

Most of us have driven a car. Driving requires skills which must be practiced until they're subconscious behaviors. The plan is that these techniques will become trained reactions, and even if we're taken aback in an emergency conditioned behaviors take over, letting us respond immediately and correctly.

While driving skills should be practiced until they're second nature, just developing certain skills as habits isn't completely practical. Cultivating deep-seated habits so we respond without thinking seems sound until we consider the idea more deeply. Suppose we've trained ourselves to repeatedly pump the brakes in an emergency stop to avoid locking up our car's wheels which would produce a skid. This habit works well unless we drive a friend's car with anti-locking brakes. Then repeated application of the brakes is meaningless at best, and at worst it won't slow the car rapidly enough to safely stop. Pumping anti-locking brakes (out of habit) doesn't work.

Some reflexes must be trained, but the mind must nevertheless stay in the moment, rapidly evaluating what's actually occurring. To purely depend on previously refined routines may not be suitable for events taking place right now. The present must be understood for what it really is. Then deep-rooted skills can be customized—or used in their original manner—whichever is fitting.

This illustration stems from driving, but it deals with a concern that has wide-ranging repercussions. We cannot wholly and lucidly experience existence through the shroud of habit or by living and responding like a robot. Simultaneously, we cannot function without memory and certain habitual behaviors.

Each of us needs to resolve this issue personally. But understanding the difference between retaining physical habits as well as intellectual concepts (as opposed to clinging to past emotions and psychological states) is helpful. Remembering which roads lead home is useful; this is an intellectual habit. Not losing the ability to ride a bicycle is likewise beneficial; this is a physical habit. However, being obsessed with a painful event from years ago, and continually reliving it in memory, is psychological and/or emotional conditioning. It's a habit of feelings, and it serves no useful purpose. It only disturbs our reactions to present day situations.

Unfortunately, countless people are attached to events from the past—positive and negative—which prevents them from living freely and seeing life for what it is now. This causes us to constantly modify our past, making us "stuck in a rut" and unable to genuinely change and grow as human beings. Instead of fully living through every moment—good and bad—and then letting the moment go, we're often attached to psychological experiences. Yet if the mind is in the present, it's never attached to its past.

Meditation involves just such a letting go of attachments and time.

The Five Methods of Autosuggestion in Review

When using the separate forms of jiko anji ("autosuggestion") bear in mind the following summarized points:

1. Renso Anji: The simplest way to implant positive elements in the subconscious is to stir up one optimistic image after another as you fall asleep. Thoughts of gratitude are especially effective.
2. Meirei Anji: A more powerful form of autosuggestion involves making a short verbal command while gazing intently at your face in a mirror. Make this your last action before closing your eyes to sleep.
3. Dantei Anji: Upon waking, pick up the mirror and use a concluding suggestion. Repeat what you said before falling asleep.
4. Hanpuku Anji: Throughout the day, verbally or mentally repeat this suggestion.
5. Shoku: Positive affirmations also alter the subconscious. They work best when repeated aloud daily, with determination.

Chapter 7

ANJO DAZA HO
MEDITATION

PRINCIPLES FOR *ANJO DAZA HO*

1. Sit with a posture that allows mind and body coordination.

2. Concentrate on the sound of a bell.

3. Mentally follow the lessening sound waves to reach muga ichi-nen.

4. As the sound waves grow infinitely small, continue listening and concentrating.

5. Let your listening enlarge, so that your ki expands into infinite space.

Most of us eventually realize that a life without concentration is needlessly difficult. We likewise grumble about our lack of composure or willpower, while doctors encourage us to relax to lower blood pressure. More and more, people are looking to meditation to acquire these important mental (and physical) traits as recently noted in *National Geographic*:

Regular meditation may increase smarts and stave off aging, according to an ongoing study.

The research is one in a string of studies that suggest some time spent getting in tune with the flow of one's breathing can complement a regimen of pills, diet, and exercise. Meditation is being prescribed for stress, anxiety, infertility, skin diseases, and other ailments.

Many medical professionals in the West remain skeptical or are against the use of meditation for therapy.

But some are beginning to endorse its benefits, said neuroscientist

Sara Lazar, who leads the research at Harvard Medical School in Boston, Massachusetts.

"Our hope is that by providing concrete evidence of [meditation's] benefits, more people will at least try it and see if it is beneficial for them," she said in an email interview.[62]

What quite a few individuals don't understand, however, is that meditation is a state of consciousness. Practicing meditation equals setting up an internal environment where we can discover meditative consciousness. Concentration, willpower, calmness, and relaxation are dramatically enhanced by meditation. But these qualities aren't meditation. They're remarkable byproducts of this mental state.

When Nakamura Tempu Sensei was in India he was exposed to meditation in Raja yoga and its eight-limbed path to spiritual realization. As noted in the Preface, Indian yoga scholars often teach that the initial five aspects of yoga lead to aspect six, which is dharana, "concentration." When dharana is experienced, yogis then move into dhyana, or "meditation," which ultimately culminates in samadhi. Samadhi is zanmai in Japanese; it indicates profound concentration in which the individual is one with the universe. Nakamura Sensei described zanmai as an ecstatic state in his paperback *Anjo Daza Kosho* (*A Booklet on Anjo Daza Meditation*).

In India he experienced dharana, dhyana, and samadhi under the tutelage of Kaliapa; yet after returning to Japan he realized the methods used in the Himalayas were designed for Indians and Nepalese living in a remote village. Citizens of Tokyo resided in a vastly more urban atmosphere. They were typically more educated and more influenced by science than the villagers of Gorkhe. In this sense they were like people in the West today.

As a result, Nakamura Sensei devised a new meditation called Anjo Daza Ho, embodying the traditional essence of dharana and dhyana, leading to samadhi. He wanted this innovative method to appeal to modern people and to be scientific in spirit. He drew on his Indian experiences, but he didn't require his students to meditate beside a waterfall as he had.

Creating *Anjo Daza Ho*

In the late 1960s, he gave a famous lecture entitled *Shin-jin Mei-go*, roughly "*The Invisible Connection between Humanity and the Spirit of the Universe.*" In this talk Nakamura Sensei explained that he spent some years developing Anjo Daza Ho. He recognized the mind can easily attain concentration—the first step in meditation—by focusing on a sound. He used the ringing of a Japanese meditation bell as the object of concentration in Anjo Daza Ho, and later he offered as an alternative the steady drone of a buzzer.

In *A Magnificent Life* he indicated:

Every day I sat for long hours and practiced yoga meditation (dhyana) from morning to night—all alone sitting on a rock by a waterfall in the mountains of India. The meditation aimed at clearing away attachments to needless thoughts.

When I came home after three years training there I wondered, "Do we really need such severe practice to get rid of delusions? The mind is the symbol of human beings as the lords of creation. Why must we practice so hard, using special techniques, just to clear the mind?"

I realized there's no special way to cure the body when tired. We just need to rest. I figured it might be the same with the mind.

It's unnecessary to practice rigorously to return to our true, original, and natural mental state. We don't need to strain to clear away mistaken and meaningless ideas, because the human mind in and of itself is something superb. We just need to find a way to do nothing and let the mind return to its original and natural condition.

This idea hit me unexpectedly.[63]

Nakamura Sensei referred to humanity as the "lords of creation" because only people display advanced reasoning, and only human beings can be consciously aware of their oneness with the universe. Plants and animals are one with the universe, but they're unaware of it, and they can't consciously act based on this realization. As I mentioned in Chapter Five, unfortunately countless individuals live more like animals than genuine human beings, possessing both reason and spiritual consciousness (reisei ishiki). We frequently fail to grasp our innate unity with the universe and suffer from this lack of understanding.

Anjo Daza Ho, like numerous aspects of Shin-shin-toitsu-do, emerged from Nakamura Sensei's quest to cure his tuberculosis. At over 90 years old, he recalled his meditation in India which eventually resulted in the birth of Anjo Daza Ho:

When my disease worsened, I couldn't help speaking to my teacher—the only person I could rely on then—about the pain and troubles I was feeling. I couldn't understand why he said without explanation, "If you want to complain about your body, go into the mountains and meditate on the sound of the waterfall."

That's a very coldhearted thing to say, isn't it? If he'd said, "Is that so? It's a pity. Shall I do something to help you? I'm sorry you're ill. It must be hard," I would have been greatly consoled. But this line of reasoning is wrong. Most people, however, think it's not. He couldn't help me by saying such things.

I first thought he was cruel and unsympathetic. But as I realized later there was nothing he could do to help me other than what he suggested.

We were in a deep virgin forest which was dark even in the daytime. It was really dark. As your eyes grow accustomed to it you can see things vaguely, but at first you can't tell a huge snake from a pine tree. It's as if you were thrown into an underground dungeon.

Sitting by a waterfall, that had been dropping tons of water for thousands of years, various thoughts about my body ran through my mind . . . at first. I thought, "What would become of me if I died here? I'm all alone, and nobody can help me, regardless of how much pain I'm in. Why did I come to this remote mountain in India? Out of curiosity?"

I was helpless. But gradually my mind, which was like a violent horse I'm ashamed to say, grew calm in the midst of the sound of the cataract. It was really a deafening roar.

My mind first experienced yuga ichi-nen ("concentration on one thought, but with self-consciousness") and then later I experienced muga ichi-nen ("concentration on one thought, but without self-consciousness"). I was aware of myself sitting by the waterfall, but I was also drawn into the roar of the falling water. Then I stopped thinking of my body and the turbulence of the mind worrying about itself disappeared. The human mind is naturally made to work this way, to be free of self-consciousness and worry.[64]

What Nakamura Sensei recalled was what we initially experience in Anjo Daza Ho. The mind first learns to focus on a single thought, in this case, a sound. This is dharana, deep concentration on one point, which Raja yogis use to release the unlimited power of the mind. Dharana is a preamble to meditation, and Nakamura Sensei later labeled it muga ichi-nen. This is to concentrate so deeply on something that it utterly fills the mind to become a single thought (ichi-nen). When this happens we forget ourselves (muga). Only the moment and the object of concentration remain.

Kaliapa asked Nakamura Sensei to sit beside an immense and ancient waterfall, while focusing his mind on its sound, to teach the intense concentration he called dharana. From dharana yogis enter dhyana, meditative consciousness, which is what Nakamura Sensei remembered experiencing next:

Then I found myself in a world where I didn't hear any sound, even the waterfall—but just for one moment. I thought, "I wasn't sleeping, but I didn't hear the water's sound for a moment. Why?"[65]

After returning to Japan Nakamura Sensei described this meditative consciousness in various ways. In some cases he referred to experiencing *musei no koe*, the "soundless sound." Other times he indicated progressing from concentrating on one thought without self-consciousness to concentration on that which is beyond both thought and self (*muga munen*). These different explanations describe the same process of moving from concentration on an objective (or sound) to objectless, effortless concentration. It's moving from dharana to dhyana, from deliberate concentration to meditation.

This sitting meditation, where I completely focused my mind on the sound of the waterfall, was one of the first practices my teacher gave me to do in the mountains in India. It continued every day for six months. The first month passed and I grasped the state of doing nothing and thinking nothing. I naturally went into a spiritual world, touching the unlimited power that is the universal ki.

The fever, which tortured me for eight years, subsided. I stopped vomiting. I felt no heart throbbing any more, however fast I walked. A flood of vigor welled up inside me. I wondered why, but my guru didn't say anything. So I talked to him at last, after two months of feeling like this. He said, "You haven't complained in days, have you?"

"Well, my body feels better now."

"If your thinking from the start was the way it is now, you needn't have suffered so much. It was nonsense. A human being doesn't think of his body when he's asleep, even when he is nearly dying."

"While he's sleeping without worry, the universal spirit gives him the power to revive. You've changed your mental state, so naturally you can receive power from nature. What's the use of worrying about yourself? If worrying helps you get better, worry all the time. But worrying makes you worse. You cannot be a strong person if you don't stop worrying. You've got it, don't you? Do you understand why I told you to go to the mountain to concentrate on the sound of the falls, instead of complaining about rubbish?"

I answered, "Yes, I've got it."[66]

More and more medical science recognizes the impact worry and emotional trauma has on physical health. A 2007 study found a connection between stress, poor personal relationships, and sickness. Lindsey Tanner of the Associated Press wrote:

Marital strife and other bad personal relationships can raise your risk of heart disease, researchers reported Monday.

What it likely boils down to is stress—a well-known contributor to health problems, as well as a potential byproduct of troubled relationships, the scientists said. In a study of 9,011 British civil servants, most of them married, those with the worst close relationships were 34 percent more likely to have heart attacks or other heart trouble during 12 years of follow-up than those with good relationships.[67]

Time magazine reports worry-relieving meditation has numerous benefits that are being scientifically validated:

At the University of Wisconsin at Madison, Richard Davidson has used brain imaging to show that meditation shifts activity in the prefrontal cortex (right behind our foreheads) from the right hemisphere to the left. Davidson's research suggests that by meditating regularly, the brain is reoriented from a stressful fight-or-flight mode to one of acceptance, a shift that increases contentment. People who have a negative disposition tend to be right-prefrontal oriented; left-prefrontals have more enthusiasms, more interests, relax more and tend to be happier, though perhaps with less real estate.[68]

To deal with interpersonal tension and stress, doctors increasingly suggest meditation to people with heart disease and hypertension, while other physicians comment on the correlation between anxiety and a weakened immune system. Though these are relatively recent developments in the West, long ago Kaliapa in India and Nakamura Sensei in Japan indicated the deep-seated relationship between concentration, meditation, and psychosomatic wellness:

> The yoga people I trained with didn't explain this as kindly and directly as I'm doing now. The principle is simple. When you are attached to some idea, image, thought, or desire, you're easily tired out. When you're not mentally fixated or upset in this way, you're not easily tired.
>
> And if you're willing to do whatever is required of you, anything you have to carry out or live with isn't burdensome. If you're not willing to lift it even a sheet of paper feels heavy.
>
> When we watch an interesting play we're never tired. But during the interval when we're staring at the closed curtain, we'll grow tired and restless in five minutes.
>
> To relieve your tiredness, restlessness, or unhappiness you'll have to change and deal with yourself. If the mind is fixated on itself or the body, you'll soon be exhausted. So a nervous person won't as easily improve in his or her disease. Some of these people may die from illnesses they could have overcome with a different attitude.[69]

In Anjo Daza Ho we discover a mind which releases its attachments to the body, the self, and the process of thought. In this condition the heartbeat slows, respiration deepens and calms, blood pressure normalizes, and worry ceases. The positive effects of meditation on physiological and psychological health are immense.

Practicing Anjo Daza Ho

Anjo Daza Ho involves bringing the mind into the present, the only moment in which the body exists. As a result, it fosters coordination of mind and body. The mental state in Anjo Daza Ho helps you become successful in Shin-shin-toitsu-do as well as transfer the insights from this discipline into life.

Anjo Daza Ho can be practiced using most postures, but I recommend the *seiza* sitting position (**Fig. 16**). In India Nakamura Sensei used the full or half lotus positions, *siddhasana* and *padmasana* respectively in Sanskrit. These asana, or "postures," are utilized in Raja yoga for stability in meditation and for developing healthy, flexible legs. Nakamura Sensei also advocated the lotus posture as does Zen (although it's easier to properly align the spine in seiza). Full and half-lotus postures are shown in **Fig. 17** and **Fig. 18**.

If you're not accustomed to these postures, copy the illustrations, but adopt the positions slowly and carefully. They're helpful for first-rate posture and balance, but they require flexibility. You can also sit erect in a firm chair (**Fig. 19**).

Forming a circle with the thumb and index finger of each hand, while interlacing the other fingers together as in the illustrations, is called an *in* in Japanese. It's comparable to the Indian term *mudra*. This specific gesture is called *Sorin-in*, and Nakamura Sensei learned it from Kaliapa. It's largely symbolic, indicating unification of opposites, and the little finger edges of the hands touch four finger widths below the navel as in **Fig. 20**. (Since this "in" is symbolic its use isn't required.)

More important than the precise sitting position is your posture. It must be upright, but relaxed—a posture in which body parts respond to gravity and settle into their appropriate place.

Meditation and Posture

During meditation a relaxed, erect, and aligned posture is essential. Nakamura Sensei noted as much in his lecture *The Invisible Connection between Humanity and the Spirit of the Universe*. He suggested a good posture, a posture allowing you to sit comfortably for a long time—a posture that's not tense and not hard to maintain long term. He indicated you can cross your legs, but don't lie on the floor. Closing the eyes was also suggested, but once you've got the knack for Anjo Daza Ho, you can either open your eyes or close them. However if beginners open their eyes they're apt to become attached to something they see. Nakamura Sensei urged his audience not to change their fixed posture once meditation starts. But he added if you feel pain or numbness changing your position a bit is intelligent, further noting that when you've practiced more seriously you'll be able to sit with no movement.[70]

In the aforementioned speech Nakamura Sensei suggested not lying down for Anjo Daza Ho, but this was due to space limitations in the lecture hall. In his book *Kenshin Sho (Polishing the Mind)* he also wrote that it was possible to meditate while reclining. Nonetheless, it's easier to avoid falling asleep when seated, and you can try the sitting positions outlined previously. Keep in mind the following details as they're important for mind-body unification in meditation.

Fig. 16. Sit lightly on your heels. The big toes cross and there is some space between the knees. The shoulders are down and relaxed. The lower back is straight, and the chest is open. This meditation position is called seiza.

Fig. 17. Sit lightly on the ground. The left leg is on top of the right, with the heel close to the lower abdomen, and the relaxed posture is erect. This is the half lotus posture.

Fig. 18. Sit lightly on the ground. Relax with an expansive posture. The right foot is on the left thigh, and the left foot is on the right thigh. The left leg is on top of the right. The heels are near the lower abdomen. This is the yogi's famous full lotus posture.

Fig. 19. Using a chair is fine for meditation. Sit down lightly. Straighten the lower back and drop the shoulders naturally. Avoid leaning against the chair's back. Keep the feet close to the chair.

In the seiza kneeling posture (**Fig. 16**) sit lightly on the heels, with the big toes crossed on top of each other and some space between the knees. Even though seiza is difficult—at first—for people who are stiff, it's practical for centering weight forward and down into the lower abdomen (shita hara).

When sitting cross-legged or in the lotus posture (**Fig. 17** and **Fig. 18**) lean forward slightly to settle the knees downward toward the floor and drop the upper body weight toward the shita hara. If this forward lean is uncomfortable try sitting on a firm cushion that's high enough to press your knees gently against the floor. Because the cushion raises your shita hara above your knees there's no need for a moderate forward lean to maintain stability.

Balancing your posture at the shita hara and focusing the mind in the same spot has a lengthy tradition in Japanese arts and meditation. It's easiest to use a spot on the front surface of the abdomen, about four finger widths below the navel, as your mental point of balance. Regard this as a natural center in the lower abdomen that corresponds to your center of balance and center of gravity.

Don't slump, which causes body weight to slip backward and away from your shita hara. Avoid lifting the shoulders, which unsettles and lifts your body upward and away from the shita hara. Sit down lightly, almost as if your bottom were sore, and retain a relaxed carriage that looks big.

Numerous times during meditation, and even in daily life, the head sags forward. Then the neck collapses, curves, and shortens. This produces a "hump" at its base (near the seventh cervical vertebra). Before long, the rest of the spine curves in on itself as well. You can change this by concentrating on the shita hara and then correcting your posture with the action of your head. Mentally release your muscles (beside the neck and spine in particular). Visualizing your shita hara as a sort of anchor, guide the top of your head up and away from your lower abdomen. Next, draw in your chin and bring your forehead and breastbone back into alignment with your shita hara. Allow the spine and neck to elongate until your posture is aligned. (Envisioning the muscles along the spine growing longer and wider is a practical method to use at this point.) If you concentrate deeply and relax, the body will move gradually into the correct position, with limited conscious effort on your part. Don't coerce your body into an overly erect posture.

By relaxing and applying visualization you can also encourage the chest to expand, while the back and shoulders widen. In most cases the ears, shoulders, and pelvis should be parallel to the ground. Your head, shoulders, and pelvis are likewise not twisted.

If you rest in a chair (**Fig. 19**) avoid sitting with legs outstretched; this causes your

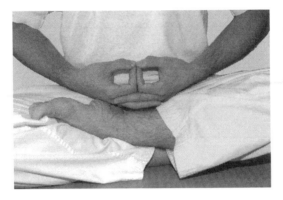

Fig. 20. This is Sorin-in, Na-kamura Sensei's favored hand position for meditation. The tips of the index fingers and thumbs touch to form rings. The other fingers are interlaced beneath the rings, and the little finger edges of the hands touch the lower abdomen.

pelvis to roll backwards and your lumbar region to curve outward in a slouch. When sitting in a chair, sit with the feet flat on the floor or tucked under the chair, roughly as your legs tuck under your hips in seiza. This maintains your natural lumbar curve, and it shifts weight toward the front surface of the lower midsection—exactly where you want to center your weight and mind in the shita hara.

Relax your face and eyes. Find the most comfortable posture within the context of the above directions. This act of "centering" causes a balanced position.

While some might feel these postural details could be distracting or confusing during meditation, this needn't be the case. Simply set up a good posture before you begin Anjo Daza Ho, and then leave your body alone during meditation. There's no need to think about your posture once you've established it (unless you start to slouch). Repeated practice of correct posture in meditation creates postural habits, which can be maintained in everyday life, resulting in a healthier tension-free life.

Starting Anjo Daza Ho

Anjo characterizes a "peaceful and stable feeling." Daza refers to a seated position, and ho is a "method" or "exercise." A Japanese bowl-shaped bell called *rin* or *kane* is re-quired (**Fig. 21**). When the edge or side of the bell is hit with its accompanying wooden striker, a mellow gong-type tone is created. This bell can sustain a lengthy resonance, de-pending on its size and the quality of the metal used. For numerous people it has a calming effect. The Sennin Foundation Center for Japanese Cultural Arts has created a CD with the sound of a ringing bell and appropriate silences for meditation. Information about the CD can be found in this book's Resources for Further Instruction and Equipment.

Fig. 21. This is a kane, a Japanese bell that can be used for Anjo Daza Ho meditation. Concentrate on the ringing until you forget yourself, and the sound is your only thought. When you no longer hear the bell, sit and do nothing.

To start Anjo Daza Ho, use the following instructions:

1. Adopt a seated pose in which you can maintain proper posture as well as the unity of mind and body. Close your eyes. Avoid shutting them firmly or abruptly as this produces meditation-inhibiting tension.

2. Hit the bell cleanly one time, and focus your attention on the tone produced. This should be relaxed concentration. Attempting to block out other sounds and thoughts only diverts you from the resonance of the bell that you're mentally following.

3. Let the bell's note fill your mind to become one thought. When your mind contains this single thought completely, while not trying to drive out other sensory impressions, your self is forgotten. Muga ichi-nen is attained; no division exists between you and the universe (in which the sound resonates.) Muga means "no self" but is more easily understood as "no self-consciousness." Ichi-nen is "one thought." Attaining "no self, one thought" is a vital first step in Anjo Daza Ho.

4. Having focused on the bell's tone, notice that the sound is gradually fading . . . growing dimmer like the image of ki traveling away from you in the orenai te exercise. This works to your benefit and here's why. If we think of the reverberation as ichi-nen, "one thought," then as the mind follows the fading tone it arrives at munen, "no thoughts." Munen is a condition that's still like a pond with no waves. All bodies of water, of course, hold some small waves. Our minds also have a brain wave pattern as long as we're alive, and so "no thoughts" or "no waves" are metaphors for calmness.

5. Once the reverberation fills your mind to form one thought, pursue the decreasing sound waves. If concentration is achieved, as the waves grow smaller, so do your brain waves. Although all brains show wave patterns it's possible to arrive at a continually smaller and calmer pattern of waves. The bell's sound leads us in this direction. Think of it as a resonance that's infinitely decreasing, like the number one which can be divided endlessly by half without becoming zero.

6. Last, as the sound waves grow infinitely small keep pursuing them mentally. Even when you can't perceive the sound, let the feeling and state of mind that's been produced continue on its own. The secret is to *do nothing*; then the condition of tranquility is unchanged. Sit as long as you find comfortable in this tranquil state.

In the late 1960s, near the end of his life, Nakamura Sensei spoke of Anjo Daza Ho simply and directly:

Your mind is drawn to the sound of the bell ringing. Gradually the tone decreases, leaving some reverberation or a lingering sound, and in that endlessly decreasing resonance you can taste a world of deep tranquility.

You hear the sound getting smaller, don't you? Keep ceaselessly pursuing it, and when you don't hear it, there is calmness. The real eternal nature of the universe has no sound and no form. It is a vast nothingness (ku). Colors, shapes, and sounds we see or hear belong to the phenomenal and transient aspect of the universe. You can mentally connect with the real aspect of life any time you like.

The world of ku, or "nothingness," is filled with a power capable of reviving your life. If your mind approaches it, your life will be linked with this unlimited power. This is a principle of nature. We can understand this principle from the viewpoint of modern physics. Similar objects always assimilate to each other.[71]

In other words, we are nature. Nature is us. The universe and the individual are composed of the same ki—a vast and all-encompassing energy that's "something yet nothing, nothing yet something." Anjo Daza Ho leads to this profound realization of our inherent unity with the universe or nature.

Fig. 22. This buzzer creates an alternative sound. When the buzzing fills your whole mind, with no other thoughts, you have realized concentration. When the sound ceases continue to concentrate on a "soundless sound." This is meditation.

Letting Go of the Object of Concentration and an Alternate Approach

Unless listening and attention remain after the sound fades, calmness fades as well. When you can't hear the bell, what are you listening to? In a sense, you're listening to the universe. At this time allow your listening to expand to fill the universe.

What if you lose concentration? Just hit the bell and begin again. Nakamura Sensei frequently addressed calmness and subsequent distraction in Anjo Daza Ho:

> At first you may only reach the state of doing nothing and thinking nothing for a brief moment. After some practice you can sense it for longer periods.
>
> But then you hear a car passing by, or you feel your back itching or a drop of sweat running down your body. And you return to your old state of mind. But once you're accustomed to this practice, you can turn your mind to the soundless sound at any time. In the beginning, however, an ordinary person or a person who's easily attached to something is drawn to whatever he or she senses—one sensation after another—and the "noisy world" returns.[72]

One day someone was vacuuming within earshot of Nakamura Sensei. He'd grown accustomed to the steady hum of the vacuum when suddenly its electrical cord was accidently pulled from the wall socket. When the sound abruptly ceased Nakamura Sensei experienced a psychological condition similar to that in Anjo Daza Ho. Seeking to take advantage of this realization, he began also using a buzzer as an object of concentration in group meditation. (You can see a Shin-shin-toitsu-do style buzzer in **Fig. 22**, and you can practice listening to its buzzing with the Sennin Foundation Center's meditation

CD, which contains this sound as well as the ringing of a bell.) This alternate approach has both advantages and disadvantages.

First, these devices are similar to a doorbell buzzer, but they aren't commercially available. Some Shin-shin-toitsu-do teachers in Japan make them and share them. The bell, on the other hand, can be purchased both in and outside of Japan.

Second, the tone of the bell weakens little by little, which helps us let go of this sound but not lose attentiveness. While one can slowly turn down the sound of some buzzers (using a knob), many click off abruptly. Sometimes the concentration of meditators clicks off as well.

Third, if you're practicing alone with a buzzer you'll have to reach over and switch it off (unless you rig up a bell with timer which automatically cuts the sound). The bell's ringing fades on its own.

Fourth, while the reverberation of the bell is regularly described as "peaceful," the buzzer's note is anything but. Numerous students prefer the bell. Consequently, in quite a few dojo (training halls) in Japan the bell is more commonly used.

Like lots of things in life, the "weak points" of the buzzer are also its strong points. Not everyone concentrates easily and the loud buzzing sound is very sharp compared to the bell, effectively holding the mind in the present. Some children at the Sennin Foundation Center liken the buzzer to a loud alarm clock, an apt analogy since both devices awaken us.

Plus, the sound of the bell dies away rapidly, with an echoing note which typically lasts a minute at best. A buzzer sustains its sound as long as it's turned on, giving beginners more time to focus completely on the hum while letting go of their attachments to everything else. Accordingly, some sensei emphasize the buzzer over the bell for new students, and still other teachers use the bell and the buzzer one after another, alternating throughout the meditation session.

Even though concentration can switch off with the buzzer, for some the sudden silence more sharply focuses the mind in the moment. It undoubtedly gets your attention. If you continue paying attention, as you did when listening to the buzzing, the unexpected cessation of sound needn't be a problem.

We can find alternate sounds to substitute for a buzzer. The aforementioned buzzing alarm clock can be rigged to work as can any similar alarm on a watch or cell phone. How loud should it be? Perhaps I've listened to too many punk bands, but my advice is: Pump up the volume! Short of injuring one's ears, a strong noise that drowns out distracting racket is useful for forgetting ourselves and focusing fully on a single sound.

It's also possible to get similar results by listening to a powerful fan, which should be situated near you, and which you should be able to turn off. Kaliapa placed Nakamura Sensei next to a massive waterfall for meditation. Nakamura Sensei was probably trying to replicate the boom of the waterfall by using a loud and steady buzz during Anjo Daza Ho.

We can employ either a bell's fading note or a buzzing noise for Anjo Daza Ho, but the main point is to actually meditate. How long you practice Anjo Daza Ho is up to you. Try starting with 15 minutes of sitting. Employing meditation before beginning your day, and again before falling sleep, calms the mind and sustains this state throughout the day.

As far as technique goes that's all there is to Anjo Daza Ho. The method is straightforward. But what takes place while engaging in this technique, and what it means in terms of meditation and life, is profound. As we practice Anjo Daza Ho, it's important to consider:

- Perception vs. thought
- Concentration vs. attachment
- The nature of time
- Genuine listening

Perception and Thought

Scores of people don't distinguish between perception and thought. The brain is designed to constantly receive various perceptions via the five senses and the nervous system. It's a survival mechanism. Any animal in the wild that ceases having immediate, clear, and accurate perceptions of what's going on around it won't live long. Human beings are similar, and it's unnatural to block out sensory perceptions in meditation. It may be impossible, too. That understood, we don't inevitably need to label our perceptions during meditation, nor do we need to cling to them, creating an endless series of largely useless thoughts.

Perception is reported to us from our environment and it's inevitable. We can't avoid smelling food cooking, hearing a bird's song, or other sensory perceptions during meditation. Nor should we try; the five senses are designed to report what's going on in our environment. If they fail to do this, then something's gone wrong.

Thought is different from perception. It's the labeling of perception based on past experiences and memories, the mind commenting on and analyzing perception. It's useful at times, but in other instances (like meditation) it serves no purpose. When we're not attached to our perceptions thought dissipates. In meditation we fully experience various perceptions, but we don't inevitably create thoughts about these perceptions.

Perceptions aren't a problem unless the mind becomes attached to what it perceives. In fact, it's when we're in the meditative state—calm and not clinging to various perceptions—that we most acutely and accurately perceive reality. Thought is also no problem when it's used as a tool for living. But for lots of us thoughts are constant, regularly unwanted, and frequently meaningless. We should use thought when needed but not be forced to continually experience thoughts when they're unneeded. Meditation allows us to discover a mind free from attachment to thought.

So if you briefly hear a bird during Anjo Daza Ho, completely experience the sound, let it go, and return to doing nothing. There's often no need to think about what you perceive during meditation, where experiencing is more important than thinking. An obvious exception is perceiving a smoke detector going off. Then thought is needed to determine the best course of action.

Attention without Attachment

The qualities cultivated to arrive at muga ichi-nen ("no self, one thought") are as meaningful as the condition that's cultivated. Although these qualities are multifaceted, one main point is learning to concentrate the mind without having it "get stuck" anywhere or at anytime. To illustrate, if we focus ki on a ringing bell we cannot arrive at muga ichi-nen without discovering how to deal with external stimuli and our thoughts—all of which can divert the mind from the object of concentration. If your mind gets stuck on an outer sound or an internal sound (a thought), it's no longer centered on the bell's resonance. If you try blocking out these noises your mind's still fighting them, and you've set up a conflict-ridden condition.

However, suppose you're sitting near a busy street. Across the street you see something which grabs your attention. As you observe the spectacle, people pass through your line of sight. Do you track each person, or do you notice the passing individuals while keeping your attention on what you're viewing?

The bell's tone is what you're "watching," while exterior stimuli and internal thoughts are "passing people." Note each thought and feeling, but don't mentally comment on it or let the mind attach itself to it. Just silently "watch" the ringing of the bell and do nothing.

Just as there's usually a space or interval between people passing on the street, a space also exists between thoughts and perceptions even if it sometimes seems small. In meditation can you find this gap between thoughts? What is this gap and does it belong to the realm of time? If it doesn't then it's unborn and undying, beyond "emotional baggage" and other forms of psychological conditioning, which is a carry over from the past to the present. When the mind remains rooted in the moment we notice everything around us and within us, but we don't become attached to these perceptions. Once the mind is stuck on something we perceive via our five senses, we're not paying attention to what's taking place in the moment. Concentration is lost, and we're stuck in the past.

In Shin-shin-toitsu-do we find a condition which accurately notes all facets of the relative world's impermanent phenomena, without becoming fixated on—or disturbed by—any of these phenomena. This lets us connect with the deeper, absolute universe that's eternal, much like the truest part of ourselves. Nonattachment was a central part of Nakamura Sensei's talks:

> In the reality of the universe, what we perceive through our senses isn't real. Are you confused to hear this? Whatever you hear with your ears, whatever you see with your eyes . . . all of this is unreal. Some of you are thinking, "Is he kidding?" No, I'm not kidding.
>
> Think more deeply. Consider the nature of water, snow, rain, frost, and hail. They're not real as well in that they don't have permanent reality. They come and go. They change form. They are phenomenal and transient, aren't they? They're water in various combinations of particles of hydrogen and oxygen. In its different combinations water changes into snow, rain, frost, or hail. That which is constantly changing is impermanent and relative—in other words, it's unreal. That which gives birth to the changing phenomena of the relative world is real and eternal; our real, eternal, and genuine self can perceive it.
>
> Most people don't understand this easily, because mistaken ideas and ignorance of the genuine nature of reality mislead their way of thinking. Why? It's because their ideas about life work effectively only within the changing and phenomenal sphere of things.[73]

Nakamura Sensei's insistence that ephemeral aspects of our relative world are not "real" is not an artifact of translation. He was redefining the use of the word in Japanese as well. As you proceed through this book, you'll discover his thoughts on the true reality of existence, and why he felt it was important to transcend attachment to all that is impermanent.

Anjo Daza Ho leads to a consciousness that's unattached to what our senses take in. In this state we connect with that which gives rise to the fluctuating phenomena in our relative world. We experience the eternal aspects of ourselves and the universe, resulting in a mind beyond suffering. And make no mistake, we suffer primarily because of our attachments to impermanent parts of life.

We may struggle for years to buy a fancy car we really want. We're unhappy until we purchase this vehicle; yet once we get it, we worry about making payments on it. We're concerned that it may be stolen. We lose sleep if it gets a door ding. Like everything, the car may someday be lost or destroyed. Then we're depressed about its fate, and we agonize over buying another similar vehicle in the future.

We suffer when we don't have what we desire. We suffer when we finally obtain the object of desire, because we're afraid of losing it. And we suffer when it's inevitably damaged or lost. When do we get to be happy?

Desires and Attachments

Due to scenarios like the above, some scholars of Eastern religion and/or meditation conclude desire equals suffering. Countless related books indicate as much, and readers struggle to live without desires. While it makes a certain kind of sense to believe living without desires produces happiness, is such a thing is doable?

Note that quite a few "spiritual authors" can't explain how to buy their book without first desiring a copy of it. Certainly some teachers of meditation try to avoid this problem with mystical mumbo jumbo and philosophical doubletalk, but deeper consideration reveals no likely circumstance within which we can get food for ourselves and work each day without the desire to do so. Seeing this contradiction, significant numbers conclude such things are impossible and continue suffering due to their attachments. Yet it is possible to distinguish between desire and attachment. They're distinct from each other, and while desires are impossible to eliminate, attachments are another animal. Brad Warner's *Hardcore Zen* discusses this same topic:

Everyone has desires. We can't live without them. Nor should we. The problem isn't that we have natural desires and needs. It's that we have a compulsive (and ultimately stupid!) desire for our lives to be something other than what they actually are. We have a world in front of us (and within us) that can't possibly match that image. The problem is the way we let our desires stand in the way of our enjoyment of what we already have.[74]

Unlike some books on Buddhism, *Hardcore Zen* confirms desires cannot be eliminated:

It's not that we force ourselves to stop having desires. That won't solve anything and it's impossible anyhow. Trying to force yourself not to desire just brings up more desires (not the least of which is the desire not to desire). You'll often hear religious-type people saying, "The only thing that I desire is desirelessness."

. . . If you have desires, leave them as they are and do what needs to be done.[75]

I think Nakamura Sensei would have appreciated this 21st century take on Zen, because he also taught it's natural to desire food to eat, clothes to wear, and a roof over our heads. Such desires are survival instincts. To deny these instincts, and countless others, is unnatural. There's a difference between the intelligent desire not to have a flat tire and being attached to never having a flat. Nobody wants to dirty their hands by the side of the road. Still, if a flat happens we can kick the car, hurt our foot, and fume while we wait for roadside repair . . . or we can approach the situation differently.

If we're not attached to our desire to avoid a flat then we remain calm while waiting for help. In a calm state we may realize that we're failing to check tire pressure regularly which can lead to deflation. We can subsequently resolve to be more diligent about this, reducing the likelihood of future blow-outs or flat tires. In this example, we didn't get angry and raise our blood pressure because of a logical desire to avoid flat tires. We became upset because we're overly attached to not being inconvenienced.

Desire isn't the problem; attachment to what we desire is the problem.

Nakamura Sensei noted this distinction. At a time when numerous religious leaders and meditation teachers in Japan preached against human desires—especially of a sexual or material nature—Nakamura Sensei taught the difference between desire and attachment. His written works aimed at freeing people from the counterproductive repression of natural desires and needless internal struggle. He further distinguished between constructive desires, which help us and others, and destructive desires which lead to our downfall. His practical advice explained the typically unexplained difference between desire and attachment, while he asked readers if their desires were working for them or against them.

Seeing the distinction between desire and attachment isn't difficult, but we still may wonder how to live free from obsessions and attachments. Unfortunately, intellectual understanding of nonattachment isn't enough. We need to experience it ourselves, and meditation gives us the chance to do just that.

Transcending attachments lies at the heart of meditation and it's within our grasp. Whatever thoughts or internal conflicts come up in meditation—*do nothing*. Do not try to force them to cease or change; if you do, you'll be attached to them. And don't "do nothing" to still the mind, quiet fears, or resolve conflicts. All of this is *doing something*, and these all amount to goals, which move the mind away from the meditative state. This only leads to more struggling and prevents you from seeing the actual nature of thought and internal conflict.

In Anjo Daza Ho, attention, or listening, doesn't involve effort or motive. Effort merely distracts you from what's taking place in the instant. A concentration exists that's not forced. We've all experienced it when we've listened or paid attention to something we truly enjoy. At that moment was effort required for concentration to take place?

Drawing inspiration from Kaliapa's Raja yoga, Nakamura Sensei promoted Anjo Daza Ho as a nonreligious means of seeing deeply into our real nature and that of life itself. He called this spiritual consciousness (reisei ishiki). His medium was effortless concentration, concentration without attachment to concentration itself. In his typically simple and frank style he explained this in one of his talks:

> Absolute consciousness exists beyond relative thought and impermanent phenomena, and it evokes an incredible power that exists in the depth of human beings. All people possess this power of mind and body unification, whether they're well educated or not, whether they are experienced in meditation or not, whether they're male or female. You are naturally given it, regardless of sex, race, or age. You certainly have it, but some people never use it.
>
> I traveled about two-thirds of the world, including Europe and the U.S.

I traveled deep into a forest in India, and I learned about absolute spiritual consciousness for the first time from my teacher Kaliapa. He said to me, "Do you know you have spiritual consciousness hidden in the depths of your mind?"

"No, I don't have such a thing."

He retorted, "You have it; you just don't know you have it. Why are we meditating in the mountains every day? Our aim is to awaken the power dormant in ourselves."

I asked, "Can't we awaken it without spending our whole lives doing these hard practices?"

Kaliapa said, "Once you've learned the correct technique to awaken it, you needn't struggle to awaken it. Unfortunately most yoga people in India think they must practice severely to find this power."

You'll understand the words of my teacher once you've heard the conclusion of this lecture. Becoming a true human being, who has realized his or her true potential, shouldn't be difficult, should it? It's difficult for a human to become a monkey or a horse. It's rather impossible. We're born as human beings, not as a baby monkeys or horses, so why do we struggle to realize our humanity and the power born of it?

Gradually we've become fake human beings, and we don't notice the existence of spiritual consciousness deep in the mind, which is the mark of a true human being. You've been too busy chasing after various desires. It's like chasing your own shadow.[76]

Based on the above, it is clear meditation involves releasing our attachments to impermanent, relative things and letting go of attachments altogether. To accomplish this we focus completely on a sound, releasing everything else but this sound. Subsequently we drop even the sound of the bell. This is like gathering up everything we're attached to and dumping it into a single bag. We then toss this bag into a bottomless pit and live free from attachments.

Suppose you actually dropped something into a bottomless pit. As you watched the object fall, the image of it would become smaller and smaller, until it was too small to see. This is like the decreasing sound of the bell in Anjo Daza Ho.

But even when you couldn't see this object, you wouldn't imagine it disappeared. You'd conclude it was still there, just too small and far away to be observed. In the same way the meditating mind releases its attachments with the fading echo of the bell, but it doesn't let go of being wholly awake and attentive.

Beyond Words

In meditation there's no necessity to attach a word or label to each thought or sensation. During Anjo Daza Ho relaxed concentration is needed, which perceives the essence of life beyond words. And while words are needed for communication they have limitations. Commonly when we label something, we don't entirely perceive its genuine, present nature. We perceive everything we already know and believe about *the word*—rather than experiencing completely what's before our eyes or ears right now.

We're translating reality rather than seeing reality as it is. That's why when two or more people view an event, more than one interpretation of what happened can occur. Each individual translates reality based on his or her prejudices, fears, and conditioning as opposed to facts. (Simple, but all too typical, examples are crude stereotypes about people of different races that some folks engage in.) Is it possible to see existence as it is, to see actual reality before interpretation takes place?

Perhaps it's when humanity evolves to see life for what it is, rather than what each individual thinks it is, or should be, that people will arrive at harmony. Certainly we can say this is impossible, but what's that statement based on? Is it our direct, uncorrupted perception of reality, or is it merely what we've heard, always believed, or how we've been conditioned to react by our past? In Anjo Daza Ho we face a reality beyond words, translations, and interpretations.

Since our ability to associate a word with a given perception stems from past knowledge and experiences, labeling during meditation keeps the mind from a direct, unaltered observation of the present. Do nothing—and say nothing to yourself—during meditation. Concentration without attachment, or doing nothing, is vital for all types of meditation. In a way, it's meditation itself.

Ultimately even the object of concentration drops away (in Anjo Daza Ho, a sound), and only uncorrupted attention without attachment remains, resting in the eternity of the moment. It's a moment outside of time, free of fixation and associated suffering, a moment having no divisions within and no barriers without.

Letting Go of the Past and Transcending Time

In Anjo Daza Ho the object of concentration fades but full attention remains—objectless concentration. Nevertheless, we have a strong tendency to be attached to past experiences. This is why we find it difficult to mentally allow the bell's tone to fade, and then do nothing, letting our full concentration remain in the present. Some people keep hearing the bell even when the ringing has become inaudible, and this interferes with their meditation. This is because even the present becomes something to cling to, reducing the present to the past. (The instant we say, "This is the present," that moment's already become the past.)

All of this is fixed in the mind's artificial creation of time. And time, at least on some levels, is contrived by humanity. Many parts of the USA have "daylight savings time," which confirms the human mind creates and manipulates time. Life is not time.

We end up being used by this self-created tool, instead of using it when needed. Then we mistake our artificial creation for reality. Reality is now. Now is beyond time.

In *A Booklet on Anjo Daza Meditation*, Nakamura Sensei wrote:

Time has no beginning, no end. Therefore it cannot in reality be measured.

Time as a utilitarian tool may be useful. However when regarded as an actuality, time is essentially an empty concept. Only the genuine self exists. That self, which is one with the absolute universe, is unborn and undying; therefore, it is beyond time.[78]

Our conditioning, fears, and suffering are rooted in what happened in the past, in time. In Anjo Daza Ho doing nothing means to carry nothing over from the past, to do nothing and arrive at a pure, unmodified perception of the instant . . . an instant beyond time. It's letting go of past psychological attachments and undergoing continual rebirth from moment to moment. Releasing the past equals experiencing a reality unmodified and unaltered by our memories of the past, which is how the past is often preserved. It doesn't exist outside of memory.

Although we may believe the past gives birth to memory, we should also know that our memories fashion the past. Lots of us are shaping our past just as we think we're giving birth to our future. This is a recognized psychological phenomenon called "memory distortion" or "pseudomemory."

History shows political leaders have repeatedly attempted to rewrite their past. Dictators forced school textbooks to be changed, governments conveniently left certain facts out of their written histories, and altered photographs no longer depict "inconvenient people." This is propaganda, and even though we think propaganda is produced by the state, we manufacture our own propaganda, modifying our pasts consciously and unconsciously according to our attachments.

Even our perceptions of events as they occur is habitually tainted by our attachments and fears, and every time we remember these modified moments we may further alter them. Our psyches are unfixed, rapidly changing, which allows the past to be impressionable and bendable. This can be avoided by letting the mind rest in the present.

We can't deny that past events lead to where we are in the present, but within the borders of where preceding actions have deposited us, we have total freedom. Our past needn't dictate what we do in the here and now. It's always our choice. Moreover, we can only really act in this instant. No genuine action takes place in the past or future, yet we obsess about the past and future as if we can actively participate in them. We can't. They don't exist.

Yet this moment is real and in this instant we can take real action to deal with where our past has lead us. The action can be positive or negative. It's up to us, but what we do now affects the future in myriad ways. Completely focusing on the present and dealing with it effectively is the most valuable preparation for the future. It's far more effective than worrying about the future. Existing in the instant, the mind moves beyond time. It also moves beyond age, because a mind in the moment is ageless.

We may long for youth, even when we realize numerous aspects of childhood were unpleasant. Maybe we'd like a younger, healthier body, but even healthy people in their twenties frequently crave a return to the past. Are we yearning for adolescence, or are we longing for a period when everything was fresh and vibrant?

When the mind clings to past emotions and experiences, the past becomes a weight to be carried into the present and future. Each time we latch onto a particular fear and/or painful occurrence—instead of living through these experiences fully and then letting them fade—we create and maintain an open wound. Eventually the mind accumulates so many "wounds" that it's scarred. Real scar tissue is insensitive, and our minds also become jaded and dulled to all but the most extreme sensations. This is why some seek extreme forms of sensation . . . just to feel something. Like other addictions, attachment to sensation keeps escalating.

For instance, as children even a trip to the park brought joy and excitement; finding an unusual flower might be wondrous. Yet for some adults, whose minds have accumulated too much, not even parachuting from a plane is enough. If our minds build up too many layers of yesterday we're unable to see life without translating it into the language of the past. Nothing's new and we find ourselves with an old mind, a mind worn down and weighed down by clinging to former experiences.

Close identification with chronological age further wears down the mind. Age is as artificial as time. Certain people are mature when technically "young," and other supposedly mature adults can barely fend for themselves. Rather than seeing who we genuinely are, or viewing a person's maturity by their actions, we see them and ourselves through the veil of age. We see an idea or representation but not reality itself.

Life is constant and ever-changing. It cannot be reduced to hours on a clock face, calendar months, or birthday candles. We invented clocks and calendars just as we invented chronological time. As for chronological age, in some cultures babies are thought to be one year old when they're born. So how old are we really? Different civilization's calendars measure the eons differently. So what month or year is it actually? Obviously sequential measuring of age and time has a practical function, but by focusing on the artificial, self-created nature of all of this, we engender a mind which focuses on image rather than fact, a mind caught in time. In Anjo Daza Ho we don't intellectually transcend time; we directly experience a moment beyond time.

A meditating mind completely perceives each moment and lets that moment die, so a vibrant new moment can be born. In listening without effort or motive, and seeing without clinging to what's seen, lies awareness transcending time and age. It cannot be measured. Being beyond time, it lasts forever without growing old.

That instant is now.

Genuine Listening

Anjo Daza Ho uses our hearing. Listening is essential in this exercise . . . but what does it mean to truly listen? We've heard that a particular person "only hears what he wants to hear," and most of us know what that's referring to. However to what degree does this phrase also relate to us—and perhaps most of humanity?

Let's try another common phrase: "He may be listening, but he's got his own agenda." When we listen, how many of us *don't* have our own agenda? If this is the case, do we perceive what's really been said, or do we perceive only our beliefs about what's being stated? Beliefs by their very nature stem from past experiences and can carry desires, prejudices, and conditioning. When we listen through this cloak of attachments and biases, we don't genuinely listen. We're only hearing ourselves. If we're listening to ourselves, carrying past emotional baggage with us, perhaps this is why so many people feel caught in a loop, incapable of transformation.

In communicating, we're commonly communicating with our image of people as much as listening to the real person. Are we listening and talking to the person in front of us, or are we listening and reacting to *our impression* of this individual? Our friend may be doing the same. Maybe this is why genuine communication is difficult for numerous individuals.

We may say we love our family or even the world. Yet this statement implies relationship. Is any factual relationship possible if our connection to the world and each other is based on former impressions and self-created ideas more than on present reality?

Meditation is an incredibly positive act, an act equivalent to intense observation of reality—an observation that's not based on the false security of past beliefs or a fear of what we might discover. Anjo Daza Ho involves direct, real perception and attention. It's a meditative state which can be sustained in every relationship, personal and impersonal.

Anjo Daza Ho in Review

When practicing Anjo Daza Ho bear in mind the following summarized points:

1. Sit with an erect (but relaxed) posture that's easy to maintain and which allows coordination of mind and body.
2. Strike the meditation bell one time and gently close your eyes. (As mentioned earlier, modify these directions when using a buzzer.)
3. Focus so deeply on the sound that you forget yourself and only the sound remains.
4. Mentally follow the sound waves as they become smaller and fainter.
5. When you can no longer hear the bell, do nothing and let your attention continue where the sound leaves off.
6. Sit as long as you like in this state of calmness. Note any perceptions, but don't cling to them, allowing the mind to instantly return to doing nothing.
7. If you lose the state beyond self-consciousness and attachment to thought, hit the bell and start again.

Chapter 8

MUGA ICHI-NEN HO MEDITATION

PRINCIPLES FOR BASIC MUGA ICHI-NEN HO

1. Unify mind and body while softly focusing your eyes on an object.

2. Do not just look but truly see.

3. Concentrate until you forget yourself and only the object remains.

4. Observe every part of the object, and then take it out of sight.

5. You should be capable of clearly visualizing it or sketching it in detail.

Dharana is the first step leading to meditation. It is roughly translated as "holding steady," implying ongoing concentration. Dharana exercises are an important aspect of classical Raja yoga, and they were a primary part of Nakamura Tempu Sensei's training under Kaliapa.

In dharana the item being meditated upon is kept in the mind without attention shifting from it. The difference between dharana (concentration) and dhyana (meditation) is that in the former, the object of concentration, the person concentrating, and the act of concentration are separate. In other words, the meditator is aware of focusing on an object and feels separate from this item. In the dhyana stage, awareness of the act of concentration and the person concentrating dissolves. Just the object of concentration exists in the mind. In Raja yoga students move from dharana to dhyana, finally experiencing samadhi. Indian yoga experts Leeza Lowitz and Reema Datta note:

Samadhi is the ultimate state of being, when the meditator merges with the object of meditation and the distinction between subject and object vanishes. In the Yoga Sutras, samadhi is "meditation that illumines the object alone, as if the subject were devoid of its own identity."[78]

Samadhi implies pure concentration resulting in union; it's often described as enlightenment. Although in numerous Indian practices the object of attention is God or the self (which some gurus see as God), Kaliapa didn't use this approach to teach Nakamura Sensei. He utilized elements of nature as objects of concentration instead of referring to Hindu gods or drawing from Indian religions. He taught Raja yoga as a science of meditation rather than as an extension of Indian religion. This allowed Nakamura Sensei to sense a universal ki, or universal spirit, which was one with nature and humanity but separate from any specific religion.

Moonlight Meditation

One evening in Gorkhe, on an especially clear night, Kaliapa took Nakamura Sensei to view the full moon. He asked him to sit in the lotus position and gaze at the moon with his complete attention. Kaliapa's final instructions were to not move or lose concentration until he returned.

When the guru did return it was near dawn. He asked Nakamura Sensei what he'd seen. Incredulous, an exhausted Nakamura Sensei silently drew a circle representing the moon in the dirt next to him.

Kaliapa shouted, "That's it?! That's all you saw?"

Shocked, Nakamura Sensei asked what else he could've seen but a round object in the sky. His teacher gently suggested looking again, pointing out variations in hue, craters, and other features barely visible to the unaided eye. He explained that Nakamura Sensei looked at the moon, but he didn't actually see it. (This was likely because he thought he'd seen it before, and because he was periodically thinking about his tuberculosis.) In Raja yoga the first step toward meditation is the one-pointed concentration of dharana. Kaliapa used the full moon as an object of concentration.

Nakamura Sensei developed Muga Ichi-nen Ho from this experience and others. But Muga Ichi-nen Ho can be practiced even when the moon isn't full. In fact, we can do it largely anyplace and anytime. It entails holding the mind in the present, the sole moment in which the body resides. Therefore, Muga Ichi-nen Ho promotes harmony of mind and body. A mental state comparable to Muga Ichi-nen Ho is also necessary in other Shin-shin-toitsu-do exercises. It leads to accomplishment in this art, and it transmits the meditative state into everyday life.

You'll recall muga literally means "no self" but is closer to "no self-consciousness." Ichi-nen is "one thought," while ho equals "exercise." Anjo Daza Ho and Muga Ichi-nen Ho are techniques Nakamura Sensei created to simply and pragmatically help people discover the esoteric Raja yoga trinity of dharana, dhyana, and samadhi:

1. Dharana was sometimes rendered by Nakamura Sensei as *yuga ichi-nen*. This is to concentrate on "one thought" but to still be "with self," to remain attached to our image of ourselves.
2. Next was muga ichi-nen, to concentrate on a single sound or object, but with "no self." We then arrive at muga munen, rising above self-consciousness and transcending thought. This is clearly dhyana.
3. Being beyond self-consciousness and beyond thoughts culminates in zan-mai, the Japanese transliteration of samadhi.

Nakamura Sensei taught Raja yoga meditation and philosophy in a new way, a way relating to modern scientific and educational principles and not dependent upon any culture's religious canon. I've continued this teaching style, not freezing Nakamura Sensei's principles in time, but adapting them to people outside of Japan and to contemporary trends and thought. This culturally adaptive approach actually began with Kaliapa.

Starting Basic Muga Ichi-nen Ho

Muga ichi-nen as a mindset can exist in any position, but for actual Muga Ichi-nen Ho practice it's traditional to use the kneeling posture of seiza, along with the full or half lotus position, as in Anjo Daza Ho meditation. You can also sit upright in a solid chair, and in *Polishing the Mind* Nakamura Sensei indicated that meditating while lying in bed is acceptable (especially if we're ill).

Making a circle with the thumbs and index fingers, while interlacing the other fingers, use the Sorin-in gesture (as in Anjo Daza Ho) for this form of meditation (**Fig. 20**). Nakamura Sensei told my instructor Sawai Atsuhiro Sensei he used Sorin-in when he

Fig. 23. You can also use this hand position, or mudra, in meditation. Place the left hand on top and form an oval with the tips of the thumbs. The little finger edges of the hands touch the lower abdomen.

Fig. 24. Placing both palms up on the knees is another meditative hand position. You can also form rings with the tips of the thumbs and index fingers. It is a mudra commonly used in Indian yoga.

meditated for hours each day in India, and because of this he still employed it in meditation. However, he told Sawai Sensei he also occasionally used two other mudra gestures. One is similar to the hand position in Zen meditation, which like Shin-shin-toitsu-do stems from Indian practices. This is *Ryaku-in*, and you can see it in **Fig. 23**. Nakamura Sensei further taught Mr. Sawai to place the back of each hand on the knees, with the palms open and upturned. This is *Hanare-in* (**Fig. 24**). While the palms are facing up, if you like, you can also place the tips of the thumb and index finger of each hand together to form a ring. You've probably seen yoga practitioners sitting this way.

    Finally, he taught Sawai Sensei that although numerous Japanese students copied his use of Sorin-in this wasn't necessary, and people should put their hands in the position which best facilitates concentration. He also indicated the position you sit in isn't as important as the posture you preserve during sitting. Although he favored the Indian lotus pose, and despite the fact that most students copied this, he told Sawai Sensei this position wasn't required. (Unlike many Shin-shin-toitsu-do teachers, Mr. Sawai didn't learn Muga Ichi-nen Ho exclusively in large public semi-nars. He received one-on-one instruction from the founder of Shin-shin-toitsu-do, and Sawai Sensei's insights into this discipline are valuable. They haven't been published in English before.)

Any erect position is acceptable. It should also be easily maintained which means an upright, but nevertheless stress-free, posture—a carriage in which all body parts react to gravity and naturally settle into their proper locations. Review the postural instructions in the last chapter to understand the posture needed in daily life and Muga Ichi-nen Ho.

Nakamura Sensei succinctly described Muga Ichi-nen Ho:

> The purpose of Muga Ichi-nen Ho is the same as Anjo Daza Ho—to create conditions within which we can discover meditation. In meditation, we can naturally direct the mind which has grown calm. The mind may be likened to the surface of a lake; when the lake's water is calm, its surface becomes like a mirror. When the mind takes on this mirror-like quality, we see and feel everything clearly, living an ideal life.
>
> In Anjo Daza Ho we listen to a sound, following it as it decreases, to hear a soundless sound. In doing so we experience deep concentration in which there's no object of concentration. We transcend our relative, imper-manent, transient self and come to our genuine self (jitsuga).
>
> In Muga Ichi-nen Ho we gaze at an object for some time, until we also forget ourselves. The distinction between the object of concentration and ourselves dissolves, leading to oneness beyond all divisions and distinctions. In Muga Ichi-nen Ho we can, if we like, close our eyes to recognize the after-image of the object clearly in the retinas of the eyes. Like the sound of the bell in Anjo Daza Ho this too will gradually fade, leaving us with object-less concentration, a condition beyond our transient self and transcending thought. With this method, just as with Anjo Daza Ho, we can discover our genuine self.[79]

Practicing Basic Muga Ichi-nen Ho

Muga Ichi-nen Ho entails looking at an object with finely tuned awareness and attention. In some Indian schools of yoga this is called *Trataka* meditation, and though a number of yogis concentrate on a candle flame, Nakamura Sensei taught that ultimately any object works, with a small dot being ideal for more advanced meditation. Trataka generally means "steady gazing." The website *Health and Yoga* offers an explanation of one form of Trataka:

> In this a regular candle is used, however any other object of choice can be used. The candle is set up at an arm's distance, level with eyes, and steady gazing is first done with the eyes open. After some time, the eyes are closed, and the after image of the flame is 'gazed at' with eyes closed at the eye brow center. Try not to move through out the practice. Relax your breath, let it lengthen, deepen.
>
> This open gazing of the flame and then with the eyes closed is alternated a couple of times before concluding the practice.
>
> If using a candle for Trataka, the gaze should be fixed at the wick tip and not on the flame.[80]

This website claims Trataka provides the following benefits:

- It improves the optic function, both external and internal, such as poor eyesight and visualization abilities.
- It helps develop concentration and mental resolve.
- Develops the ability to maintain one-pointedness amid the noise and distractions of daily life.
- Develops the psychic eye, that is the ability to "see" or understand what is inside and beyond the obvious. It develops the power of Intuition.[81]

I'm not implying Muga Ichi-nen Ho is identical to Trataka. I am, however, asserting a historical relationship between Nakamura Sensei's teachings and those of classical yogis. While several benefits of Trataka are familiar to students of Shin-shin-toitsu-do, Nakamura Sensei included his own list of benefits in *A Booklet on Anjo Daza Meditation*:

Muga Ichi-nen Ho has many benefits. They're not the goal of this form of meditation; they are the byproducts of meditation. Here are just some of these benefits:

- If we enter into Muga Ichi-nen Ho, we can become skilled at any martial art. Martial arts require concentration and willpower, qualities discovered via this meditation. Plus, as long as we worry about ourselves, and whether or not an opponent will hurt us, we cannot focus attention on the opponent. We need to forget ourselves and let the opponent become the one thought . . . just like in Muga Ichi-nen Ho.
- If we enter into Muga Ichi-nen Ho, our willpower and determination become stronger. Focusing the mind deeply on one thought, for extended periods of time, cannot be done without realizing the nature of the will and strong resolve.
- If we enter into Muga Ichi-nen Ho, we unearth hidden talents, becoming better at anything we try. The enhanced willpower and concentration required for regular Muga Ichi-nen Ho contribute to this, but of equal importance is the fact that this meditation gives rise to reiseishin, which is always present in the depths of the mind.

These are just a few examples of how Muga Ichi-nen Ho is helpful in life, leading us beyond worry. The true human being (shinjin) has no worries, no trouble.[82]

Clearly Muga Ichi-nen Ho, Nakamura Sensei's no-nonsense gazing meditation, offers numerous advantages. The website *Yoga Basics* likewise discusses using the gaze for concentration training and meditation:

A drishti (view or gaze) is a specific focal point that is employed during meditation or while holding a yoga posture. The ancient yogis discovered that where our gaze is directed our attention naturally follows, and that the quality of our gazing is directly reflected in the quality of our mental thoughts. When the gaze is fixed on a single point the mind is diminished from being stimulated by all other external objects. And when the gaze is fixed on a single point within the body, our awareness draws inwards and the mind remains undisturbed by external stimuli. Thus, the use of a drishti allows the mind to focus and move into a deep state of concentration. And the constant application of drishti develops ekagraha, single-pointed focus, an essential yogic technique used to still the mind.[83]

Regardless of terminology differences, both Trataka and Muga Ichi-nen Ho allow us to move from concentration (dharana), to meditation (dhyana), and finally to enlightened union with everything (samadhi). The main point is to first clear and concentrate the mind which Nakamura Sensei also noted:

Clear consciousness and concentration are important for liberating oneself from attachment and obsession. Most people lack this clear consciousness and have at least some attachments. I'm not the first to say this. In my studies, I've seen how teachers of Zen Buddhism and Sennin-do ("the Way of the Sennin") also advocate making "the mind's mirror like the calm water's surface" (shinkyo shisui), a metaphor for clear consciousness.

Most people have many delusions, so it's impossible for them to reach muga munen, the state transcending the impermanent self and thought. It is like trying to jump to the top of a high tower directly from the ground, with no stairs or steps in between. Before we reach muga munen we have to prepare the first step of clear consciousness and concentration. We can do this with Muga Ichi-nen Ho.[85]

Before Muga Ichi-nen Ho begins you need a correct posture, regardless of whether you use the lotus position, kneel in seiza, or sit in a chair. Start with aligning your body.

First, sit erect—no slouching—but don't be overly stiff and straight. Your spine and body should be like your arm in the orenai te exercise. When your arm was correctly unbending, it wasn't ramrod straight; the elbow had a slight, relaxed bend to it. Nonetheless, your arm wasn't limp. Probably the feeling was flexible, without undue stiffness or floppiness: positive relaxation. You want the same sensation in your entire body. Your spine is erect but not excessively straight, just like the gently curved arm in orenai te. Like the supple muscles in orenai te, your neck and muscles along the backbone aren't floppy; they're firm but not tense.

Second, softly focus your eyes on a chosen item. Place it where you can gaze at it comfortably and not disturb your aligned position. Your eyes rest on it gently and naturally. If you're looking at something a few feet away on the floor, your eyes adopt a stress-free, half-open position. Don't stare; this creates tension which weakens unification of body and mind. It also dissolves the flow of ki from the eyes that's aimed at the object. (A tense arm in orenai te is equally ineffective.)

Third, bring your awareness into the moment, and let the article of concentration completely fill your psyche. Actually *see* this item, as it truly is, instead of just glancing at it. This concentrates your mind in the present, where the object and your body reside. It consequently aids in harmonizing mind and body, and when the mind is in the present there is no worrying.

Moreover, mind-body accord only takes place in a natural, comfortable condition. Although it's imperative to genuinely see the object of attention, your attentiveness shouldn't be overwrought. Aim for relaxed concentration.

To arrive at this condition center the mind strongly on the object, and yet, don't try to drive out perceptions and sensations. By striving to keep out different perceptions, you end up thinking more about these sensations than the article of attention. You furthermore set up a paradox in which you're concentrating on the very noises, smells, or thoughts you're struggling to ignore. This is fighting with nature, because nature is everywhere. It's rough to relax while scuffling with every sensory impression which isn't the object of concentration.

Nakamura Sensei used this story to explain concentration in meditation:

A teacher of archery once lectured his students: "When you put an arrow on your bow, I can see you're already attached to something. You wonder if you'll hit the target. That's why you can't hit the target, especially when you participate in an important tournament. Don't grow attached to any thought or to any thing. Just unite with the target and become one existence."

In Muga Ichi-nen Ho the object of concentration is the target to unite with.[85]

Testing Your Concentration

As long as we're attached to thoughts like, "I want to concentrate," or "How long have I been sitting here?" we aren't fully focusing on the object of concentration. If this item fills the mind to become a single thought, we're not thinking about ourselves. If we're thinking about ourselves, the object of concentration isn't really concentrated on. This is one way to determine if the first step in meditation—concentration—has been arrived at. Are you still thinking about yourself?

You can also shut your eyes and see if you can vividly recall the details of the article you were observing. Lots of people can't clearly visualize the object once their eyes close, or they can't remember several details. This is another simple way to evaluate and develop attention.

Start by using objects with few details, which makes them easier to picture once the eyes shut; there are fewer facets to recall. Then progress to more complex items. Can you nevertheless summon up every detail once your eyes close?

Have a companion pose questions about the minutiae of the article after you've closed your eyes. It's an excellent assessment of attention and mind-body unification. (The mind must actually observe what the body's eyes see.)

Don't have anyone to work with? Hashimoto Tetsuichi Sensei suggests after some time goes by turning away from the article of attention and trying to draw it without looking at the original item. Don't worry about artistic aptitude; just see if you've absorbed all the details you were looking at.

This is the fundamental form of Muga Ichi-nen Ho, the basis of which is summarized in the five principles at the beginning of this chapter. It's simple, but regular training results in dramatic increases in concentration and willpower. With that understood, what's outlined above is nearer to contemplation or a concentration exercise than meditation. However, Nakamura Sensei also taught Sawai Sensei a more advanced meditative version of this technique that's comparable to Anjo Daza Ho.

Advanced Muga Ichi-nen Ho: A Single Dot

In this type of Muga Ichi-nen Ho, use a piece of plain white paper with a dark dot on it around the size of a penny. First, tape this to the wall at eye level, place it on the ground, or actually lay a penny on a sheet of paper a few feet ahead of you on the floor. Any location you can comfortably see it is fine, but if it's below eye level, don't let your head nod forward. Keep the neck and back erect. Just lower the eyes to see the dot or coin.

Second, as before, concentrate so deeply that the division between you and the dot dissolves. Concentrate until you forget yourself.

Third, when you arrive at "no self, one thought," or when your eyes get tired, let the eyelids shut softly.

Fourth, notice that the reversed image of the dot appears on the retinas of your closed eyes. The dark dot now appears light in color. Continue concentrating on it with your eyes shut. It will fade visually, just like the ringing in Anjo Daza Ho.

Fifth, as with the decreasing sound, follow the vanishing image without losing concentration. In a sense, as the dot diminishes the brain wave pattern also becomes "smaller," more and more still.

Sixth, when the reversed figure of the dot is too faint to see, do nothing, and keep the same feeling of attention as when you were looking at the actual dot. Move from concentration on an object to concentration with no object of focus, without any motive or anything to be attached to.

If you daydream or lose your composure, open your eyes, look at the dot, and start again. Watching the dot for a longer period makes it easier to see the reversed image when your eyes are closed. But don't strain to see it. Tension is counterproductive in meditation, which should slow the heartbeat and breathing as it lowers blood pressure.

Buying a home blood pressure kit is a fun way of testing your health and meditation. Some of these devices also record pulse rate, and you can check yourself before and after 15 minutes of meditation. If your heart rate and/or blood pressure go up, you're not arriving at relaxed concentration. Fortunately, most folks find that with a bit of training, meditation slows the pulse and benefits their blood pressure. And these are just a few of the profound profits of meditation.

That's about it for the technical side of Muga Ichi-nen Ho. Like much of Shin-shin-toitsu-do, this meditation is simple. Nonetheless, how we engage in it, what we realize, and what all of this means has tremendous depth. The remainder of this chapter focuses on more fully understanding Muga Ichi-nen Ho and transferring these insights into daily living.

Attachment and Attention

During meditation we aren't fixated on any thought or feeling. Once the mind is trapped in this way, it ceases flowing with the continuous movement of life. It's stuck in the past. In short, when the mind's obsessed with a particular thought or sensation, this distracts us from the present, and attachments stop us from adapting to life's fluctuations. Based on this we might conclude aloofness and indifference are the ideal means of handling life and meditation. Regrettably, detachment is a response. It's still "doing something," a response to the pain the self feels when it's powerless to have, achieve, or hang onto whatever it's attached to. By trying to not be fixated on various desires, we've just formed another obsession: an attachment to detachment.

Muga is the transcendence of a simulated self, a self which thinks it's a real solitary being, disconnected from the rest of the cosmos. This personality, being the invention of recollections, previous thoughts, and the impressions others have had concerning it, has no reality. Being supposedly independent from life, it won't survive death. To handle the terror of nonexistence it attaches itself to property, individuals, attitudes, inflexible conclusions, and even feelings. Yet all of that's transient too, and this false self continues desperately clinging to things and desires, fashioning a circle of misery.

The disconnected, false self clutches after fixed opinions, feelings, and possessions in a stab at permanent stability. When this fails the same transient self looks toward aloofness and disinterest. That kind of detachment is the defensive reaction of a self with no enduring reality.

However, meditation uncovers why we cling to thoughts, memories, and ideas, even as it lets us realize how attachment locks up the mind. This is crucial as a fixated mind has trouble finding continuous attention that adapts to each new moment. Freeing the mind from attachments, in turn, relates to concentration in Muga Ichi-nen Ho.

Muga and Attention

Instead of strained concentration, allow your mind to rest naturally on the object of concentration. Pay attention to each part of it until you forget yourself and only the item remains. At this time no barriers exist between you and the article of attention, between you and everything that's not you. Your sense of division is transcended. The mind is serene, in harmony with nature, and typical perception of time stops.

Quite a few of us have experienced something so powerfully engaging that we forgot ourselves and time ceased. When we unite the mind and body in the instant, while focusing intensely, no shyness or self-consciousness exists. The action taking place engulfs our mind, we transcend images we've created about ourselves and worry ceases. Nakamura Sensei discussed this in his talks:

> Many of you still don't know what doing nothing and thinking nothing means. Some people think it's something dreamy, illusionary, or chaotic. That's a mistaken understanding. When you don't worry about yourself, you're already in the world of doing nothing and thinking nothing. People, who are suffering from something or attached to something, always think about their mind or body. They're self-conscious or self-obsessed.
>
> You're always thinking about or feeling your mind or body, aren't you?

You're in the state of doing nothing and thinking nothing only once or twice a year and it's by accident. Most people don't notice it and say, "I'm a human being, so I have a body, and I think about it when it's in disorder, and I worry about my mind if it's in trouble. It's natural, isn't it?" It is not, and we don't have to live this way.

You have often switched off your connection with nature, with the result that you've fallen ill or are in trouble. When you enter into the state I call "doing nothing and thinking nothing," you switch on the source of life. Especially when you're ill or having some difficulty in your life, you have to take in more of the unlimited power of the universal ki. However, usually you've been doing the opposite—blocking the stream of life.[86]

Simply stated, when we're happy and calm, we rarely focus on ourselves. Even on a physical plane, we infrequently spend hours being conscious of our heads (for instance) save for having a headache. When the head feels okay, we don't pay much attention to it. This, of course, doesn't indicate that we can't or shouldn't be capable of sensing parts of our bodies. Rather, it suggests we're more functional when we aren't worrying about our bodies, when we're not anxious about ourselves, and when we let go of whatever self-image we've created. Self-image leads to psychological pain.

You may find the last sentence a bit strange, and it makes sense to wonder if it's true. There's no need to agree with anything in this book because a supposed expert has authored it. Instead, let's examine the genuine self, self-image, and muga ichi-nen.

Muga and Self-Image

Most individuals have experienced fear, but we haven't all reacted to it in the same way. Instead of running from fear, try letting it become the one thought. Pay attention to it.

When we're afraid, what really causes fear? We often blame fate, factors outside of ourselves, and other people. Fear is a reaction to something, but not everyone in the same situation is afraid. Thus, the experience of fear is actually determined by the individual and what the individual thinks and believes.

Suppose an acquaintance says something offensive and false about us. This can produce fear and anger. But why?

For many it's because their self-image has been assaulted. If so, then the picture we have of ourselves connects to fear and anger. In other words, we're afraid what was said might make us appear in a way other than how we want to see ourselves (especially if it's true). Self-image is tied to fear in this case.

We can say the same for envy, apprehension, and other troubles. If self-image is also the source of these problems then why bother to construct (and labor incessantly to maintain) this image of ourselves? And for much of humankind, their self-image is them.

Most people's self-image is based on past experiences that they remember. These recollections can be good or bad; they tend to be memories of what others said about us or what we thought about ourselves. The problem is that these recorded emotions and encounters amount to *what we were* instead of *what we presently are*. They're frequently the beliefs of others, who ultimately don't know us, and they are fixed in the past . . . even if that past was a couple seconds ago.

We're constantly changing. Our cells die and new cells are born. In a year's time biologically speaking, we don't even have the same body we had before, not to mention the effect of new experiences on the mind. This is reality.

Look at a snapshot of yourself as a child. Do you look the same? I hope not or your life's gone in a very unnatural direction.

Do you still want to eat nothing but candy? Are you still the person in the picture? Realistically, that little kid is gone. Sure, remnants of the past exist in that you may have a scar from childhood, but even the scar has faded and changed. We are, of course, an accumulation of past events but just in the most superficial, relative sense. And even this accumulation of the past only exists right now. The past is gone; the future's unwritten. Just this instant exists.

If we see what we truly are at this second, a remembered self-image is meaningless. We build an image or representative symbol of something when either the real thing isn't at hand or when we don't know the real thing. Since countless people don't recognize their genuine self and the universe (which aren't ultimately different), they respond with rage or terror each time they believe the image they're trying to preserve is attacked. This image may be all we know, which diverts us from the actuality of our genuine self and genuine existence. Nakamura Sensei, in his usual blunt style, said the same to powerful Japanese business leaders:

Look, we all die when the time comes. Don't be discouraged to hear this. Even though I talk of important matters, I also have to leave this world some day. You do, too. We don't know which of us will go first.

We all die sooner or later. If so, which is better, to relax and enjoy this short life fully, or to not enjoy yourself because you're constantly worrying about power and your image? It's better to always live with smiles, even though people may laugh at you. Don't you think so?

When I'm at home, I'm like a kid. My daughter calls me Father but treats me like her son. She says to me, "Dad, what do you want to eat, my son?" It's funny, isn't it? And it's contradictory but I don't mind.

Do you also put on airs and try to act important when you go to the toilet? The way you sit on the toilet is natural and childlike. Nobody is arguing on the toilet, nor are most people engaging in abstract logic to make the whole process take place. It's something very natural.

What I'm getting at with this analogy is simple. Don't be conceited, don't pretend, and don't be vain. Lead is lead, and gold is gold. Don't pretend to be gold when you're lead. It's good enough if we do our best with whatever ability and knowledge we presently have. That's all anyone can do, and we must not lose touch with the real nature of our mind, which is what happens when we lose touch with sincerity. We always suffer when we're attached to our desire to be something other than what we really are.[87]

When we know the truth about ourselves, nobody can genuinely distress us. But if we're acting as if we're something we aren't or if we're trying to be what others think we should be, then our self-image can seem damaged by a single comment. Fear is one outcome of this imagined damage to an imagined self.

Growth comes from seeing what's really going on in our lives. If I'm a fearful individual to be told as much by someone else is to hear the truth. Until I genuinely observe the truth for what it is no transformation of fear is likely.

We can change, but I'm not sure an artificial, preserved, and protected collection of memories we identify as "my self" can truly grow (except in our imaginations). Meditation is seeing reality, including us, and it has nothing to do with self-created images. If we drop our self-image to meet life as it is, does our genuine self surface? Meditation gives us an opportunity to answer these inquires and to discover what the "no self," in Muga Ichi-nen Ho refers to. Numerous individuals reside in a realm of concepts, symbols, and recollections. Muga Ichi-nen Ho lets us penetrate reality, to center the psyche on *what is*.

As you concentrate on the object in Muga Ichi-nen Ho, attempt to identify the line dividing the self observing the object and the object itself. Is this separation concrete or artificially created? The late Indian spiritual teacher Jiddhu Krishnamurti asked his audiences if they could divide "the observer from the observed." His question was important, and it ties into everything in this chapter. We act as if a rock-hard line splits the human race from the universe and one person from another. But is this real or a contrived distinction of convenience that makes language and science possible? Is there ultimately a difference between our genuine self and the universe? Muga Ichi-nen Ho lets us directly experience the answers to these questions in meditation.

Realizing our innate unity with all creations is characteristic of Nakamura Sensei's meditative teachings and ancient forms of Raja yoga. The Indian magazine *Life Positive: Your Complete Guide to Holistic Living* explains a traditional yogic view of nondualistic meditation paralleling Anjo Daza Ho and Muga Ichi-nen Ho:

> During dharana, the mind becomes unidirectional, while during dhyana, it becomes ostensibly identified and engaged with the object of focus or attention. That is why, dharana must precede dhyana, since the mind needs focusing on a particular object before a connection can be made. If dharana is the contact, then dhyana is the connection.
>
> Obviously, to focus the attention to one point will not result in insight or realization. One must identify and become "one with" the object of contemplation, in order to know for certain the truth about it. In dharana the consciousness of the practitioner is fixed on one subject, but in dhyana it is in one flow.[88]

This flow of attention allows us to notice if a true distinction exists between the observer and the observed. It lets us experience nondualistic perception in which subject and object are one and conflict ceases. *Life Positive* indicates this relates to samadhi:

> When we succeed in becoming so absorbed in something that our mind becomes completely one with it, we are in a state of samadhi. Samadhi means "to bring together, to merge." In samadhi our personal identities completely disappear. At the moment of samadhi none of that exists anymore . . .
>
> . . . During samadhi, we realize what it is to be an identity without differences, and how a liberated soul enjoys a pure awareness of this pure identity. The conscious mind drops back into that unconscious oblivion from

which it first emerged. The final stage terminates at the instant the soul is freed. The absolute and eternal freedom of an isolated soul is beyond all stages and beyond all time and place. Once freed, it does not return to bondage.

The perfection of samadhi embraces and glorifies all aspects of the self by subjecting them to the light of understanding. The person capable of samadhi retains his/her individuality and person, but is free of the emotional attachment to it.[89]

This isn't just an apt description of samadhi; it ties into Nakamura Sensei's references to muga: "no self." Certainly Indian yoga experts quoted in this book and Nakamura Sensei's teachings are different in tone and technique, but he nevertheless aimed at a new approach to the primordial truths he encountered in Gorkhe. It is an approach drawing on science and medicine, religion and yoga, yet it's not any of these disciplines. It's wholly unique, but its history is entwined with the yogic traditions of India.

Nothingness and No Self

In India muga is sometimes termed *anatman*, but both ideas are essentially the same; both are rarely understood and often misinterpreted. Their basis lies in *shunyata*, or "emptiness," which is rendered as *mu* in Zen meditation. Instead of mu, Nakamura Sensei preferred a slightly different expression, which wasn't so closely tied to Zen—*ku*, "nothingness."

He suggested the real, absolute, timeless nature of existence was beyond form, an infinite void, while the forms our senses perceive are just the momentary parts of life. Ku is a void, but the void is filled with an unseen power—ki—that gives birth and sustenance to everything in the void. Through meditation we tap into this power, but to do so we must arrive at a similar state of emptiness, of doing nothing. Like attracts like.

When the mind lets go of itself and we do nothing, we understand the reality of nothingness. Yet something cannot come from nothing. Thus, this nothingness is a void filled with a creative potentiality or energy. It's nothing and everything, just as a mirror only reflects because it is empty, yet the mirror always reflects something. It's empty/full.

So is meditation. Meditation releases self-consciousness and thought, arriving beyond self and beyond thought. In that state—and this is important—we connect with "something," which Nakamura Sensei called ku: "nothingness." The source of the absolute universe, ku is filled with ki: "energy." We're ultimately one with this infinite void, emerging from it like all aspects of the relative world, and merging back into it at death.

Nothingness is things as they really are, before our prejudice, attachments, and emotional baggage colors them. To perceive this unaltered reality we let go of the artificially created, seemingly independent, self. We experience muga and mu—uncolored truth—at the same time. In *Hardcore Zen*, Brad Warner explains:

> Emptiness is not a nihilistic concept of voidness. Emptiness is not meaninglessness. Emptiness is that condition which is free from our conceptions and our perceptions. It's the world as it is before we come along and start complaining about the stuff we don't like.
>
> Nishijima translates the famous line: "Form is emptiness, emptiness is form," as "Matter is the immaterial, the immaterial is matter." John Lennon expressed the same idea in Everybody's Got Something to Hide Except Me and My Monkey. "Your inside is out and your outside is in." The world we perceive and the thing that perceives the world are one and the same.[90]

Therefore we have no independent reality, no self, except what we construct for easy communication. But we're not alone; we're all that exists. It's in "emptiness" that the interpenetration of the universe and individual becomes possible and knowable. And science might be making similar discoveries.

Fred Alan Wolf, a PhD in theoretical physics and the National Book Award-winning author of *Taking the Quantum Leap*, writes in *Forbes*:

> Quantum physics is the theory of the behavior of matter and energy, particularly at the level of atoms and subatomic particles. It is nearly impossible to imagine the strange behavior of matter at this level. An electron in an atom, for example, performs a trick much like the crew on Star Trek when it "beams" from one energy level to another without going in between. But if we aren't watching it jump, we have no control as to when it will happen.
>
> But suppose we do watch? Well, if current experiments in quantum physics are relevant to our everyday experiences, we will actually be able to alter the matter—and thereby the crapshoot of life.[91]

Scientists like Dr. Wolf seem to be extrapolating a profound relationship between us and everything else, but further research is needed before scientists can move his ideas from the realm of conjecture to that of verified scientific theory. Still, classical physics assumes that all matter affects all other matter, that nature is interrelated. This inter-relationship exists in scientific terms because all matter exerts a force of some type on all other matter.[92] The same concept is considered true in quantum mechanics in many, if not most, situations. Muga Ichi-nen Ho gives us a chance to similarly sense the connect-ed nature of the universe, but in a nonintellectual manner, outside of a laboratory setting.

Wolf's work in quantum physics is not without critics, but it caused him to deduce that intent—positive or negative—may have the potential to alter the course of our lives due to the interrelationship of elements in nature. Nakamura Sensei surmised much the same thing. Wolf writes:

> To make what you desire come true you need to pursue your vision vigorous-ly, not passively dream about it and hope it will come true. If this "watched-pot" theory turns out to be correct at the human level, then our desires and accompanying actions are what actually govern our daily lives. Luck has nothing to do with it.[93]

Of course, the observation of systems operating in the realm where quantum me-chanics plays a significant role isn't necessarily the same as altering the properties of these systems to conform to one's intent. Nonetheless, Wolf's sometimes controversial ideas form an interesting parallel with Nakamura Sensei's teachings. In fact, Nakamura Sensei expressed an interest throughout his life in the connection between science, medi-tation, and the effects of the mind on living.

Other mind-bending discoveries in physics might also relate to nothingness, the universe, and the lack of truly separate identity. For example, if the nucleus of an atom was in front of us, it'd be so minute that even if it was magnified a million times, it would still only be as big as a grape. And the electron circling it would be as tiny as a dust mote. What's more, it would be moving a half mile away.[94]

Essentially, atoms are incredibly small and more than 99 percent "emptiness." Buddhism similarly holds that material forms are empty. Nakamura Sensei's student Tohei Koichi Sensei explained the ki of the universe doesn't increase or decrease, but it continually alters itself. He indicated this universal ki is an immeasurably vast gathering of immeasurably tiny particles—more tiny than an atom. It is "something yet nothing, nothing yet something." And while I'm not a scientist, and although to some degree the jury's still out, quantum physics may be making related proclamations.

Yet these are just words . . . complex words at that. Thus, Nakamura Sensei simplified centuries of yogic lore, offering Muga Ichi-nen Ho and Anjo Daza Ho as concrete methods whereby ordinary folks can experience an extraordinary consciousness: a state beyond self and thought, a state linked to the very essence of the universe.

Retaining Knowledge and Information

When we gaze at an object in Muga Ichi-nen Ho, are we seeing the real object or just our knowledge of this object? There's a difference.

Actual awareness, taking place in the moment, is unlike our knowledge of something which is rooted in the past. Nakamura Sensei indicated meditation leads to a deep silence. In Muga Ichi-nen Ho we concentrate in a state transcending internal dialogue. Intensely observing an item doesn't mean observing our opinions and knowledge of this object. It isn't talking to ourselves about the perceived item; it's simply seeing the object as it is. What we think, believe, or remember about this article is of little use in Muga Ichi-nen Ho. The article of concentration isn't really important nor are our opinions about this object. To observe with full alertness is what's vital in this meditation. Meditation is entering into untainted, unaffected consciousness of the universe at this second.

Of course we must retain past information about different things in life. Nevertheless, this information should be employed as a tool, when and where we want to utilize it. Our tools shouldn't take over and/or control the mind, preventing us from seeing each new moment.

When the mind is in the moment, life is bright, fresh, and vibrant. The mind never grows decrepit or world-weary. This is different from our typical assumptions about life, which recreate our past over and over again. We're so accustomed to vaguely glancing at life, using the eyes of the past, we're not sure if we are concentrating on what is or if we just imagine we're paying attention. Meditation in daily life involves really seeing life as it is in the moment.

For instance, we may alter our appearance only to have this go unseen by family and coworkers. It might be simply changing hairstyle, but our associates fail at first to perceive this change. In this example our friends are looking at their surroundings with the eyes of the past, instead of genuinely seeing what's occurring here and now.

Letting Go of the Article of Attention

When we start Muga Ichi-nen Ho we're focusing on a solitary subject. This is concentration with an object. When you close your eyes to watch the fading dot, you determine how to preserve this wakefulness without depending on the dot itself. In short, as the reversed image of the dot fades your concentration then takes in everything. It isn't restricted to the dot you've been gazing at. This is concentration without an object.

Once objectless concentration is grasped you can open your eyes, walk away from the dot you were looking at, and each thing you see or feel is completely attended to. You concentrate in association with every moment in life and every occurrence, regardless of how rapidly the experiences follow each other. Every second is lived completely, and when the next instant comes it too is wholly experienced, with no shadow of the previous moment diluting your focus.

To move from concentration with an object to concentration without an object is essential, which is what should take place when we close our eyes in Muga Ichi-nen Ho or when the bell dies away in Anjo Daza Ho. Yet, explaining how to achieve this change—and how to maintain it—is difficult. Each of us needs to find out how to do this via personal experimentation, and Muga Ichi-nen Ho gives us a structure within which to experiment. That noted, we can change from concentration with a motive to concentration with no motive. Maintain attention; just drop the feeling of focusing on a particular item for a specific purpose. Try also changing from concentration that's exclusive to attention which excludes nothing.

We can also learn objectless concentration using negation. While you continue looking at the object, notice if something is causing or encouraging your attentiveness. Concentration with a cause isn't objectless concentration. Any attachment to concentration or to what you're directing ki towards isn't it either. Feelings of exclusion equal attempting to block out everything but the object of concentration; and this creates a fight, a sense of separation, which creates meditation destroying tension. And by trying to divorce ourselves mentally from everything but the object of attention, we become attached to the thing we're employing to lead us beyond attachment. The same can be said for looking for results from meditation: it only encourages fixation and creates tension. Determine what objectless concentration *is not* to reveal what it is.

When awareness is motivated by ambition, we experience attachment to an objective, and as mentioned previously, attachment leads to suffering. Is it feasible to lead the mind with immense intensity in a specific direction, but with no ending target, without stopping concentration and ki at any spot? Can we concentrate completely without attachment to whatever we're concentrating on?

These are significant questions because scores of us pay attention exclusively by clinging to something. It can be an individual, a conviction, or even a dot. Trouble is, most things aren't permanent, so when our object of attachment is gone we're unhappy and uncentered. We attempt to resolve this unhappiness by clinging to something else. Then we're incapable of living fully and without restraints, because we are continually determined to get something, the thought of which we're obsessed with, and/or we're living in dread of losing some article of attachment. Though attention in the instant is necessary for living wholeheartedly, if this attentiveness is forced by obsession, it's counterproductive.

Concentration without an object isn't something to lust for or be fixated on. In doing so we're replacing one obsession with another. And the cycle begins once more.

Practice Anjo Daza Ho, then do Muga Ichi-nen Ho. Approach it from the viewpoint of what you've been doing in the other meditation. In the end these two forms are identical. They just use different senses to lead to objectless concentration and mind-body unification. Regardless of method, according to Nakamura Sensei, the primary point is to practice correctly, and we needn't sit long. It's the quality of meditation that's important. Even if we only experience meditation and oneness with the universe for a few seconds, if we actually grasp what we've experienced that's all that matters.

How deeply we feel the absolute stillness of meditation is what's important. But if you're a beginner, this depth of feeling may not take place at once. Sitting for 15 to 20 minutes is probably a good idea, but even much shorter periods repeated throughout the day can lead to a new way of seeing the world. Regardless of time, the main point is still to look deeply into the mind and personally discover the meaning of absolute stillness and deep calmness.

Nakamura Sensei further suggested in *A Booklet on Anjo Daza Meditation* to not be impatient to reach this ideal state. Impatience is an obstacle on the road to realization. So Nakamura Sensei urged his readers to practice Anjo Daza Ho and Muga Ichi-nen Ho "patiently, innocently, without seeking an instant effect." When we forget about progressing toward a future point of perfection, we enter into a state beyond time.

He also mentioned that people often do well at what they have confidence in, because they arrive at concentration stemming from that confidence. But concentration must exist, and can exist, in anything we do and at any moment. We can learn to concentrate even on things we're not accomplished at and things we're unfamiliar with. Both Anjo Daza Ho and Muga Ichi-nen Ho lead to concentration.[95]

The Term "Meditation"

The word "meditation" represents different things to different people. In fact, its meaning varies so significantly from person to person as to make communication complicated. Don't assume your characterization of meditation is the same one utilized in *The Teachings of Tempu*, and this suggestion holds true for definitions and communication between people in general.

People frequently call the Sennin Foundation Center for Japanese Cultural Arts for information about Shin-shin-toitsu-do. I take many calls personally, and it isn't unusual for some version of the following to take place:

Caller: "I'm interested in your classes."

HD: "Thanks for calling. What we're practicing is called Shin-shin-toitsu-do, which refers to unifying mind and body. To aid in this unification, we practice stretching exercises, breathing exercises, and meditation. In Shin-shin-toitsu-do meditation involves . . ."

Caller: (Interrupting) "I know what meditation involves. I've been practicing meditation for years."

HD: "Have you studied Shin-shin-toitsu-do?"

Caller: "No."

HD: "Have you read books about what we're studying, or have you visited a class?"

Caller: "No."

HD: "Have we met or have you talked to someone about meditation in Shin-shin-toitsu-do?"

Caller: "No, but I think I understand what you're practicing and what you mean by meditation."

HD: "How is that possible?"

Our representative caller assumes something he's never encountered is the same as what he thinks he knows. Assumption makes genuine communication, understanding, and awareness of reality unworkable. However this needn't be the case.

Knowledge, which relates to our recollections, only becomes awkward when it's no longer a device, and it overrides our instant-to-instant awareness of what's actually occurring. My suggestion is to practice meditation as if you'd never heard of this word or read anything about it. Discover it anew each time you sit in Muga Ichi-nen Ho or Anjo Daza Ho, and understand it not so much in theory but through personal experience.

To clasp onto the expressions and experiences of others concerning meditation (particularly when techniques differ so much), and to compare your actions with such words, isn't direct understanding of meditation. It's imitation. Although copying is helpful for learning certain exercises or methods, meditation isn't an activity to be duplicated. It's an experience, an experience which can't be copied, bestowed, or borrowed from others. This consciousness I'm calling "meditation" exists solely in the moment. It's an immediate experience that's not based on previous understanding or fixed in the past.

Meditation is diving into the undiscovered instant, jumping into the ever-changing present, stripped of assumptions, hardheaded beliefs, and anything clinging to days gone by. It's to meet life without preceding psychological experiences modifying the here and now. Such modifications trap us in a loop, powerless to move past what we've formerly experienced. Meditation isn't a projection of ideas, intellectual constructions, or one's self. We can't create it or recreate it, but we can set up an internal environment within which it can flower. That's the idea behind Muga Ichi-nen Ho and other forms of meditation in Shin-shin-toitsu-do.

The Timeless

Our viewpoints, prejudices, judgments, and the like stem from previous experiences, which we've preserved as memory. Memory only becomes awkward when it stops us from perceiving life as it is. Yet many see only with the eyes of long-ago, with the eyes of memory. Then memory becomes conditioning, which prevents us from discovering freedom and from observing the real nature of living, along with the significance and worth of our lives.

When this conditioning isn't understood for what it is we're caught by our past. Sooner or later, we feel "stuck." We have the same difficulties—in changeable variations—over and over. Autosuggestion offers immediate techniques for modifying especially negative conditioning. Though this is helpful, we must still wonder if it's feasible to have efficient memory and yet not be hardened by our past.

Certain trained reflexes aren't problematic. Typing without looking at the keyboard is useful. The habituation of techniques and physical responses isn't a concern. On the other hand, psychological and emotional conditioning *is* a problem. Is it possible to experience life completely and remain free of emotional baggage, to not be conditioned psychologically by our experiences?

Muga Ichi-nen Ho is an occasion to discover ourselves by ourselves. What we realize must by definition be new, or it's not a discovery at all. By clinging to previous experiences we end up discovering only what we want to unearth or what we've experienced beforehand. We merely modify our past.

We long for safety, and we try finding it through fixed viewpoints or by hanging onto "property." Favorite books, a dream house—even a spouse—become property to own, the possession of which we hope will give us a refuge from the changeability of life. Our upbringing, the social order, and even we have habituated us to think this offers security. But views can be challenged, houses catch on fire, and books get lost. When we meet such problems we bump into fear as we're required to gaze at how much of a fantasy security is. Seeing this, we may ignore whatever challenges our conditioning, hoping against hope that the next house will remain perfect forever.

Ultimately life is beyond our complete control. While we can influence life, the only thing we fully control is our reactions to events. This reaction can be positive or negative. The choice is ours.

Security is wanted by memory, which desires to maintain the known or earlier periods. A mind fixated on yesteryear is conditioned. Our past shifts into the present, and after that the future, using this habituated psyche. It is this mind which longs for absolute safety—even when it's seen to be fantasy—so it can continue itself. Each of us, who have branded this conditioned intelligence as our genuine selves, thinks that dropping this conditioning, this carry-over of past familiarity, is to drop our very selves. Some of us, comprehending that we're ensnared by what went before, seek to jump out of time, to hit upon liberation in constant change. Afraid and caught by our habituated view of ourselves, we look for the timeless.

However even attempts at transcending time come from familiarity with what's happened to us in earlier periods. It's a search that's still based on locating a state beyond fear: in other words, a condition of security. It is clutching at one more form of defense, and this grasping which stems from fear can't show the way away from fear. Therefore it's not walking into the unknown, an act transcending time, recollections, and the illusion of security.

So how do we arrive at meditative consciousness beyond time? It can't be coerced or created. Any premeditated effort comes from what we imagine meditation should be, which is founded on what we've formerly read or believed about meditation. This isn't so much meditation as a re-creation of our past.

Trying to safeguard permanence is being fixed in time. Reality is now and so is life. We can say the same for meditation. In the present we can realize reality and discover if permanence is truly taking place. It's the supposition of continuity that stops the mind from observing what actually occurs—just as it is—in a condition transcending time. Only a mind which identifies continuity, but that doesn't search for or predict continuity, can truthfully recognize the immediate present, a present that's not inexorably a continuation of earlier patterns and which is eternal. This mind exists in meditation beyond time.

Advanced Muga Ichi-nen Ho in Review

When practicing Muga Ichi-nen Ho bear in mind the following summarized points:

1. Get a piece of plain white paper with a dark dot in the center.
2. Place it where you can look at it comfortably.
3. Sit with an erect, but relaxed, posture that's easy to maintain and which allows coordination of mind and body.
4. Focus so deeply on the dot that you forget yourself and only the dot remains.
5. Eventually, close your eyes softly and watch the reversed image on your retinas.
6. Mentally follow the dot as it becomes fainter.
7. When you no longer see the dot, do nothing and let your attention continue where the image leaves off.
8. Sit as long as you like in this state of calmness. Note any perceptions, but don't cling to them, allowing the mind to instantly return to doing nothing.
9. If you lose this state transcending self-consciousness and attachment to thought, open your eyes and start again.

Chapter 9

MEDITATION
& THE FIVE SENSES

PRINCIPLES FOR TRAINING THE SENSES

1. Don't just look but truly see.

2. Don't just touch but truly feel.

3. Don't just sniff but truly smell.

4. Don't just eat but truly taste.

5. Don't just hear but truly listen.

In Gorkhe, Nakamura Tempu Sensei sat for hours each day beside an immense waterfall, resting on a flat rock Kaliapa selected for meditation. One of his first tasks, mentioned in Chapter One, was to hear "The Voices of the Earth." Once he could perceive the faint sounds of insects and birds, despite the roaring cascade nearby, then he attempted to sense "The Voice of Heaven," a soundless sound equaling the essence of the universe. In the end, when he stopped trying and let go of his attachments, when he did nothing, he experienced a unity with the universe which was absolutely still and peaceful. It changed his life.

What he realized in India helped him create Shin-shin-toitsu-do, the name he gave his teachings. It continues positively changing the lives of people even today.

Training the Senses

Nakamura Sensei's teachings are both practical and esoteric. Before he could experience the profound stillness and essence of the universe beyond the five senses, Kaliapa asked him to train these very senses to be more acute. In listening for the Voices of the Earth, Nakamura Sensei learned to concentrate deeply, an important first step in having fully functional sensory capacity. Without refined concentration we look but we don't often see; we listen but we rarely hear.

Part of concentration is tied to nonattachment, which is why Kaliapa emphasized that to genuinely hear and sense what was going on around him, Nakamura Sensei couldn't be distracted by the cascading falls. He had to let go of his resentment and irritation toward this roaring cataract that was preventing him from sensing other parts of life. Once he heard the waterfall, but wasn't attached to what he heard, then his senses became more acute. This unattached state isn't just the heart of concentration; it's the fundamental nature of meditation.

Kaliapa next asked him to hear the Voice of Heaven, i.e. the essence of the universe. Just as in Anjo Daza Ho, for Kaliapa "hearing" was really an expression of pure and refined awareness. To accomplish this awareness Kaliapa encouraged him to transcend the same senses he'd worked arduously to train.

Nakamura Sensei developed his awareness by teaching himself to hear minute sounds even in a noisy environment. This relates to the evolved concentration of dharana. Enhanced attention has innumerable practical and obvious benefits in everyday affairs, but it's easy to get obsessed with goals and benefits, which causes our growth to stop. Thus, one more step was needed.

This step occurred when Nakamura Sensei let go of all effort and tension, falling on his back to lie in the grass. When he forgot himself he merged with the shifting clouds and experienced dhyana, "meditation," which resulted in the harmony of samadhi. He was one with the universe.

A Practical Spirituality

The absolute nature of the universe is one. We can call this ki, and it exists beyond divisions, beyond distinctions. Yet this singular, nondualistic energy paradoxically gave birth to our relative, transient world, which is made of seemingly conflicting elements. Hot/cold, strong/weak, hard/soft, and every other duality cannot exist apart from each other. We only recognize health because of the existence of sickness, sunshine because of shade, and so on. These opposites define the relative aspect of existence, but they're inseparable, with night giving birth to day and day transforming into night.

All impermanent dualistic elements in life are born of, and disappear back into, a universal ki that's absolute. It doesn't increase, it never decreases; it isn't born, and it doesn't die. In the end we can say the same for the transient and outwardly opposing aspects of the cosmos, including us. They constantly change form, but their ki doesn't vanish.

The ki of the universe, when viewed in a relative way, consists of an endless number of parts that seem opposite from each other. If we don't look more deeply into life our world appears to be one of perpetual conflict between opposites. And this is as far as many people ever get.

Thus even the spiritually inclined tend to choose sides. If the average person thinks the world consists of a conflicting dualism, or constant fighting between differing forces, then the spiritually disposed may declare relativity is an illusion, rebuffing the varied impermanent aspects of life. Yet, by choosing this over that, we actually display the same relative, dualistic thinking we aim to reject. We're little different from our contrary counterparts. We're opposite from them but trapped in the same way.

A relative, dualistic viewpoint gives birth to a fighting mind which anticipates, sees, and creates conflict everywhere. A mindset that refuses to acknowledge relative differences, that rejects anything transient as delusion, cannot function in our relative world of contrasting phenomena. Taken to its ultimate conclusion this outlook leads to insanity.

Yet this is avoided via Nakamura Sensei's realization that the absolute ki of the universe is the origin of our relative realm of contrasting elements, just as hail, snow, and frost are variable impermanent facets of water. With this understanding we see that the relative world and the absolute universe each have their own reality, and most importantly that they aren't separate from each other. We can't genuinely choose one and reject the other.

Similarly, Nakamura Sensei indicated he'd experienced a consciousness in meditation that transcended every transitory part of the world, an awareness of something beyond the five senses, which still recognized the ephemeral and relative components of living. He accepted that as long as we're alive we must interact with these impermanent parts of creation, and to do so effectively we need to cultivate our senses. This outlook that values and efficiently uses the senses, but which isn't attached to what they recognize, results in practical spirituality. Along with Shin-shin-toitsu-do meditation, which teaches us not to cling to changeable parts of life that are perceived by our senses, Nakamura Sensei created simple exercises allowing us to cultivate extraordinary levels of smell, taste, touch, sight, and hearing. He called these exercises *Kanno no Keibatsu*.

Shikaku: *Sight*

Kanno no Keihatsu refers to "developing" (keihatsu) the "functionality of the body" (kanno). In essence, it's training the five senses, one of the most important of which is sight. Many of us glance at the world, but we don't genuinely *see* it. This isn't so much a problem with the eyes but more a problem with the mind. We think we see with our eyes, but this is only partially true. The mind sees through the eyes, the mind hears through the ears, the mind tastes through the tongue, and so on.

Case in point, I once heard of a man who had a daily routine. He'd come home, open the door to his house, walk across his living room, and go into the bedroom to put away his coat. He'd then walk back through the living room to get a drink in the kitchen. Finally, he would return again to the living room, where he'd sit—drink in hand—in front of the television. One weekday, when he was working, someone broke into his house and stole his rather oversized TV. This television occupied a prominent and lofty place in his living room, but when he opened the front door that night he didn't see it was missing. He walked through his living room twice, and on the third time entering that space he sat down in front of where his TV had been. It was only when he tried to use the remote control that he finally saw a gaping expanse, which was once filled by a television.

In this story the problem isn't the sense of sight, but the way in which this sense is hampered by a mind that sees life through the eyes of the past. It's a mind that isn't paying attention, because attention takes place in the present. When this happens we glance vaguely at the world, but we don't fully experience what we're supposedly seeing. We sleepwalk through life.

This was dramatically pointed out to Nakamura Sensei when his guru asked him to concentrate on the moon, only to discover after several hours of looking at it he'd failed to see its details. Muga Ichi-nen Ho developed from this experience and others, with the basic version relating to training our ability to truly see. Here are a few similar ways of cultivating concentration and eyesight:

1. Place several objects in front of you. Pick items with multiple details. Focus your eyes on them gently. Don't stare as this weakens your capacity to see and creates tension in the eyes, which blocks the movement of ki toward the objects. After concentrating deeply on these objects for a few minutes, close your eyes, and have a friend ask you questions about what you saw. See how many correct answers you give, and gradually shorten the time you look at the aforementioned items. Nakamura Sensei could quickly gaze

at a significant number of items, turn away, and recall virtually every minute feature he saw only briefly.

2. Try the same exercise with a photo. Pick a picture with numerous elements in it. Look at the image for several minutes, then close your eyes and see how many details you remember. Progressively shorten the time you look at the photo, and gradually use photos with more complexity. Have friends ask you about what you saw, or just try to recall the particulars yourself. You can also turn away and endeavor to sketch the picture in as much detail as possible.

3. Some American newspapers publish comics showing two seemingly identical drawings. However, the second cartoon has several tiny differences from the first. The viewer's job is to spot all the alterations in the second drawing; the correct answers are printed at the bottom of the page or upside down beneath the cartoons. This is similar to what Nakamura Sensei taught for training one's sight and powers of observation. It's fun, too.

Regardless of which method you use arriving at muga ichi-nen is vital. Remember, this is when you're not self-conscious, and as the result you can profoundly concentrate so that what you're looking at becomes the only thought in your mind. Previous chapters give hints to accomplish this.

Shokkaku: *Touch*

Nakamura Sensei was fond of an ancient Japanese game called *Go*. It's played on a four-sided board divided into 361 crossing points or 324 squares. Two players take turns placing small black or white stones on the board. The objective is to enclose as much area as possible. The person who surrounds the biggest section wins.

Black and white Go stones are identically shaped and similarly smooth, but they're made from different materials. (Black stones are made from ebony colored rock called *nachi guro*, and good quality white stones are produced from clam shells.) There's a very subtle difference in texture between the two, but most folks never notice any dissimilarity.

Nonetheless, Nakamura Sensei trained himself to feel the nearly unidentifiable textural differences between the black and white stones. He'd periodically demonstrate his heightened tactile sense and mental focus by distinguishing between the two varieties while blindfolded. The muga ichi-nen mindset was crucial for accomplishing this.

225

These are some ways we can likewise cultivate our sense of touch and concentration:

1. Lay out several different coins. Pick up each coin, rubbing it between your fingers, noticing every detail and sensation. Next, gently close your eyes and reach out to mix up the coins. Wait a moment and then pick one up. Holding it in your fingers, can you tell if you're touching a penny, a nickel, a quarter, or a dime?
2. Nakamura Sensei could also shut his eyes and feel variations between different weight sheets of paper, some of which were thicker, while others were thinner. Amazingly this ability extended to even paper of varying colors, which probably differed slightly in composition and/or method of manufacture. We can do the same for a more challenging tactile test.

Despite what we touch we need to fully concentrate the mind and relax the body. We don't want to merely touch the world; we want to actually *feel* it.

Kyukaku: *Smell*

Japanese culture has an old and respected aesthetic discipline called *kodo*. Brought to Japan in the sixth century by Buddhist monks, who used mysterious aromas in their purification rites, the fragrant *ko* ("incense") became entertainment for aristocrats in the Imperial Court during the Heian Era 200 years later. What Japanese call kodo, "the Way of incense," has long been a wellspring of spiritual sustenance in their society. Part of kodo involves identifying what variety of incense one smells and ascertaining as much information about this particular incense as possible with just a sniff. Comparable to wine tasting, this part of kodo is largely practiced as an aesthetic ceremony today, but taken to its ultimate level kodo is a Do ("Way").

To correctly sense delicate features of a given fragrance requires attentiveness and calmness, qualities that are also helpful in daily life. In this context developing the sense of smell in kodo cultivates useful mental traits that can be carried into everyday living, making kodo a Way of life like judo, *sado* (tea ceremony), shodo (brush calligraphy), and other Japanese Do forms. Nakamura Sensei suggested using an approach similar to kodo to refine one's sense of smell and awareness.

We can do better then dimly sniff; the goal is to accurately *smell*. Unlike our Japanese counterparts not every Westerner has access to a large variety of fine incense.

Therefore Sawai Atsuhiro Sensei suggests using the following methods to develop our olfactory sense:

1. Get several bottles of different perfume. Lay them in front of you, and smell each one, memorizing what you smell. Then shut your eyes, jumble up the bottles, and pick one at random. With your eyes closed, try to identify the perfume by smell alone.

2. For a more advanced test buy several types of tea in bag form. Pick up each tea bag, hold it close to your nose, and calmly smell it. Forget yourself, and let the smell completely fill your mind. After doing this for some time, close your eyes, and mix up the tea bags. Then pick one and determine the type of tea you smell without looking. (You can write a number or name on each bag if you like.)

Mikaku: *Taste*

We eat but do we really *taste*? Somehow I doubt people who eat breakfast while simultaneously reading the newspaper, watching TV, and texting their buddies are genuinely tasting their food. This type of activity discourages mind and body coordination, and it's better to just eat if we have a meal. By not sleepwalking through breakfast we cease eating unconsciously, and we learn to keep the mind in the present. We start to concentrate.

More than this, we may consider the living things which die so we can live. This often results in gratitude, which in turn leads to a positive outlook. It can also result in a deeper consideration for plants, animals, and our planet as a whole.

Here are a couple of easy ways to refine your taste buds and power of attention:

1. Remember my reference to wine tasting? This is a classic Western approach for developing the sense of taste. It takes knowledge and concentration. But unless you like the tang of cheap wine, it also takes money. Since I don't drink alcohol, and because I'd rather spend my cash on other things, I've substituted different types of fruit punch or other drinks. Various companies produce fruit punch, but not all of it tastes identical. Using the eyes closed approach described above you can cultivate your sense of taste. Ac-

tually, any food or beverage works and some people like trying to recognize varying sorts of tea.

2. You can have fun with friends by asking them to bring various foods to a party. Blindfold a guest. Have other party goers lay out their food items on a table, and feed them one at a time to the sightless person. His or her job is to make out the taste. No nasty stuff, please.

None of this is complicated. However, it won't work for us if we don't practice it. Even when Nakamura Sensei was alive he noticed quite a few of his students didn't practice Kanno no Keihatsu regularly, mistakenly believing it was "too simple to be effective." Yet simple doesn't always mean easy, and if we actually try the exercises repeatedly for several months we notice real changes in ourselves.

These drills can, nevertheless, become thorny because we frequently have trouble holding the mind in the moment. If you put something in your mouth how long can you truly focus on the taste before you're distracted? For the majority it's only a few seconds, which may not be long enough to discern subtle variances in (for instance) different varieties of tea. If you have trouble with the preceding exercises, first work on simply allowing what you taste or touch to fill your entire awareness to become one thought. Learn to sustain this and you're also learning about dharana, the ancient yogic art of concentration.

Chokaku: *Hearing*

I've mentioned Nakamura Sensei's experiences listening to faint sounds of birds and insects beside a thundering cascade. In accomplishing this, he gained initial insights into not only concentration and meditation but also hearing. We may not sit by a waterfall, but most of us have experienced the difficulty of trying to listen to something in a noisy office or restaurant. We assume loud background noise makes it impossible to hear fainter sounds. This might occasionally be true, but attachment to louder noises may also be a problem. The more you struggle not to hear a noise, the more you hear it. If you've tried meditation, you've probably already figured this out.

You may have also noticed that quite a few of us more or less hear, but we don't in fact *listen*. Anjo Daza Ho is—at least at the outset—tied into our auditory sense. It provides insights into the nature of truly listening, but its ultimate aim is to transcend attachments to what our senses perceive. This doesn't mean our senses aren't functioning. Just the opposite is true.

Here are a few exercises for refining hearing and attentiveness:

1. Listen to the ticking of a clock or watch in a quiet room. Pick a relatively loud clock. Once you forget yourself and stay focused on the sound for awhile, move the timepiece a little farther away. Concentrate intensely on the noise for a bit and then move it farther again. As you continue you'll not only keep your mind on the ticking for longer periods, but you'll be able to hear it when it's farther away.

2. Next, add some noise. Turn on a TV, but still listen intently to the sound of the clock. Add a radio to the mix. Can you still hear and focus on the ticking? (Naturally if the radio is exceptionally loud it can drown out the clock regardless of how well you concentrate.)

This is a straightforward method to train ourselves to legitimately hear and concentrate. It obviously ties into Nakamura Sensei's experiences in India, but it also offers useful clues about how to focus during the hubbub of modern life.

To keep our mind on a ticking timepiece, we shouldn't try to block out the TV or radio. Such attempts only attach the mind to these sounds. We don't need to be in conflict with the varied background noises in life, we just have to not be fixated on them. The secret is to *do nothing* when you hear these noises. As the result, your mind immediately returns to the ticking clock. You'll clearly perceive the TV, but your mind won't cling to what you hear, allowing you to concentrate on the clock.

Maybe this sounds tough to do. It is if you think it is. Yet most people have concentrated on one thing while several other things were going on at the same time. Proof positive, we commonly drive in the rain with the windshield wipers on. While we notice the wiper blades when we initially turn them on, most of us are soon able to remain focused on the road. We know the wipers are going back and forth, but we aren't stuck on them, which allows us to pay attention to what we see down the road. And we rarely try hard to not think about the windshield wipers, which is why we can be aware of them but still focus on driving.

In Kanno no Keihatsu internal thoughts and external sounds are like the windshield wipers and whatever we're listening to or tasting is the road. In Anjo Daza Ho and Muga Ichi-nen Ho our varied perceptions are akin to the wipers, and the state beyond the senses and self-consciousness is the highway. Don't try to stop your thoughts or perceptions. Just do nothing.

Develop the Senses to Develop the Mind

We think our senses are physical, but that's only half of what they are. The other half is the mind. To refine these senses we must refine concentration. Certainly people who have trouble with a particular sense could be suffering from a physical disability, but lack of attention may also be the culprit.

I've spent most of my life teaching Shin-shin-toitsu-do and martial arts to young children. I once had a child in my dojo who responded to nearly every command or request with "Huh?" I wondered if he had a problem with his ears, and I asked his mother if his school was checking the hearing of their students. She thought they were, but she took him to a doctor anyway. The verdict was OK ears, not OK attention.

I began encouraging him to "Wake up!" each time he responded to something I said with "What?" It became a game where I tried to catch him off guard, and he attempted to stay alert. Eventually his "hearing" improved.

Nevertheless, I still tell parents to have the hearing of their children checked if they seem inattentive in class. Usually the problem has nothing to do with the ears, but this isn't always the case. Yet even if we have a physical problem with one of our senses, this is all the more reason to learn to concentrate using the above drills. In doing so we may offset certain disabilities.

Some may think this is going to be rough, since they can't focus well to begin with. But I wonder how many who claim they're unable to pay attention are as bad as they think. If we do something we truly enjoy are we unable to concentrate on it? If so, then we may have our work cut out for us, but I'll bet most people can occasionally concentrate, and when they do it's in conjunction with an activity they like.

As an example, I enjoy sports cars and classic automobiles. My wife and I were once driving a new and especially nice BMW sports coupe when I got a funny feeling. I asked her if the car seemed strange to her, but she felt nothing. After a few minutes of uneasiness, I told her I was pulling to the side of the road. Just as I finished crossing several lanes of busy California freeway, one of the BMW's new rear tires exploded. I avoided an accident because of where I'd positioned the car. My wife was dumbfounded that I'd noticed something she couldn't feel and also that this sensing took place long before the tire actually blew out. I can't say any one sense played a role in this; it was more a combination of senses. She credits this to my training in Shin-shin-toitsu-do, and I do as well. But beyond this, I love cars far more than she does, so I more easily and effectively pay attention to what they're doing . . . even on very subtle levels.

We all have this capacity for sophisticated sensory ability and profound concentration. We can learn more about concentration by noticing how we feel, and what we're doing mentally, when we engage in an action we enjoy. Why can we easily concentrate on a favorite movie but not on a college textbook? Again, a positive attitude and concentration are interrelated as is concentration and the five senses.

Kanno no Keihatsu and Sound Judgment

In his classic work *Polishing the Mind*, Nakamura Sensei wrote:

All of us understand that good judgment is important, but few know it can be consciously developed. . . . I'd like to discuss cultivating and training the five senses, which correlates to perceiving life deeply and with clarity of awareness. Unless all senses work at peak capacity they won't clearly and effectively take in information from our environment, making it impossible to correctly judge what to do in a given situation.[96]

We frequently say common sense can't be taught, but if common sense is equivalent to sound judgment, perhaps this needs to be reconsidered. Nakamura Sensei further wrote:

Cultivating judgment and clear perception makes it possible to intelligently and rationally control actions and reactions. When the functioning of our five senses is heightened discernment improves, perception becomes better and more precise, the sixth sense, intuition, and inspiration arise . . .

But modernists are sometimes unaware of the importance of cultivating their senses and clarity of perception; they're often too busy cramming their brains with knowledge and information, not all of which is particularly useful. The result is that they create their own failures, problems, and afflictions.[97]

Nakamura Sensei was versed in several languages, he attended top schools, and his personal library was enormous. He was an extremely knowledgeable person. His comments above aren't condemning learning. They simply indicate that the mere memorization of facts does not equal understanding, and it doesn't lead to happiness. Likewise, Nakamura Sensei's observation about "modernists" needs to be understood in its historical context. He lived through a period in which Japan repeatedly rushed to embrace anything new and Western in origin, regularly forgetting its traditional values and culture, while racing headlong toward materialism. He wasn't against technological progress. He just didn't believe it could ultimately solve the problems of humanity. In *Polishing the Mind* he indicated two elements are required for effective judgment:

    1. Improved functioning of the five senses
    2. Cleansing and evaluating information received through the five senses

Nakamura Sensei offered sound advice and commentary on the correlation between the senses and efficient discernment:

Improving the five senses means training and sharpening these senses so they function better. Suppose you lost your five senses. What would become of you? If you couldn't see, hear, touch, smell, and feel, how well could you think, discern, or enjoy life? You'd fall into very deep and dark hell.

Some mistaken scholars think human thought can work at a high level without any relationship to the senses. If we observe life more closely, we see any idea or thought arising in the mind relates to materials we've received from the outside world through our five senses. We give birth to one idea, or one series of thoughts, by reacting to impressions from our environment through the windows of the senses. We then modify these impressions and manufacture original ideas.

These sensations that we take in from outside are to the mind as food is to the body. The body takes in nourishment via the mouth; the mind receives sustenance through the senses. So the impressions obtained from outside are very important to the mind. They're the mind's food. But we usually forget this simple fact.

We're fussy about the food we eat every day. We remember precise information about the nutritional content of various foods and different cooking methods, but we often know little about training our senses and increasing our capacity for clear perception of the external world. And this is why I emphasize that the first principle for obtaining good judgment is to heighten the perceptive abilities of the five senses.

Yet we also need to consider the content of what comes into the mind and what we do with it, and this is the second principle for effective judgment. When our five senses receive impressions from outside, we have to be conscious enough to notice which images are positive and which are negative. Embrace positive impressions and let go of negative ones. When we eat we're often careful to choose healthy food. Why don't we also choose what we want to embrace in terms of sensations coming to us from the outside world? There's so much negative information, in the form of destructive desires and violence that comes to us through the media.[98]

Awareness of difficulties in the world through the media isn't a problem. On the other hand, clinging to these difficulties and being negatively influenced by them *is* a problem for numerous people. A mind that's depressed and withdrawn will not be capable of good judgment.

Kanno no Keihatsu and Meditation

In 2003, Marc Kaufman, a staff writer for the *Washington Post*, reported on exciting new research into meditation and the brain:

Brain research is beginning to produce concrete evidence for something that Buddhist practitioners of meditation have maintained for centuries: Mental discipline and meditative practice can change the workings of the brain and allow people to achieve different levels of awareness.

Those transformed states have traditionally been understood in transcendent terms, as something outside the world of physical measurement and objective evaluation. But over the past few years, researchers at the University of Wisconsin working with Tibetan monks have been able to translate those mental experiences into the scientific language of high-frequency gamma waves and brain synchrony, or coordination. And they have pinpointed the left prefrontal cortex, an area just behind the left forehead, as the place where brain activity associated with meditation is especially intense.

"What we found is that the longtime practitioners showed brain activation on a scale we have never seen before," said Richard Davidson, a neuroscientist at the university's new $10 million W.M. Keck Laboratory for Functional Brain Imaging and Behavior. "Their mental practice is having an effect on the brain in the same way golf or tennis practice will enhance performance." It demonstrates, he said, that the brain is capable of being trained and physically modified in ways few people can imagine.[99]

Scientists used to believe the reverse—that connections amongst brain nerve cells were set near the beginning of life and didn't change later in life. But from roughly 1993 to 2003, this hypothesis was disproved with the aid of advances in brain imaging and other methodologies. Now scientists are tending to embrace the idea of potential constant brain growth and what Davidson terms "neuroplasticity." In the *Washington Post* article, Davidson stated his latest results from the meditation study published in the Proceedings of the National Academy of Sciences take the notion of neuroplasticity a step further by showing that mind training via meditation—and apparently other disciplines—can transform the internal mechanism and circuitry of the brain.[100] Shin-shin-toitsu-do meditation may not be identical to the version of meditation in Davidson's study, but it seems reasonable to suppose that since most meditation involves concentration, a number of the techniques in this book might similarly have a positive effect on the brain. In fact, the NCBI website, a service of the U. S. National Library of Medicine and the National Institutes of Health, reports that an Emory University study of Zen meditation also showed positive results relating to the brain:

> In this study, we examined how the regular practice of meditation may affect the normal age-related decline of cerebral gray matter volume and attentional performance observed in healthy individuals. Voxel-based morphometry for MRI anatomical brain images and a computerized sustained attention task were employed in 13 regular practitioners of Zen meditation and 13 matched controls. While control subjects displayed the expected negative correlation of both gray matter volume and attentional performance with age, meditators did not show a significant correlation of either measure with age.[101]

The effect of meditation on gray matter volume was most noticeable in the putamen, a structure associated with attentional processing. These findings imply that the ongoing practice of meditation may have neuroprotective effects and decrease the cognitive decline linked with typical aging.[102]

Nakamura Sensei's exercises for training the senses clearly involve concentration, but depending on how we approach them, they have elements in common with meditation. Like meditation they bring the mind into touch with reality. In a way they awaken us, making us more sensitive to the world. The late Tohei Koichi Sensei, one of Nakamura Sensei's senior students, sometimes described the lives of typical people as "*suisei mushi.*" His phrase means to live as if drunk and to die still dreaming. This isn't pretty, and Shin-shin-toitsu-do allows us to heighten our senses while also feeling what lies beyond these senses.

Obviously the senses can only identify various parts of reality in the present moment, which ties into meditation as well. Concentration occurs when the mind remains in the present, and this lets us perform the above drills effectively. It simultaneously awakens us to the only moment that truthfully exists, an instant beyond time and with no space for worry. Time stops, eternity is encountered, and the mind grows calm. Sound similar to earlier chapters on meditation? It is.

Try holding an object between your fingers. Focus your mind totally on the sensation of touch. Do this correctly and you'll experience a moment in which only this feeling fills the mind, in which you stop worrying about your life or your self-image. This is when the distinction between the observer and the observed dissolves resulting in oneness. When Nakamura Sensei's exercises for the senses progress to this point, they move toward the Raja yoga trinity of dharana, dhyana, and samadhi—from concentration to meditation to realization of our unity with everything. In this context, the drills in this chapter relate to meditation.

Kanno no Keihatsu and Aging

In the USA the Baby Boomer Generation (1946-1964) is aging. Many predict with such a huge percentage of the populace growing old the health care system and society as a whole may be overwhelmed with Alzheimer's cases, senior dementia, and elderly-related maladies, resulting in a severe drain on the economy. It's a reasonable concern, and Kanno no Keihatsu can help aging people.

Actually, concentration exercises and meditation in general have numerous physical benefits that apply to people of any age. Joel Stein, in an article for *Time* magazine, wrote:

Contentment and inner peace are nice, but think how many Americans would start meditating if you could convince them they would live longer without having to jog or eat broccoli rabe. More than a decade ago, Dr. Dean Ornish argued that meditation, along with yoga and dieting, reversed the buildup of plaque in coronary arteries. Last April, at a meeting of the American Urological Association, he announced his most recent findings that meditation may slow prostate cancer.[103]

Clearly exercises like Kanno no Keihatsu have the potential to benefit both young and old on psychological and physiological planes. Bottom line: We needn't lose the acuteness of our senses as we become older.

While it may be true that sight and hearing can decrease with age, how much of this is physical and how much is mental is hard to determine. By training our five senses frequently our hearing, eyesight, and other senses remain functional even when we're senior citizens. Nakamura Sensei never lost the sharpness of his senses even as his final moments approached. He remained fully conscious until the end, choosing his last words and perhaps even the moment of his death.

I teach Japanese calligraphy to a number of senior citizens from Japan. These women, who've been regularly practicing brush writing for some time, seem younger than their years, and I'm convinced their shodo training contributes to this. In calligraphy and ink painting eyesight is trained, concentration is utilized, and hand-eye coordination is involved, while intellectual capacities are used. Some members of our small shodo group are over 90 years old, and yet they live alone, walk without canes, and take the bus to the Buddhist church we rent space from. The old adage "If you don't use it, you lose it," may apply to the physical functionality of senses just as it does to muscles.

Some might claim our sense of smell isn't a muscle, so it can't be developed. This could be the case, but I doubt numerous scientific studies have been done to confirm that the senses can't be improved. Others may argue that Kanno no Keihatsu isn't training the senses on a physical level as much as it is training the mind. Mind and body are one, so I agree it's hard to separate senses from psyche. But again, I doubt abundant medical studies have definitively determined how much these sensitivity exercises involve the mind and to what degree they relate to the senses.

However, quite a few scientific studies have shown that meditation and concentration training is useful for combating physical ailments. Dr. Jon Kabat-Zinn, Professor of Medicine Emeritus and founding director of the Stress Reduction Clinic and the Center for Mindfulness in Medicine, Health Care, and Society at the University of Massachusetts Medical School, has conducted clinical trials relating meditation to the alleviation of pain and the treatment of illness:

> Lately Kabat-Zinn has been studying a group of patients with psoriasis, an incurable skin disease that is often treated by asking patients to go to a hospital, put goggles on and stand naked in a hot, loud ultraviolet light box. Apparently, many people find this stressful. So Kabat-Zinn randomly picked half the patients and taught them to meditate in order to reduce their stress levels in the light box. In two experiments, the meditators' skin cleared up at four times the rate of the nonmeditators. In another study, conducted with Wisconsin's Richard Davidson, Kabat-Zinn gave a group of newly taught meditators and nonmeditators flu shots and measured the antibody levels in their blood. Researchers also measured their brain activity to see how much the meditators' mental activity shifted from the right brain to the left. Not only did the meditators have more antibodies at both four weeks and eight weeks after the shots, but the people whose activity shifted the most had even more antibodies. The better your meditation technique, Kabat-Zinn suggests, the healthier your immune system.
>
> Meanwhile, the evidence from meditation researchers continues to mount. One study, for example, shows that women who meditate and use guided imagery have higher levels of the immune cells known to combat tumors in the breast. This comes after many studies have established that meditation can significantly reduce blood pressure. Given that 60% of doctor visits are the result of stress-related conditions, this isn't surprising. Nor is it surprising that meditation can sometimes be used to replace Viagra.[104]

If Kanno no Keihatsu actually develops our senses, or if it only cultivates concentration and clear awareness, the practical results are the same. We're more alert, more functional, and we live better lives.

Kanno no Keihatsu in Review

When practicing Kanno no Keihatsu, bear in mind the following summarized exercises:

1. Place several objects in front of you. Pick items with multiple details. Focus your eyes on them gently. Then close your eyes, and have a friend ask you about what you saw.

2. Try the same exercise with a photo. Look at the image, close your eyes, and see how many details you remember. Progressively shorten the time you look at the photo, and use photos with more complexity. Have friends ask you about what you saw, try recalling the particulars yourself, or turn away and sketch the picture in detail.

3. Some newspapers publish comics showing two seemingly identical drawings. The second cartoon has tiny differences from the first. Spot the alterations.

4. Lay out several different coins. Pick up each one, rubbing it between your fingers, noticing every detail. Next close your eyes and mix up the coins. Pick one up. Can you tell what you're touching?

5. Shut the eyes and feel the difference in weight between various sheets of paper, which you've numbered. Also try this with paper of varying colors, with slightly different composition and/or method of manufacture.

6. Get bottles of different perfume. Smell each one, memorizing what you smell. Then shut your eyes, jumble the bottles, and pick one. While your eyes remain closed, identify the perfume by smell alone.

7. Buy several types of tea in bag form. Pick up each bag and smell it. After this close your eyes, and mix up the tea bags. Then pick one and determine the type of tea you smell.

8. Using the eyes closed approach above, cultivate your sense of taste utilizing various foods and drinks. Any food or beverage works, and some people like trying to recognize varying sorts of tea.

9. Lay out assorted foods. Blindfold yourself. Have a friend feed food items one at a time to you. Make out the taste and identify the food.

10. Listen to a ticking clock or watch. Move the timepiece farther away. Concentrate on the noise for a bit, and then move it farther away again. Can you still hear it?

11. Next, add a bit of noise from a TV and/or radio, but still listen intently to the clock.

Chapter 10

INTEGRATING
SHIN·SHIN·TOITSU·DO
& DAILY LIFE

Shin-shin-toitsu-do is more than mere philosophy. What we often think of as philosophy may degenerate into abstract concepts with slight application in life. Instead, Nakamura Tempu Sensei's teachings—if they are "philosophy"—are a philosophy with a physical expression. As the result, we see no substantial difference between mind and body unification as practiced in the dojo (training hall) and as applied in everyday existence.

Shin-shin-toitsu-do is first and foremost a system of universal principles, which are easy to integrate into life. For example, if we lose composure in a meeting, it may not be possible to calm down via an exercise, but we can unobtrusively recover calmness by focusing ki in the lower abdomen. This is a principle more than an exercise. Nakamura Sensei's exercises and forms of meditation are practiced as much to understand the principles they're based on as for mind-body benefits. In his work *Searching for Truth in Life*, Nakamura Sensei clarified integrating Shin-shin-toitsu-do with life when he explained the third and fourth of the Four Basic Principles to Unify Mind and Body. You'll recall these principles are:

- Use the body obeying the laws of nature
- Train the body progressively, systematically, and regularly.

In Chapter Four I wrote about the essential aspects of these two principles such as correct relaxation, proper posture, centering ki below the navel, and other points. However in *Searching for Truth in Life*, under the heading of these principles, Nakamura Sensei also clarified how to develop our minds and bodies during everyday actions. He sought to make daily activities mental and physical exercise, letting us more easily "Train the body progressively, systematically, and regularly."

We typically think of meditation as something done in church or alone in a quiet room, but the consciousness realized in meditation can be carried into life. In other words, we can experience *do chu no sei*, "calmness in activity." Similarly we may believe physical training must occur at a gym or on a sports field, but Nakamura Sensei aimed to make the way we live physical development. This allows us to more easily and economically maintain our health.

While detailing all of Shin-shin-toitsu-do is beyond the reach of this book—especially the intricate types of physical exercise—we can still discover how to train the body (and mind) in life. That's the primary focus of this chapter.

Waking Up

Our minds control not only our bodies, but also the course of our entire lives. So how we begin an action is important. If we commence with a negative attitude or an upset mind we sabotage our endeavors before we start.

Japanese culture places a heavy emphasis on the onset of the New Year, with celebrations and rituals to kick the year off on the right foot. For instance, in traditional brush writing *kakizome* (the first calligraphy in the New Year) is of significant concern. However, understanding the magnitude of an upbeat start isn't limited to Asia. In America we describe depressed and/or ineffective individuals as "having gotten up on the wrong side of the bed," indicating a similar realization that the beginning of something is important.

I encourage people to practice meditation when they first wake up. It's excellent for clearing and arousing the mind in preparation for the day ahead. If we start each day by calmly and positively coordinating mind and body, we have a better chance of sustaining this condition throughout the day. At the least, we'll be awake while driving to work. Nakamura Sensei in his writings similarly offered four ways to positively start every day.

First, recognize that waking up isn't guaranteed in life. Someday the sun will rise, and our bodies won't rise with it. This is true even if we ignore this fact. By facing this we get up feeling grateful for being alive. In the most profound sense, every morning we wake up is a good day, a day filled with potential and possibilities. Simply realizing and remembering this starts the day with a positive attitude. To quote Nakamura Sensei:

Every new day alive is a gift from the universe, but some people begin what could be their last day by complaining. This not only wastes the day, it weakens the subconscious mind.[105]

Second, upon waking perform *kokyu ho*, "breathing exercises" (pranayama in India). Deep breathing stimulates us mentally and physically, and since it involves both mind and body it ensures we start the day with mind and body coordinated. Nakamura Sensei emphasized that even three to five complete breaths clear the mind, awaken the body, and trigger positive elements in the subconscious. (Later I'll explain a few of the easier Shin-shin-toitsu-do techniques of breathing.)

Third, make your bed each morning. As noted, Nakamura Sensei taught a nondualistic philosophy which doesn't inevitably divide the world into separate components. Everything—animate and inanimate—is connected to everything else through ki. Thus, gratitude extends to nonliving things. If we're thankful to the bed we used last night, a bed which provided us with rest, we shouldn't leave it for someone else to put in order. Nakamura Sensei made his bed daily. Even when staying in a hotel he didn't leave this for a maid, and unlike scores of Japanese men of his generation he didn't expect his wife to make the bed for him. His independent approach can also help us start every dawn in an optimistic, disciplined manner, while it cultivates self-reliance.

Fourth, like numerous people Nakamura Sensei washed at least his face after he got out of bed. It awakens mind and body, clearing the mind for the day ahead. He also suggested stripping to the waist while doing this and washing the upper body too if possible. This trains the skin to adapt to changes in temperature even as it prevents the body from being weakened by such changes, increasing its ability to avoid illness. Like Indian yogis he advocated "training the skin," but surprisingly there seems to be little medical research relating to this reasonable idea. Therefore it isn't at present scientifically clear if by doing the above we're training the *skin*, or if we're conditioning other parts of our body through the temperature stimulus on our skin. Regardless, the results among the thousands of Shin-shin-toitsu-do students for nearly 100 years are fewer colds and better health. In fact, Tohei Koichi Sensei, one of Nakamura Sensei's senior students, advocated dumping a bucket of cold water over the body (or a quick dose of chilly water in the shower) each dawn to train the skin and influence the mind to awaken completely and immediately every morning.

Deep Breathing Exercise

Shin Kokyu Ho, "Deep Breathing Exercise," easily and positively starts the day. It also calms the mind and relaxes the body before we begin something significant. It restores composure when we're nervous or angry, and we can do it to recover energy when fatigued.

At the Southern Illinois School of Medicine researchers verified that deep breathing produces significant and positive changes in the mind. They realized tension can negatively impact student performance, but few medical schools offer students a consistent chance to cultivate and perform stress reduction techniques to assist them academically. To address this they designed a curriculum component intended to aid 64 post baccalaureate minority students in developing and practicing a stress-management technique. This was put into practice on an ongoing basis from June 2004 to April 2006. Students participated in "Deep Breathing Meditation exercises" in two classes and completed pre-, post-, and follow-up surveys every school year. These students reported less test anxiety, apprehension, self-doubt, and attention loss. They used breathing exercises outside of the two classes, and most seemed to believe it assisted them scholastically and that it would help them as doctors.[106]

My students report a similar reduction of tension through breathing practices. Yet, lengthy sessions of deep breathing aren't inevitably necessary to simply recover equanimity. Just three to five times can be enough. Here's how to practice and integrate Shin Kokyu Ho into your life:

1. Begin by breathing out slowly, smoothly, and calmly through either the mouth or nose. Initially getting rid of waste products, like carbon dioxide, is important. Exhale 100% of the carbon dioxide but don't strain unnecessarily.

2. Pause, stopping your breath briefly, at the conclusion of exhaling. At this time maintain kumbhaka as detailed earlier.

3. Now inhale. Make both exhalation and inhalation calm, long, and deep. Inhaling through the nose warms the air before it reaches your lungs and filters impurities from the air, but you can inhale with the mouth if your nose is congested. Mentally aim the breath toward your shita hara, "lower abdomen," while keeping the shoulders down and relaxed. Avoid excessively lifting your chest as you inhale. As professional singers confirm, deep breathing is abdominal breathing.

4. Pause, stopping your breath for a few moments after inhaling. Maintain kumbhaka at this time. This concludes one breath cycle in Shin Kokyu Ho. Start by exhaling and end on an exhalation.

In *Searching for Truth in Life* Nakamura Sensei suggested visualizing ki flowing out while exhaling and absorbing ki when inhaling to unify mind, body, and breath:

> Visualize receiving vital life energy (ki) from the infinite universe when inhaling, and releasing ki and carbon dioxide into the universe when exhaling, to become one with the universe. Breathe with a feeling of gratitude to the universe.[107]

Clothing and the Skin

Once we're out of bed, and we've practiced meditation and/or breathing exercises to start the morning positively, we need to put on clothes. Nakamura Sensei typically wore traditional Japanese clothing which is rarely tight. Whatever clothes we dress in, regularly wearing excessively snug garments is problematic. Tight pants or a tight bra makes full, relaxed, and natural breathing harder. We can go days without food and quite some time without water, but even a few minutes without oxygen means trouble. Of our life functions breathing is perhaps most important and most ignored. Avoid clothing that inhibits breathing, especially abdominal breathing.

Skintight attire may lessen "skin respiration" and the skin's adaptability to temperature changes, unless it's made of a breathable sports fabric. We can say the same about too many layers of clothing. In India Nakamura Sensei learned the skin needs to breathe and be trained to quickly adjust to temperature variations.[108]

Shin-shin-toitsu-do stresses correct and natural breathing for living well, but it emphasizes that breathing isn't restricted to the lungs. The need for healthy "skin respiration" is well documented in science. Dermatologists will agree because breathing is how cells exchange carbon dioxide, a waste product. (Other waste products aren't removed through cellular respiration but by additional processes.) "Skin breathing" delivers oxygen to the upper layers of skin cells before the oxygen is gone.

Nakamura Sensei also encouraged practicing Shin-shin-toitsu-do exercises and meditation while wearing minimal clothing, and old pictures show him leading class clad only in shorts. He wore little more even when training outdoors in cold weather, and he wrote that allowing the body to feel heat and cold, without always protecting it from extremes in temperature, strengthens the skin, which he believed helped people to more easily avoid illness. On the other hand, if we aren't used to exposing the body to heat and cold we should do so gradually. According to Nakamura Sensei a sudden change when training the body, regardless of the type of physical training, isn't beneficial.[109]

Our skin protects our internal organs and tissues from injury, exposure to sunlight, and invasion from infective agents like bacteria. Nerves and capillaries running underneath the skin regulate body temperature by altering blood circulation. When this fails to occur efficiently it's easy to fall ill. That's why Nakamura Sensei emphasized strengthening the skin.

He taught my teacher Sawai Atsuhiro Sensei additional methods to fortify his skin and promote health. As mentioned, Sawai Sensei was encouraged to start the day by washing himself to reinforce the skin's ability to respond to changes in temperature. This took place before turning on the heat in the house. He was urged to bathe in cold water, and if this wasn't possible to massage his skin with a wet cold towel (even in the winter). Both techniques gradually train the subconscious to become fully awake immediately upon rising and increase blood circulation while strengthening the skin. Nakamura Sensei told him, "Once you decide to do this, don't give it up. If you do it some days, and don't other days, the effect on your health is small." Nevertheless, whether washing with a cold damp towel or bathing in cold water, avoid this if you're unhealthy. Practice other Shin-shin-toitsu-do methods and begin cold water training as your health improves.

Sawai Sensei was also urged to shun numerous layers of clothing, regardless of the season. He didn't do this suddenly, and as he gradually reduced the clothing he wore his skin and body easily adapted. Nakamura Sensei told him as well to avoid the then common Japanese practice of wearing wool underwear (and wool long johns in the winter), encouraging the use of cotton instead. Japan is humid, and when the body sweats cotton absorbs perspiration more effectively. Nakamura Sensei probably also felt wool underwear would be too hot, not allowing the body to learn to adjust to temperature changes and inhibiting skin respiration.

I hope you'll consider the experiences of Sawai Sensei and the advice of Nakamura Sensei, adapting it to your culture and life. The primary points are allowing the lungs and skin to breathe well while training the skin to acclimatize to temperature changes.

Eating and Drinking

Correct and effective respiration is important, but it isn't enough to sustain life. We, of course, need to also eat and drink. What to eat or drink, when, and how much are questions I'm asked at my dojo and in seminars. Yet I'm reluctant to give a firmly established response.

We have different bodies, are of differing ages and sexes, and we may live in different geographic locations. As a consequence it's difficult, and probably a mistake, to prescribe one rigid diet for everyone. And constantly worrying about food isn't good for our psychological or physical wellbeing. That said, general recommendations can be made regarding dietary principles and eating. In Shin-shin-toitsu-do these recommendations stem from science and Nakamura Sensei's life experiences.

He stated that while in India he suffered from tuberculosis and initially worried about how much meat he had in his diet. In Gorkhe he was served vegetarian meals and complained to Kaliapa about the lack of meat and eggs. Kaliapa replied that many people in his country (and even large Indian elephants) ate no meat and were still in good health. Eventually Nakamura Sensei conquered his illness, and he came to feel this was due, at least in part, to the vegetarian diet he ate in India.

Diet

Nakamura Sensei consequently followed, and encouraged students to adopt, a vegetarian or (at least) semi-vegetarian diet. He arrived at this idea from studying medicine and yoga. In *Searching for Truth in Life* he wrote, "Vegetables, grains, nuts, and fruit are best."[110] This is simply stated but based on sound reasoning.

He indicated meat and fish can make blood acidic—acidosis—while vegetables and fruits tend to create alkalosis, a barometer of health. If our blood inclines toward alkalinity we aren't prone to disease, and we more easily resist bacteria. Blood is naturally slightly alkaline[111], so Nakamura Sensei's statements about blood alkalinity are generally recognized by medicine. All the same, true alkalosis is as bad as acidosis. When the pH of blood deviates from its norm it's characteristically a sign of underlying disease or stress. High alkalosis is thus dangerous as well.

Modern science also recognizes Nakamura Sensei's claimed link between blood chemistry and diet. Meat and fish create acidic byproducts when digested, while fruits and vegetables normally (but not always) generate alkaline byproducts. The body needs both types of food (acid forming and alkaline forming), but alkaline forming food should outweigh acid forming food.

What's more, recent studies have shown a link between consuming meat and cancer:

> Eating meat boosts the risk of pancreatic cancer, which almost always is fatal, says a new study by the Cancer Research Center of Hawaii and the University of Southern California.
>
> Researchers tracked 190,000 people, ages 45 to 75, for seven years. Those who ate the most processed meat (bacon, ham, cold cuts) had a 68% higher risk of pancreatic cancer than those who ate the least. Eating the most pork or red meat boosted odds 50%.[112]

As usual, Nakamura Sensei's fruit, grain, and vegetable-based diet was ahead of his time. He further indicated that if we don't adopt a vegetarian diet, at a minimum, we should:

> . . . eat vegetables, nuts, grains, and fruit as 70% of the whole meal, with meat or fish making up no more than 30% of what we eat. Some people worry that without the protein in fish and meat their bodies will fall ill. This is a mistaken idea; remember plenty of protein is found in vegetables, beans, and other foods.[113]

Like everything in life, diet should harmonize with nature. Along these lines, Nakamura Sensei avoided eating too much out of season food. Once again, respecting nature makes sense. Eating with respect for nature and the changing seasons is natural and intelligent. Although science hasn't presently reached an ultimate conclusion regarding consumption of out of season foodstuffs, it's scientifically provable that most foods need time to develop completely. By eating foods out of season we may ingest items which haven't developed all their important nutrients (or foods that are past their prime).

For example, fruit is frequently picked before it's ripe so it keeps in supermarkets. This means the fruit hasn't developed all the nutrients required to make it whole. Consequently food that's in season, regionally grown, natural, and unprocessed may offer a more ideal diet.

Mastication

Nakamura Sensei also suggested chewing food as much as reasonably possible. Mastication (chewing) is how foodstuff is mashed and compressed by our teeth. It's the initial step in digestion, and it increases the surface area of foods to permit more effective break down by enzymes.

In mastication food is placed between the teeth for grinding with the cheek and tongue. As chewing continues food softens and warms, and enzymes in saliva break down its carbohydrates. Chewing also supports the production of saliva which promotes digestion and health. Well-chewed food becomes well-digested food; better digestion is important for better health. And if we chew thoroughly we eat more slowly. As a side-effect we don't feel like eating as much. This is an easy way to become slimmer, and since obesity is at a high in the West, especially in the USA, this advice is noteworthy.

Cooking

How we cook food is likewise important. Food that's not overcooked is better for us which Nakamura Sensei noted, too. Naturalness in eating is important. Some cuisine is regularly so overdone it's less nutritionally sound. Simply put, Nakamura Sensei indicated overcooking food destroys its nutritional value.

This is valid scientifically since heat obliterates nutrients in foods. Of course, countless foods (especially meats) must be heated to destroy bacteria within them, so heating food is often part of food preparation. Still, cooking causes chemical changes within food that can lead to nutrient loss. We need balanced moderation when heating food as some foods shouldn't be eaten raw, but overcooking is also a bad idea. Nakamura Sensei aimed for constant naturalness, one part of which is balance.

Another facet of balanced cooking lies in avoiding massive amounts of spice, chili, pepper, mustard, salt, and similar seasonings when cooking. This isn't to say food must be bland, but extremes in seasoning can cause problems. Not everyone reacts the same way to different spices, and people with high blood pressure should shun large quantities of salt. (My sensei Hashimoto Tetsuichi, like other health experts, recommends sea salt when salt's desired.) Notice how salt and spices affect you, avoiding or limiting what you don't have a good reaction to.

Quantity

Nakamura Sensei also offered this crucial suggestion: "Don't eat too much!" Japanese enjoy one of the world's longest life spans, and certain diseases which are all too common in the West are little known in this island nation. Nonetheless, as Japanese adopt a more Western diet, with fast food chains and more meat, fat, and refined sugar than before, they're developing health problems widespread in the United States. What's more, they're getting fatter.

Japan's indigenous diet is grains and vegetables, with a modest amount of fish. This diet, combined with frequent walking to mass transportation and a cultural distaste for excess and obesity, has resulted in a populace that's rarely overweight. While this may be changing for the worse, Japan still has a lower obesity rate than the USA. Virtually each day new scientific evidence ties being overweight to everything from hypertension to splitting your pants—it's a huge problem in America (pun possibly intended), where bigger is better (pun sarcastically intended).

Nakamura Sensei offered ready and effective counsel. He advised to simply stop eating when we feel "80% full," also mentioning that obesity is a major cause of illness and overeating is a major cause of obesity. Learning when to stop eating is a simple way of controlling weight.[114] We should listen to and respect what our bodies tell us. Nakamura Sensei taught that we don't inevitably need three meals per day, at the same time daily. We should eat when we feel hungry, not out of habit, social conventions, or boredom. This helps to maintain proper weight, and eating multiple smaller meals daily, instead of three big meals, has been shown to produce weight loss. Eating less makes the stomach feel better, the brain clearer, and we're inclined to live longer and fall ill less. This isn't suggesting that we starve ourselves. We have hunger impulses, and we feel these in our stomach. To assimilate food our stomachs use digestive enzymes and muscular contractions. When blood's low in nutrients the brain generates messages that make us hungry. With the right foods we get nutrients back into the bloodstream, and this makes the stomach feel better. The brain also needs nutrients (especially glucose) to function properly. When these are depleted we feel groggy or have trouble concentrating, because the brain isn't working at full capacity. Nevertheless, overeating makes the stomach feel bad because it's overworked. This leads to overcompensation by the digestive system in terms of enzyme production and muscular contractions which upsets the stomach.

Nakamura Sensei didn't eat overly large, heavy meals in the morning, feeling that moderation is best. Quite a few of my students tell me too big a breakfast makes them sluggish, and although this is anecdotal evidence, maybe a modest breakfast is better for vigorously starting the day in a positive manner. We can also speculate that stuffing the belly causes the body's blood supply to move toward the stomach to aid digestion, drawing blood away from the brain, limbs, and muscles. Perhaps this contributes to the sluggishness some people feel if they overeat at breakfast. With that understood, if we engage in heavy manual labor for a living, a bigger breakfast makes sense because we'll burn more calories than office workers.

Nakamura Sensei further counseled against forcing sick people to eat what they don't like. Their bodies naturally tell them what's best for their current condition. However loads of us aren't calm, and the mind isn't in the present, resulting in us forgetting how to listen to what our bodies tell us. Bearing this in mind, and remembering how meditation can rectify this situation, pay attention to your innate tendencies and allow others to do the same.

Attitude

How does the mind factor into what to eat, how to eat, and how much to eat? It is prominent.

Quite a few of us have been so afraid we vomited or had diarrhea. If you haven't experienced this, feel lucky and ask an actor, musician, or other performer what it's like. Scores of them can give you an earful.

Ever been so angry while eating that you got a stomachache not long after? It's common, and the psychosomatic relationship to digestion prompted Nakamura Sensei to write about this topic. He pointed out that since the mind influences the body and digestion people should be as cheerful as possible when taking a meal. Smile when you're eating. If you're angry or sad don't eat at all as such emotions can upset proper digestion. Eat a bit later when calmness and cheerfulness have returned.[115]

Drinking

After oxygen, water is the most necessary consumable for sustaining life. Water is lost during exhalation, perspiration, and urination. It's important to drink enough, and by the time you're really thirsty, you're somewhat dehydrated. When we're tired sometimes all we need is a quick gulp of water to re-energize:

"A significant number of people who come to me complaining of fatigue are actually dehydrated," says Woodson Merrell, M. D., executive director of the Continuum Center for Health and Healing at Beth Israel Medical Center in New York City. One study found just a 2% dip in hydration levels—the point where you start to feel a little thirsty—decreased short-term memory as well as the ability to add and subtract. Another study found that dehydrated exercisers tired out 25% sooner than those that sipped water during workouts.[116]

Everyone realizes dehydration leads to illness but not all grasp how better water consumption helps us in other ways. For instance, researchers at the University of North Carolina found people who knock back seven cups of water per day eat almost 200 fewer calories than people who consume less than a glass of water a day, and they're less likely to eat high-fat food.[117] Ever notice how thin, uber-beautiful Hollywood stars are regularly photographed holding a bottle of water? They may be on to something Nakamura Sensei also advocated: the oft unrealized health benefits of water.

Nakamura Sensei, again cautioning balance, avoided drinking extremely hot or cold drinks which might cause stomach upset. Avoiding ice water and exceptionally cold drinks is a widespread belief among older generations in Japan. As an adolescent practicing judo I remember teachers admonishing us not to drink lots of icy water after sweaty classes in the hot summer. They told us combining exceptionally cold water and very hot bodies wasn't bright, but many of us ignored them, gorging on chilled water as kids sometimes do. I still vividly recall my stomach pain after one such episode.

While not every culture agrees ice water has drawbacks, some schools of thought concur. Avoiding excessively cold or hot fluids is addressed in Native American medicine, where they believe extremes are bad for wellbeing and body organs. This is relatively intuitive; Nakamura Sensei felt the same way. Additionally, some scientists agree that drinking markedly hot or cold fluids aggravates heartburn (i.e. causes stomach upset). It isn't at present medically clear if this exacerbates a pre-existing condition as opposed to *causing* the upset stomach.

Nakamura Sensei especially recommended drinking plenty of water and green tea. According to his writings, tap water is good enough . . . "as long as you can trust that the local government is providing clean and healthy water."[118]

As mentioned, he felt alkalinity was good for the body. Note most foods Americans overindulge in (meats, fatty foods, etc.) are acidic. Moreover, green tea is alkaline, and if the average person typically eats a diet that's too acidic, alkaline drinks may balance out the acidity. It's also medically recognized that we should drink ample amounts of water since our bodies consist mostly of water. Other drinks, such as soda, typically contain sugars that can damage teeth and digestive systems. Soda and alcohol actually dehydrate the body due to ions within them, which draw water from body fluids. This is the osmotic effect in action. Salts and ions in general suck water out of your system and act as a diuretic. So given the multiple well-known drawbacks associated with soda and alcohol, water and green tea may be better drinks, with decaffeinated tea always being an option.[119]

In recent years the Western medical community has investigated the possibility that green tea consumption may be linked to lower risk of cancer, strokes, and cardiovascular disease. The National Cancer Institute in the U.S., as of 2006, was funding studies to probe a link between tea extract and the prevention of several types of cancer. A recent newspaper article by The Associated Press stated:

> Tea contains substances called antioxidants that can help keep cells healthy. Green tea has more of them than black tea and studies in animals have shown that tea antioxidants called catechins seem to shrink cancerous tumors. Some studies in humans have suggested tea can also help keep arteries and cholesterol healthy.[120]

Some medical experts also suggest a possible link between green tea consumption, vegetarianism, and a lower risk of disease:

> However, heavy tea drinkers in the study also tended to eat more fruits and vegetables, and such a diet might reduce cardiovascular disease and cancer risks, said John Folts, a professor of medicine at the University of Wisconsin.[121]

In a scientific study funded by the Japanese government green tea drinking seemed to guard against stroke:

> Green tea appeared to work best against clot-related strokes. Among the five-cup-a-day group, women had a 62 percent lower risk of dying from these strokes than women who drank little tea, and for men the reduced risk was 42 percent.[122]

Medical theory evolves and is revised; it takes time for a hypothesis to be regarded as fact within the scientific community. While studies point to the healthful advantages of green tea, not every physician agrees and presently the case for green tea hasn't been fully decided. But the evidence seems promising.

Nakamura Sensei had more to say about tea. In 1947 he wrote that avoiding excess black tea or coffee is best. Unwarranted caffeine has a detrimental effect on the body. According to his book *Searching for Truth in Life* putting excessive sugar in these drinks is also inadvisable as too much refined sugar has little nutritional value and puts unneeded weight on the body.[123]

While his comments were made years ago, contemporary science indicates the validity of quite few of them. Certain ideas, like his recommendation of green tea, have only more recently made headlines but are still worth considering.

Housing

During our day we'll leave the building we live in and typically go to another building to work. At day's end we return to our house, and we may wonder if Nakamura Sensei had suggestions concerning housing. He did.

They're simple, logical, but not always considered. He indicated that getting enough fresh air is important for good health as is sufficient exposure to sunlight. Consequently, ventilation and sunlight are significant factors to consider when having a house built, buying a house, or renting an apartment.[124]

This is sound advice, but sadly times have changed and how much ventilation we want may depend on where we live. Case in point, air quality in Tokyo and Los Angeles is notoriously bad, and there we may be better off inside a building that's climate controlled with air filters. However, as long as air quality is acceptable, then both science and Shin-shin-toitsu-do indicate to get plenty of fresh air. Without appropriate circulation and ventilation the air within structures becomes stagnant and concentrated with waste products our bodies expel (i.e. carbon dioxide), so fresh air is an excellent idea. (In a major city check the news for a daily "air quality index" before opening doors and windows.)

As for sunshine, modern medicine recognizes lack of sunlight causes sickness and fatigue:

"One reason for the fatigue that is rampant in our society may be light deprivation," says Micheal Terman, director of clinical chronobiology at the

252

New York City State Psychiatric Institute in New York City. Research suggests that exposure to bright light in the morning can boost energy throughout the day. One theory: Light stimulates neurotransmitters in your brain, such as serotonin and dopamine, which improve your mood and increase motivation.

Exposure to any sunlight can provide a little boost, but Terman says that "the dawn signal has a particularly strong therapeutic effect." So take a morning walk or quick stroll during your coffee break; even a cloudy day offers enough light to have a stimulating effect on the brain.[125]

Sunlight has an emotional effect, and it's a positive one. Studies reveal people are less apt to get depressed in warm and sun-drenched locales. Sun deficient illness and depression can stem from reduced Vitamin D and changes in hormone levels. In fact, in the Arctic Circle people use UV lamps for short periods to prevent sunlight-deprivation sickness. We'll get into deriving maximum advantage from the sun shortly.

Air

We've seen the importance Shin-shin-toitsu-do places on breathing exercises, so it's no surprise Nakamura Sensei discussed using the air surrounding us for maximum health benefit:

Deep breathing has a beneficial effect on the body, and doing breathing exercises in fresh, clean air is best. Likewise bathing in refreshing, cool air strengthens skin resistance and respiration. We have no reason to fear and hide from cold air, and I'd suggest engaging in both practices above.

Doing almost anything outdoors in the fresh air is good for our health. Maintaining an intimate connection with nature by walking, gardening, playing outdoor games, etc., is vital.

Within the home open the windows, and let stale air out and new air in. Even in the cold of winter do this from time to time.

Some people are afraid of night air, thinking it will make them ill. This is a mistake, because at nighttime air is often cleaner and fresher than during the daytime. Dirt and waste particles in the air drop to the ground at nightfall, and pollution from cars and factories lessens as they're less active at night. Indian yogis sit in meditation at nighttime in the outside air, and I recommend the same practice. Nevertheless, it's better to go to bed by 12 o'clock at night, because energy from the sun is gone by around that time.[126]

Again, sunlight has considerable worth in terms of our physical condition. If we're awake all night and sleep later into the day, then we receive less exposure to sunshine. This means less vitamin D and altered hormone levels. Of course too much sun is destructive, leading to sunburn and cancer, but we need daylight to function properly.

Sunlight

India has a long tradition that stresses the benefits of being closely tied to nature. Japan and its indigenous Shinto religion have a similar emphasis. Predictably Nakamura Sensei discussed absorbing ki from food, water, air, and sunshine. It's an emphasis that's unfortunately less common in the West, and it may be waning in the East. Nakamura Sensei commented that ultraviolet light from the sun has valuable effects on the human body. Sunshine helps produce vitamin D, which promotes generation of red blood cells. Even so, he advised against being in the sun too long. Excessive exposure might cause the blood to be oxidized, and it can also lead to skin cancer.[127]

UV radiation is a source of free radicals which can oxidize cells. This damages them and has been implicated in cancer and aging. Huntington's Outreach Program for Education at Stanford University indicates:

Free radicals are atoms or molecules that are highly reactive with other cellular structures because they contain unpaired electrons. Free radicals are natural by-products of ongoing biochemical reactions in the body, including ordinary metabolic processes and immune system responses. Free radical-generating substances can be found in the food we eat, the drugs and medicines we take, the air we breathe, and the water we drink. These substances include fried foods, alcohol, tobacco smoke, pesticides, air pollutants, and many more. Free radicals can cause damage to parts of cells such as proteins, DNA, and cell membranes by stealing their electrons through a process called oxidation. (This is why free radical damage is also called "oxidative damage.") When free radicals oxidize important components of the cell, those components lose their ability to function normally, and the accumulation of such damage may cause the cell to die. Numerous studies indicate that increased production of free radicals causes or accelerates nerve cell injury and leads to disease.[128]

In the biological field oxidative stress is a hot topic because of its involvement in these processes. This is why antioxidants are booming in the health and diet industry (because they may slow oxidative damage). Considering this, avoid excess sun, which can also cause headache, fatigue, dizziness (due to dehydration) and premature aging of the skin. Although extreme sun exposure is damaging this doesn't mean we can't gain from moderate and intelligent exposure to sunlight. Actually, because the dangers of excess sun have received tremendous publicity in the last few years, some experts are labeling this as possible overkill. A *Medscape Today* article touts the benefits of ultraviolet-B induced vitamin D production indicating:

> The health benefits of UVB seem to outweigh the adverse effects. The risks can be minimized by avoiding sunburn, excess UVR exposure and by attention to dietary factors, such as antioxidants and limiting energy and fat consumption. It is anticipated that increasing attention will be paid to the benefits of UVB radiation and vitamin D and that health guidelines will be revised in the near future.[129]

Infrared rays, ultraviolet rays, and the seven visible colors (red, orange, yellow, green, blue, indigo, and violet) make up sunshine. Shin-shin-toitsu-do exponents regularly practice meditation, breathing techniques, and physical exercises in the sun while wearing little clothing. In this way they let their skin breathe as they train it to adapt to varying temperatures and expose it to sunlight.

How much sun should we get? Unfortunately too many variables, such as time of day, geographic location, and individual physical condition, exist to offer a specific answer. Even so, common sense indicates to get a reasonable amount of sunlight each day while avoiding sunburn. Plus, in the United States we can consult the National Weather Service's UV Index online, which predicts the next day's ultraviolet radiation level and how long someone can be exposed to the sun before sunburn occurs. All and all, Nakamura Sensei's proposal to get enough sunshine still holds true.

Earth

The earth has great strength. Chemical wastes can be decomposed and neutralized in soil, indicating its potential power, and Nakamura Sensei encouraged students to remain connected to the earth. In the West studies have shown plants in your office or home may result in reduced stress, weariness, and sickness.[130] Humans thrive—like most living things—when they're in touch with nature.

In Gorkhe Nakamura Sensei lived in intimate contact with the earth, sitting in the grass or on a flat rock each day in meditation. Even after returning to the big city life of Tokyo he maintained close ties to the earth and wrote that mud baths have helped some people suffering from neuralgia, rheumatism, and other troubles. He urged his readers to consider gardening with ungloved hands touching the soil and walking on sandy beaches with bare feet. He felt both are healthful. Nakamura Sensei believed the earth has energy to revive us when we're fatigued, and he mentioned that all animals and plants maintain a constant connection to the earth and its varied elements. When human beings lose this connection they often grow weak and suffer in different ways.[131]

Even though we may intuitively agree with Nakamura Sensei that we feel healthier or more natural when contacting the earth, it's hard to scientifically study this concept. That understood, in a strictly scientific sense all material things in the universe have energy simply by being made of physical matter and having mass. The earth is no different.[132] Material things are also connected as they're made of the same universal building blocks (i.e., atoms). As a consequence, one could speculate that energy in human beings reacts to the energy in the earth (for instance), but more research is needed before this is provable. At this time we'll have to arrive at our own conclusions, but for millennia in Asia people have sensed an exchange ki (or prana) between themselves and elements in nature, including the earth.

Exercise

Nakamura Sensei strongly believed in exercise, frequently leading his students in jogging even as a senior citizen. With every passing year medicine seems to get closer to indicating that if anything is a medicinal magic bullet or panacea it's intelligent exercise. Sarah Arnquist, writing for the *Daily Republic* newspaper, affirms this:

> Regular physical activity has been proven to lower the risk of cancer, heart disease and even increase life spans by up to four years. Despite reams of

research supporting the health benefits of exercise, 60 percent of U. S. adults are not sufficiently active on a regular basis. Almost one in four do not exercise at all, according to the Centers for Disease Control and Prevention.

Battling those statistics, more and more primary care doctors are prescribing exercise.[133]

Dr. Irwin Barr, an internist at Kaiser Permanente in California, makes the case even more succinctly:

"If exercise was a drug, it would be the biggest wonder drug to ever hit the market," he said. "People would be clamoring for it."[134]

While physicians have always recognized the advantages of exercise, this recognition is more profound in recent years, as clinical evidence piles up. Yet Nakamura Sensei explained the same thing decades ago, writing that in order to maintain a proper metabolism exercise is essential. But moderation in exercise should be considered, too. Over exercise, just like overeating or overdoing anything, isn't ideal for the body.

We can get exercise in the course of our everyday lives by being more self-reliant. In daily life we can cook our own food, walk instead of depending on a car, climb the stairs instead of relying on elevators, and mow our lawns instead of hiring someone else to do it. If we personally take care of matters in life we'll automatically get more exercise.[135]

Although many in the West once thought only relatively severe exercise was valuable, most doctors and studies today indicate a modest amount of moderate exercise, engaged in regularly, is ideal for wellbeing. And walking, even more than jogging, is now touted by numerous physicians as perhaps the best exercise for average people. Nakamura Sensei, more than 50 years earlier, also advised brisk daily walks. 30 to 60 minutes of walking is ideal, and though some forms of exercise are too severe for the elderly and infirm, most everyone can walk. It's free, and it evenly exercises the body as a whole.[136]

Researchers have found daily walks are nearly as effective as jogging for promoting heart health and blood circulation. University of Texas studies confirmed a 30-minute walk also improved "mood, energy, and mental look in people with serious depression."[137]

Nakamura Sensei also promoted the importance of blood circulation. *Yodo Ho*, which involves four different moving drills, and *Hitori Ryoho* (a kind of "self-massage") are physical exercises found in Shin-shin-toitsu-do. He designed them to stimulate circulation, among other benefits. (These techniques are outlined in *Japanese Yoga: The*

Way of Dynamic Meditation.) Especially for the middle-aged and elderly, it's important to get enough exercise to maintain blood circulation. Nakamura Sensei explained that enhanced circulation of blood helps distribute oxygen more efficiently to the cells in the body, and it aids in effective elimination of carbon dioxide that's produced by the metabolic process in these cells. It helps the skin and body to function well.[138]

Clearly exercise has profound physical advantages, but not everyone realizes exercise is also linked to mental wellbeing (despite the aforementioned University of Texas research). Studies show links between lack of exercise and propensity for dementia:

> Older adults who exercised at least three times a week had a 30 percent to 40 percent lower risk of developing dementia compared to seniors exercising less often, according to a new study.
>
> "Even those elderly people who did modest amounts of gentle exercise, such as walking for 15 minutes three times a week, appeared to benefit," said Eric Larson, director of the Group Health Cooperative of Seattle's Center for Health Studies and lead author of the report, published Tuesday in The Annals of Internal Medicine.[139]

The above newspaper quote not only asserts a link between mind and body, it shows the impact physical activity has on the psyche. It also appears to affirm Nakamura Sensei's recommendation of walking as excellent exercise and his beliefs that exercise needn't be severe to be beneficial.

Cleansing the Blood

Not only did Nakamura Sensei advocate exercise for enhanced blood circulation, he advised "cleansing the blood." This may sound esoteric, conjuring images of rock star Keith Richards in Switzerland having blood transfusions. It's actually simple and sensible.

Nakamura Sensei counseled to keep the blood "clean" by having regular bowel movements. Proper elimination of excrement is needed for cleansing our blood. At least one bowel movement a day is ideal.[140]

Our digestive system breaks down food and allows nutrients within that food to pass into the bloodstream. Simultaneously the lining of the digestive tract prevents waste products and toxic chemicals from passing into the blood. When our digestive system works properly, it keeps blood "clean" through this selective material transport into the blood. Having regular bowel movements maintains an optimally working digestive system. Without normal bowel movements the lining of the intestinal tract could possibly become coated with a thick layer, which might prevent absorption of nutrients into the bloodstream. Some feel this could lead to health problems, including perhaps a condition in which harmful chemicals (the ones normally prevented from entering the bloodstream) leak through the intestinal lining and into the blood. Daily bowel movements could prevent these problems. Though bowel movements don't "cleanse the blood" directly, they may prevent the bloodstream from becoming "poisoned."

In essence, we have four forms of excretion that maintain health: exhalation, perspiration, urination, and evacuation of the bowels. Anything inhibiting these four processes should be avoided.

Deep breathing exercises are central to Shin-shin-toitsu-do. In deep breathing fully exhaling eliminates waste products; Shin-shin-toitsu-do physical training and everyday exercise do the same through perspiration. Ingesting plenty of healthful liquids, like green tea and water, promotes urination. Nakamura Sensei also taught that sufficient water is needed for normal evacuation of the intestines. He made a habit of drinking one or two glasses of water every morning when he washed his face, indicating that he also drank plenty of water throughout the day as well for cleansing the blood.[141]

Drinking water helps the bowels move freely, preventing the nasty things listed previously from happening to the intestinal tract and blood. As for cleansing the blood, fluids we drink and foods we eat directly effect the composition of our blood. Nutrients, ions, and other elements are exchanged between our bloodstream and fluids in our digestive tract. After these materials pass into the bloodstream, the blood passes through the kidneys which filter wastes and extra water.

Remember how certain fluids (like coffee, tea, or alcohol) dehydrate the body because of the particular ions they contain? This is because the kidneys filter blood using ionic concentration gradients. So drinking water flushes out unwanted wastes in the blood by way of the kidneys. Of course, excessively drinking water isn't smart.

Health conscious individuals often ponder what they put into themselves, but they sometimes forget the importance of efficiently eliminating wastes from their bodies. Making sure our lifestyle supports excretion via effective bowel evacuation, respiration, perspiration, and urination is important.

Sexuality

Nakamura Sensei grew up when quite a few educators counseled people to avoid having very much sex. Meditation instruction available during his lifetime was largely tied to religions which were also frequently sex phobic. This was true in both Japan and India.

Sadly, even today in some circles not much has changed. Physicians and psychologists are presently quite clear that human sexuality isn't something to be feared, and sexual release is usually good for us. The same can't be said for some religious zealots, in the East and West, and it's unfortunate that many still imagine meditation must be tied to religion. A quick perusal of the San Francisco phone book under "Meditation Instruction" reveals several listings, the majority of which are coupled to an organized religion, usually of Eastern descent. For certain people this connection is favored, but it would be nice if non-religious meditation was widely accessible for individuals preferring to find their own spiritual answers.

This is what Nakamura Sensei offered. He bravely advocated an affirmative view of sexuality, based more on science than religion, in a place and time when this was potentially controversial. He distinguished between innate human desires and being attached to these desires. He insisted that the former cannot—and should not—be eliminated. This freed generations of his younger Japanese readers from unnecessary religious guilt, letting them experience a practical spirituality that distinguished between desires and attachments, with the transcendence of attachment leading to freedom from suffering.

In *Searching for Truth in Life*, considered by some his most basic textbook, he wrote:

In the old days many doctors and religious scholars warned against having much sex, but I propose a moderate sexual life is good for our health and shouldn't be repressed or forbidden. Sex is natural, but because some religions emphasize the mind over the body, they encourage their followers to repress sexual urges. This is unnatural or perhaps impossible. Even if doable it results in internal conflict and tension.

However when we're exceptionally tired or intoxicated it makes sense to abstain from sex. And when we experience anger, sorrow, or fear it isn't the best time for sex either. Sex cannot be genuinely enjoyed at such times, and it shouldn't be used as a crutch to hide from depression or anger. We need to encounter such feelings and transform them. Distracting ourselves with sex will not lead to understanding and resolving the roots of fear or sorrow.

All the same, when we feel both mentally and physically fine it's natural to enjoy making love. A healthy sex drive is, in fact, an indication of a strong life force (ki).[142]

Staying Healthy

Quite a few look to Nakamura Sensei's teachings as a way of recovering health, and an explanation of Shin-shin-toitsu-do in everyday life would be deficient without mentioning his views on health maintenance. As usual he dispelled common myths:

Many people wrongly believe that if they're exposed to cold air, they'll catch a cold or the flu. Viruses, not coldness in air temperature, cause colds and flu.

We can catch cold, however, if our skin resistance is weak from not regularly and systematically training the skin to adapt to changes in temperature. Under such circumstances, if the body is exposed to unusual cold for a lengthy period of time, the immune system can be weakened. Then, if the person is exposed to a virus, a cold can result. But viruses are nevertheless the cause of colds and influenza.[143]

Currently, the above point isn't fully decided by the medical community. Although this is debatable some hold that frosty weather constricts blood vessels (especially in the nose), leading to lowered resistance to infection, possibly because of reduced blood flow and reduced immunological molecule flow to that area. If this is true we could intelligently speculate, like Nakamura Sensei, that conditioning the skin to cold prevents this blood vessel constriction. This is why he suggested that folks who don't wear multiple layers of clothing are less likely to catch cold. Despite what some might believe people working outdoors less frequently come down with colds than individuals working indoors do. It's easier for bacteria to be transferred from person to person indoors, and being outside in cold temperatures has little to do with getting sick—provided we've gradually strengthened the skin and built up our tolerance for cold weather.[144] Numerous physicians also surmise cold weather causes people to spend more time inside, helping spread colds faster, which roughly agrees with Nakamura Sensei's ideas above. Doctors also indicate bacteria may proliferate in warm circulation systems indoors, again approximating his statements.

If we've caught a cold or the flu, aside from seeing a doctor, Nakamura Sensei offered five easy suggestions for speedy recovery. First, he advocated rest, encouraging his friends to sleep as much as they wanted, insisting that sleep was one of the best ways to absorb new ki from the universe. More sleep initially sometimes means less time spent in bed overall.

Second, he advised keeping warm. Warmth encourages blood circulation, which is advantageous for treating most illnesses and even injuries.

Third, he suggested being especially positive. At this stage in *The Teachings of Tempu* it should be clear that both psychosomatic sickness and psychosomatic cures are real.

Fourth, Nakamura Sensei urged his readers to avoid fever reducing drugs when intelligently feasible. Fever isn't common, although it's possible, with a cold. If we get a fever it's more likely the flu. Some physicians state that fever is a natural reaction to certain illnesses and part of our immunological response for dealing with viral infection. By reducing fever with medication we may actually prevent healing mechanisms, lengthening the course of the illness. Allowing a fever to run its course might shorten the time we're sick. Note however that fevers above 103 degrees can be dangerous and should be lowered.

Fifth, he counseled making the body hot so it perspires fully. Nakamura Sensei (although he rarely caught cold) was fond of putting minced ginger or leek in hot water and drinking it, which makes the body sweat. By perspiring we can sometimes cause a fever to break.

It's a medical fact that sweating is a natural reaction, used to cool the body, but which also releases toxins. When a fever breaks it is frequently accompanied by perspiration. All of this is helpful to the body, but little scientific research exists for how this relates to colds. That understood, Nakamura Sensei also mentioned Japanese have traditionally mixed baked plum or horseradish in hot water. They'd drink this when they had a cold. *Kakkonto*—kudzu vine root in hot water—is another time-honored Japanese cold remedy he discussed. Numerous Japanese of his generation believed these treatments were effective, more natural, and better than aspirin for reducing fever.

Healing with Ki

Even though the preceding is straightforward, sound advice for treating colds and influenza, it obviously doesn't cover every illness, and treating injuries wasn't mentioned. Common sense tells us to visit a doctor or emergency room if we're seriously ill or injured. Nakamura Sensei agreed, feeling that Shin-shin-toitsu-do can harmonize with conventional medicine. Indeed in Japan a number of doctors are prominent teachers of Shin-shin-toitsu-do.

Nonetheless, even though Western medicine possesses advanced diagnostic skills, it can be prohibitively expensive and prone to side effects. It isn't invariably ideal for less serious and/or chronic injuries. This is often cited as contributing to the mushrooming alternative medicine industry.

Though useful, not all alternative therapies are the same, few are regulated by any established agency, and no universal standards exist for training of such therapists, who can sometimes create their own litany of side effects. I advise my students to get a doctor's opinion and diagnosis, and then decide if they want to fill the prescription, use Shin-shin-toitsu-do healing, or a combination of the two. We should also appreciate that healing with ki may take time, so if your appendix is about to burst get to an emergency room rapidly.

Healing with ki has a simple premise: Ki equals life energy, and directing it toward weakened body parts (areas "lacking in life") stimulates ki in these spots. Several methods to arouse ki in injured or debilitated body parts are covered in Shin-shin-toitsu-do. Nakamura Sensei taught massage-like healing techniques which stimulate ki and blood distribution, but they're beyond the capacity of this book. Instead I'm presenting two simple methods for healing injuries and illnesses using ki. Like much of *The Teachings of Tempu* these two techniques appear here for the first time in English.

First up is *Katsuryoku no Iso Ho* ("Method for Transferring Life Power"). Nakamura Sensei stated that this method focuses ki from the universe in a specific part of the body to promote healing. It's simple and easy to use unobtrusively in daily life.[145]

If you've sustained injury, slowly and smoothly inhale air, while visualizing also bringing ki into your body. Concentrate on sending that ki to the weakened muscle or organ. Then hold the breath while in the kumbhaka posture for a moderate amount of time and focus on the received ki healing the selected muscle, tendon, bone, or organ.

Next, gradually and evenly breathe out. At the conclusion of the breath, again make sure you're in the state of kumbhaka, which takes place easily when the breath is suspended. Have the feeling of breathing not just from the top of the lungs, but from the whole body, especially the diaphragm and lower abdomen.

We naturally stop breathing when threading a needle or engaging in great concentration. Breathing tends to likewise stop when we suddenly experience pain or when struggling to move something heavy. Briefly holding the breath makes it easier to coordinate mind and body. However of equal importance in Katsuryoku no Iso Ho is the power of visualization, concentration, and belief. It's essentially psychosomatic healing.

Do Katsuryoku no Iso Ho in clean, fresh air. How long you do it is your decision, but the duration needn't be unusually long—even five breath cycles produces results if we sincerely concentrate. We can use it several times daily, but if we feel tired resting after we do it is intelligent.

A slightly different (but related) form of healing also involves deep breathing. In this case again visualize ki entering your body while gradually inhaling, but think of it filling your entire body. Imagine this ki working to heal your whole body while unhurriedly inhaling. Continue this visualization when you briefly hold your breath. Then slowly and smoothly exhale as you picture the illness leaving your body along with your breath. Do this as long as is comfortable, several times each day. It's designed for less specific purposes than the preceding technique. It's helpful for "breathing out depression," too. Treating specific injuries is more readily accomplished with the initial method.

In *Searching for Truth in Life* Nakamura Sensei wrote this about Katsuryoku no Iso Ho healing:

> The Sennin practicing Taoist yoga deep in the mountains of ancient China,
> and later Japan, developed this method to cure illness and wounds. It is a
> Senjutsu, or one of the "arts of the Sennin."[146]

You'll recall the Sennin were the Japanese and Chinese equivalents to the Indian yogi. Being equal parts man and myth they're associated with esoteric Taoist meditation and healing. Some of my teachers think Nakamura Sensei may have been exposed to these methods during his early years in China, although this isn't universally agreed upon.

Another method of healing with ki is advocated by Hashimoto Tetsuichi Sensei, one of Nakamura Sensei's senior students. It's *Kan-i Jiko Ryoho* ("Easy Self-Healing"), and Nakamura Sensei didn't mention it in his books, but he did teach it to Mr. Hashimoto. I learned it privately from Hashimoto Sensei during one of my visits to Tokyo, and I'm presenting it for the first time now.

Kan-i Jiko Ryoho is uncomplicated but effective. Right before falling asleep take several deep and slow breaths as described previously, remembering kumbhaka. Then when you're calm and ki is flowing strongly, place your palm on the injured or weakened body part. Relaxing completely, visualize ki flowing out of your palm and into the damaged area. Give your subconscious the suggestion that no matter how you shift during sleep, your palm will remain on this spot, transmitting ki until you awaken.

At first the hand may move during the night, but with ongoing effort it will stay in place for longer periods. Once you learn this method well some injuries can be healed in a single night. It works for several reasons.

First, calm and deep breathing puts us in the right state to send out ki. The more we coordinate the mind and body while relaxing, the stronger ki flows. Next, whatever we concentrate intensely on right before sleep continues to work throughout the night in the unconscious. This includes subconscious hints of healing and suggestions that one's hand will stay in place through the night. Every night we make these suggestions they have a powerful accumulated impact on the subconscious. Finally, sleep is the only time some people genuinely relax and their minds grow calm. This allows them to more effectively receive ki from nature, which makes slumber an efficient time for healing.

True, it's hard to reach certain parts of the body, but quite a few places can be comfortably touched during sleep with creative positioning. Although the method is uncomplicated it takes practice, and it only works to the degree we unify mind and body. Such unification of mind and body is the culmination of enhanced concentration, calmness, willpower, and positivity, which are byproducts of Shin-shin-toitsu-do disciplines. Without sincere practice of these exercises and forms of meditation, it's hard to develop the needed traits to genuinely transmit ki from the palm or fingers as in Kan-i Jiko Ryoho. The same can be said for numerous techniques of healing in Shin-shin-toitsu-do. So if you skipped the initial chapters, or if you haven't correctly practiced what was outlined in those sections, the preceding healing arts may prove difficult.

Going to Sleep

We've looked at how Nakamura Sensei's teachings relate to:

- Beginning each day
- Deep breathing to start the day positively
- The clothes that we wear everyday to work and training the skin
- Eating and drinking during the course of the day
- The buildings we work and live in each day
- Absorbing ki from the air, sunlight, and earth during the course of the day
- Incorporating exercise into our day by day routine

- Proper daily excretion and water consumption to cleanse the blood
- Integrating healthy sexuality with everyday existence
- Staying fit in daily life and free from colds
- Healing with ki in everyday living

This covers numerous topics coming up daily but one—ending the day. Just as an endeavor's start is important for success later on, how we end said endeavor is also critical. Simply explained, focusing on a superior beginning and a superior ending produces a superior middle.

We commonly get to the end of a project, or the close of the day, and feel like we're home free. Unfortunately that's when we may trip on the way to home plate.

It's not unusual to primarily use unification of mind and body principles to accomplish a goal. Even though nothing's inherently wrong with that it can nurture an attitude which turns this state on at the start of a project and off at the end. Trouble is, we don't always know when things are really over, and if we stop coordinating the mind and body too soon, we screw up. Far better is regarding Shin-shin-toitsu-do as a path through life and incorporating it into every branch of our lives on a continuing basis. This means unifying mind and body not so much to "be strong" or to "be successful," but purely because it's right and natural. We can nevertheless deliberately harmonize mind and body at specific times in life, but training to do this throughout the day—as a habit—is more important. Which brings us back to ending each day positively and that comes down to how we go to bed. I advise students to meditate before bed, just as they meditate after waking up. These dual "bookends" of mind and body unification support the middle of the day.

Getting into bed with a relaxed body and calm mind makes for fine sleep, something crucial for first-class health. Regrettably poor sleep and/or lack of sleep not only makes us woozy at work, it also makes us more susceptible to obesity. In Quebec, University of Laval researchers demonstrated that women sleeping seven to eight hours nightly were on average 11 pounds lighter than women sleeping six to seven hours a night.[147] Other studies indicate "sleep disruption may increase your risk of breast cancer."[148]

According to the U.S. Department of Health and Human Services roughly one-third of adults have insomnia, while 10% have chronic sleep difficulties.[149] We may think sleep deprivation only affects insomniacs, but quite a few Americans are sleep deprived. Dr. Tedd Mitchell indicates:

Short-term sleep deprivation (say, staying up to see the ball drop on New Year's Eve) can lead to decreased alertness, impaired memory and cognitive ability, and increased stress. The effects of long-term sleep deprivation are even worse: high blood pressure, strokes, heart attacks, psychiatric problems, and weight gain.[150]

Baby Boomers make up the majority of sleep deficient zombies, just as they remain the majority in most facets of life. In the 1960s we were quite vocal as a group, denouncing our parents' addiction to work and materialism. Yet most Boomers are just as materialistic as their parents, albeit in new ways, and they're working more than their parents did. This means less time to snooze, and it means minds running overtime, even when trying to fall asleep.

The U.S.-based Better Sleep Council states that 66% of Americans blame their lack of sleep on "worrisome thoughts."[151] What are we so worried about? Getting a new SUV, the modern equivalent of our dads' gas guzzling giant cars and station wagons (sometimes bigger and thirstier), getting a job promotion, getting our grandkids into a top kindergarten, getting the latest cell phone, the list goes on for some time. And we nonetheless wonder about the attraction of punk rock as a reaction to 60s musical and lifestyle influences, and why at least one cartoon kid on the South Park TV show "hates hippies" . . . but younger folks also suffer from insomnia like their parents and grandparents. Maybe Baby Boomers are as bad an influence as their parents. Or maybe every generation suffers due to its attachments, and a revolution in consciousness is in order.

Meditation seems the likely candidate to lead humankind toward evolving consciousness, one more reason to meditate before falling asleep. Nakamura Sensei offered excellent, easy advice for sleeping well:

> Sleep is vital for healthy living. Nevertheless, countless people have trouble sleeping.
>
> This is often due to worry, and in some cases, an extremely sedentary lifestyle. People who get no exercise and oversleep each day may eventually be unable to sleep. More exertion during the day and sleeping less can sometimes restore normal sleep patterns.
>
> We need to listen to and respect the body, not forcing it to sleep when it isn't genuinely sleepy and not trying to keep it awake when sleep is needed.

Being natural is important in life, and my advice is to sleep when we really feel the need to sleep.[152]

This is another example of Nakamura Sensei's constant emphasis on naturalness. He also tied insomnia to psychological disturbances linked to attachment:

Nervous people tend to become fixated on some obsession, which ties into their propensity toward insomnia. The more difficult the individual finds it to sleep, the more he or she strains to sleep and therefore cannot do so. Psychologically speaking, this is because of obsessive compulsion.

Because some nervous individuals can't sleep, they turn to sleeping pills. This isn't the best idea as sleeping pills can have damaging side effects, and they can become addictive.

So what can we do when we can't sleep? The answer is do not sleep! It's natural to become sleepy sooner or later, so we'll eventually fall asleep. Human beings can't help sleeping in the long run. This realization can help us to stop worrying about sleep when we lie down each night.

The more we try to sleep, the more we obsess over our lack of sleep and can't rest. As the body reflects the mind, if the mind worries about lack of sleep the body cannot relax enough to fall asleep.

In fact, if we can't sleep resolving to go one night without sleeping sometimes takes care of the problem. When the next evening comes we'll be truly ready for sleep. But struggling to sleep a few hours each night gives us just enough rest so we can stay awake for another night of tossing and turning. If we can't sleep we could perhaps even try to see how many nights we can go without sleeping. In doing so we cease worrying about sleep. Once our obsession with sleeping ceases, sleep comes naturally.

In summary, to avoid insomnia be more active in the daytime. Don't oversleep during the weekend or on holidays, and avoid worrying about anything—especially sleep—while lying in bed.[153]

As usual his counsel about sleeping was simple, to the point, and easily understood. Contemporary studies bear out much of what he advised long ago.

Yes, it's getting close to 100 years since Nakamura Tempu Sensei returned from India a changed man. Some might wonder what significance such "musty teachings" have in the new millennium, and in the next chapter we'll consider that topic.

Chapter 11

SHIN-SHIN-TOITSU-DO
IN THE NEW MILLENNIUM

A human being is a part of the whole called by us "Universe," a part limited in time and space. He experiences himself, his thoughts and feeling as something separated from the rest—a kind of optical delusion of his consciousness. This delusion is a kind of prison for us, restricting us to our personal desires and to affection for a few persons nearest to us. Our task must be to free ourselves from this prison by widening our circle of compassion to embrace all living creatures and the whole of nature in its beauty . . .

— Albert Einstein, (A letter from 1950 as quoted
by The New York Times, March 29 1972)

Truth is eternal, and Nakamura Tempu Sensei's discoveries in the 1900s until his passing in 1968 remain as vital today as when he was alive. Some of his students created diverging versions of these teachings, but all their methods recognize the correctness of mind and body coordination and his Four Basic Principles to Unify Mind and Body. Increasingly science and medicine are also advocating ideas similar to Nakamura Sensei's, a point I've established throughout this book. For teachers of Shin-shin-toitsu-do this is a happy development, which has taken place with greater frequency since Nakamura Sensei passed away.

Unfortunately, even when he was alive the average person in Japan and other nations didn't deeply understand Shin-shin-toitsu-do. Despite his books being widely available in Japan, and despite worldwide distribution of *Japanese Yoga: The Way of Dynamic Meditation*, the situation hasn't changed much in the 40 years or so since his death. But this situation isn't exclusive to Nakamura Sensei. Doctors tout the benefits of maintaining healthy weight, yet Americans grow heavier every year. The truth is out there, but we've got to want to find it.

The Teachings of Tempu aims to not only make Shin-shin-toitsu-do concepts and meditation accessible to the average non-Japanese, it intends to show the universality and timelessness of Nakamura Sensei's ideas. In this final chapter we'll consider what these principles and exercises offer humanity as we enter the 21st century.

The Impact of Aging and a Revolution in Lifestyle

Humankind faces numerous challenges in the new millennium, more than I can detail in The Teachings of Tempu. One significant problem, however, can still be resolved before it's out of control: the financial and social impact of aging Baby Boomers. Boomers represent a huge segment of society, and Shin-shin-toitsu-do can help them realize a new way of living, keeping them productive and mobile as they become senior citizens. But that's not the only reason I'm addressing the Baby Boom generation at the start of this chapter.

Many authors direct their writing toward whatever group represents the majority of their readers. I'm no different. For that reason and others this section is (at least partially) aimed at Baby Boomers, their impact on the 21st century, and how Shin-shin-toitsu-do relates to this topic. However, my comments also definitely apply to generations that are a smaller percentage of society, but who nevertheless have elements in common with the biggest U.S. generational group to date.

It's clear Boomers represent a huge number of people in the US and other nations. It's just as clear that they're getting old. Japan also has an expanding elderly population, with numerous Japanese living over 100 years. What's more, people in the know in Japan are worried. According to an Associated Press story:

> While experts say that there are more active centenarians than before, the rapidly graying population adds to concerns over Japan's overburdened public pension system.
>
> Its centenarian population is expected to reach nearly 1 million—the world's largest—by 2050, according to U.N. projections.[154]

How will Japan, the USA, and other nations deal with a gigantic and unprecedented population of senior citizens? Not well, according to numerous pundits. With old age can come disability and dementia, and with infirmity can come retirement. Who will fill their jobs when Boomers can't work, and who'll care for a potentially massive number of feeble and addled seniors? Where's the money going to come from?

Hard questions all, and while some look to the government for answers to these dilemmas, like many Boomers I'm reluctant to trust governments periodically marred by corruption and other problems. For the sake of our nations, for the sake of our children and grandchildren—really for our own sakes—we must take matters into our own hands and ensure our health and well-being. Problem is, not everyone knows how to do that.

This is where Nakamura Sensei's techniques are especially applicable. Nakamura Sensei and scores of his students lived not only exceptionally long lives, they retained (or still retain) most of their faculties. This is significant: We needn't associate age with disability and dementia if we coordinate mind and body and live naturally.

Shin-shin-toitsu-do encourages a remarkable self-reliance. Why depend solely on an impersonal health care system and platoons of physicians to maintain health and sanity? Each of us who's aging, and that's all of us, can apply Nakamura Sensei's simple principles of mind-body unification, breathing, exercise, autosuggestion, and meditation to sustain our psychophysical health well into our senior years. A large percentage of the people practicing Shin-shin-toitsu-do in Japan consists of senior citizens, most of whom are vastly more vital than the average elderly person I encounter.

Yet this vitality is available to everyone, whether or not we're "officially" studying Shin-shin-toitsu-do and regardless of nationality. Numerous important activities for remaining healthy as we age have been outlined in *The Teachings of Tempu*. Yet these disciplines offer more than fitness for the aging. They represent a chance for all of humankind to evolve spiritually, which in turn is an opportunity for bona fide and lasting social change.

Toward an Evolution in Consciousness

One contribution made by Baby Boomers relates to individual freedom. Boomers were prominent in the civil rights movement, feminism in the 1970s, gay rights, disabled rights, and the right to privacy. Certainly we're to be applauded for working to institute such changes, but numerous old problems still exist. We may have "Turned on, tuned in, and dropped out" in large numbers, but many dropped back in just as quickly. Hippies aimed for a less materialistic culture based on love—a noble ideal—but present society is far removed from this state.

Though Baby Boomers made major contributions to the social order the problems of previous generations—war, racism, poverty, environmental destruction, materialism, hate, and attachment—remain. Without a doubt positive developments occurred due to the upheaval of the 1960s, but few of these changes resulted in an actual change in the consciousness of the majority. And since we are society, society remains fundamentally the same.

A change in consciousness isn't a new idea, a new style, or a new agenda. No genuinely new ideas, new governments, and the like can come out of the same consciousness. What arrives is a modification of the old.

It's different, but it's not really new. Newness arises from a mind existing in the eternal present transcending time. It springs from a consciousness that's beyond attachments, beyond conditioning, and thus capable of embodying not just new ideas but a new spirit as well.

In meditation we discover a consciousness free from attachment to chronological time, resting in the eternal moment. The mind in meditation is perceiving, but never clinging, not even to its thoughts or itself. As a result it's constantly letting go of its past, constantly leaping into the unknown, and constantly capable of an unconditioned newness. This childlike mentality is ever new, a psyche not bound by what it already knows. This is a gateway to the unknown present, an instant outside of our perception of time and utterly fresh. Nakamura Sensei's meditation gives us an opportunity to let go of attachments to past, present, and future, to experience life in the now—the only real perception. In doing so, we let go of time.

Time cannot calculate timelessness, eternity, or the absolute universe that's without beginning or end. Historically most people's minds have been shackled to the past, present, and future, and using that self-constructed artificial gauge they've attempted to experience the unknown and break free of old patterns, to calculate what isn't calculable. When we struggle to gauge something which isn't quantifiable we get trapped by words . . . thus Nakamura Sensei's insistence that "how to do" is more important than "how to say."

Accordingly, a mentality which grasps the nature of attachment, that's let go of its past pain and conditioning, experiences an endlessly fresh and innocent present. From this emotionally unconditioned innocence we give birth to new and creative accomplishments. This action is forever in the dynamic present, and only a psyche which lives this active instant can receive the new. Only this mentality can create a new society and way of life because only this mind is in constant creation.

As a majority generation Baby Boomers still have the capacity to realize an evolution in consciousness, which due to their large numbers could transform the world. The same can absolutely be said for smaller generational groups, but this evolution/revolution must emerge from an awareness unconditioned by its past, free of attachments and thus fears and prejudices. It is this mindset that can escape from peer pressure and social conditioning to reveal something genuinely new.

Nakamura Sensei's life is an example of authentic progressiveness which sees beyond "us and them." In recordings of his lectures the simple and extremely blunt speech Nakamura Sensei was famous for is evident. His seminars were popular with Japan's top executives, CEOs, and politicians, partly due to his own early success in business. Yet in these lectures Nakamura Sensei frequently, strongly, and fearlessly chastised some of the then most powerful people in Japan, where he's known for adamantly rejecting racism, nationalism, and fighting.

When much of Japan geared up for war in the 1940s, believing in the divine infallibility of its Emperor, he openly questioned this direction and indeed any sort of nationalism. One of few Japanese to widely speak out against Japan's wartime activities, he was followed by plainclothes police, his lectures were disrupted, and he was finally jailed. Due to having high-ranking politicians and policemen among his students he was eventually released. Nakamura Sensei never wavered and began lecturing again, opposing Japanese imperialism and involvement in WWII. Toward the end of the war, when most Japanese were filled with fear and hatred for their enemies, he saved the life of a downed American pilot, who villagers were beating. This later lead to him teaching Shin-shin-toitsu-do to officers associated with the U.S. Army General Headquarters in Japan.

Not merely interested in the welfare of his countrymen Nakamura Sensei held a lifelong affection for the Chinese people, leading to his support of Dr. Sun Yat Sen (1866-1925, a.k.a. Sun Wen). Sun lived when China was repeatedly conquered by foreign powers and shamed by unequal treaties, and he decided it was time to oust the corrupt Manchu Dynasty. Supporting Dr. Sun's ideals of democracy and better social conditions for the Chinese populace, Nakamura Sensei was at his side for part of his campaign to reform China. But as Nakamura Sensei aged his politics moved further toward nonviolent change.

He cared for the Indian people, and he was an early advocate of Mahatma Gandhi's sovereignty movement in India. Like Gandhi (1869-1948) he believed in *Satyagraha*, overcoming tyranny through civil disobedience based on *ahimsa* ("nonviolence"), which led India to independence and inspired movements for civil rights around the globe. Rash Bihari Bose (1886-1945), a leader of the Indian independence movement, once lived in Japan after escaping British intelligence. Nakamura Sensei was at one point his bodyguard, although he's believed to have parted ways with him philosophically when it became clear Bose was moving toward violent military revolution in India.

Nakamura Sensei questioned the common Buddhist emphasis on transcending desire, insisting that desires are natural and attachment to what we desire is the real problem. More than this he questioned religious prohibitions concerning sexuality, maintaining sex is similarly natural and positive.

He taught that the way of the universe could be found and followed by anyone, regardless of gender, social class, or race. He did this at a time when Japan (and other nations) discriminated based on race, class, and gender.

Long before antismoking forces gathered steam worldwide, Nakamura Sensei quit smoking. He stopped in an era when countless men—especially Japanese men—smoked. And this was before medical studies expounded on the dangers of tobacco. He, likewise, advocated vegetarianism before this movement was well-known or even trendy.

In recorded talks his powerful rejection of materialism is poignantly palpable, especially considering some of the audiences attending these lectures—company presidents and executives. Listening to his speeches additionally makes clear his disdain for social elitism, male chauvinism, fortune telling, occultism, and superstitions.

Nakamura Sensei came from a wealthy and well-established family, but he rejected the trappings of wealth and status. Considering the era he was raised in and the cultural climate when he gave seminars his progressive thoughts on materialism, interaction between societal classes, discrimination against women, blind adherence to religious and cultural traditions, and interaction between the sexes was remarkably far-sighted.

It's still remarkable today when we're beset with the collective and personal ills he saw beyond. Various social programs seek to eradicate these problems, and though these programs are needed, they've been tried before and obviously aren't solely enough to create deep change. Such change must also come from within each person comprising society. Just as Nakamura Sensei changed from the violent boy, the spy and soldier, and the dying man, as individual members of society we can also evolve through meditation. Indeed we must if the world is to truly evolve.

In this sense, Nakamura Sensei's teachings are applicable to any generation, because we all face the same challenges in the 21st century. Ecological destruction, war, poverty, new illnesses, and other societal tribulations aren't generation specific. Shin-shin-toitsu-do offers every age group an opportunity to progress beyond these problems and find new approaches to living through meditation.

A Meeting of Spirituality and Science

The discoveries of Galileo, Newton, Einstein, and others altered humankind's perception of the universe, creating major changes in lifestyle through technological advances. For some, science replaced old folk beliefs and religions, but for others empirical inquiry was at odds with religious faith. And for most the deeper realms of science remain mystifyingly complex. Many feel science and spirituality are in conflict, but in the 21st century there's no escaping the influence of science on technology we use. Resolving the seeming battle between rationality and spirituality may be a hallmark of the new millennium. Since technology born of science has an increasing role in global society, this resolution is of real importance.

Although some suppose a rift must exist between science and spirituality, reason and emotion, Nakamura Sensei didn't agree. He examined reality using every form of inquiry—scientific and mystical—and concluded both logical and meditative avenues of analysis must be pursued to arrive at a true picture of reality. While unusual, Nakamura Sensei wasn't alone in this viewpoint. Renowned scientist David Bohm, Indian spiritual thinker Jiddhu Krishnamurti, and the Fourteenth Dalai Lama are just a few well-known individuals who have espoused parallels between meditative and scientific examinations of the universe.

In my classes, books, and seminars I also advocate a meeting of science and spirituality. However like most of you, I'm no scientist.

But I am a capable researcher, and in writing *The Teachings of Tempu* I've drawn from the ideas of qualified scientists. Kyle Kurpinski (PhD genetics), Boris Faybishenko (PhD earth science), Stephen Fabian (PhD anthropology), Srinivasan Sethuraman (MS physics), and other scientists have reviewed the contents of this book. Like Nakamura Sensei, they don't believe a rift must exist between rationality and meditation. Nakamura Sensei envisioned a global community in which scientific and spiritual approaches to comprehending ourselves and the universe meet to serve humankind. His Shin-shin-toitsu-do represents one of history's earliest mergers of science and meditation, East and West. For quite a few people it's their first exposure to truly practical and rational spirituality.

He studied science, medicine, psychology, meditation, religion, and philosophy throughout his long life, using these disciplines as tools but not defining himself by them. By this I mean he didn't pledge exclusive allegiance to any approach to understanding life, and thus no single methodology formed a rigid framework which limited him.

For instance, Karl Popper, one of the most influential philosophers of science in the 20th century, is noted for clearing up the roles of deductive and inductive reasoning in the creation and proof of a scientific hypothesis. With the Popperian falsifiability thesis, he clarified that a valid theory must have within it circumstances under which it can be proven to be untrue. ("Falsifiable" doesn't, however, mean false.) Based on this, the hypothesis that God exists and created the cosmos isn't scientifically acceptable, since it cannot contain an explanation of the circumstances under which this thesis can be disproven. If God is unobservable and transcendent then we can't disprove his existence via observation. Quite a few theists agree God is "unfalsifiable," and even that the idea that God exists isn't scientific but is solely an issue of faith. While Popper's elucidation of what is and isn't a valid hypothesis is useful in some realms applying this standard to every aspect of living suggests numerous questions relating to the value of our existence, spirituality, and aesthetics remain separate from science. Yet for countless people these are crucial topics that they'd like to resolve in their lives. As the result, Nakamura Sensei didn't restrict his search for truth to scientific analysis; it included his experiences in meditation.

In Shin-shin-toitsu-do we see a difference between something which isn't found literally versus something proven to not exist. To clarify, not seeing a spider on your wall is proof no spider exists in that place since you'd see the bug if your eyes are functional. On the other hand, not seeing lead which might exist in paint on your wall isn't the same as concluding the paint's lead-free. Seeing lead in paint requires more than mere eyesight. We can't see the lead, but this doesn't prove no lead exists.

Similarly, we haven't found human-like life on other planets, but this doesn't scientifically mean no such life exists. Nakamura Sensei appears to have understood this distinction, realizing the fact that science hasn't proven the existence of the ki of the universe doesn't mean ki doesn't exist, especially for those embracing this idea. There's a difference between something negated by reasoning and something not yet validated by reasoning. Since Shin-shin-toitsu-do encompasses a unity of rationality and feeling its meditation and theories help us see where science and spirituality meet, where they differ, and how they benefit each other.

New Science, New Spirituality

In the new millennium a meeting of science and spirituality could open new doors causing a useful alteration in world culture. One such shift is the emerging field of neurotheology, which scientifically determines the physiological impact of meditation and spirituality. Joe Lindsey, in a magazine article called *The Science of Belief*, explained this developing discipline:

> Andrew Newberg, M.D., is an associate professor of radiology at the University of Pennsylvania and the author of the book Why We Believe What We Believe. He used a brain imaging technology called single photon emission computed tomography (SPECT) to examine brain activity in meditating Buddhists and Franciscan nuns in deep prayer.
>
> In his experiments Newberg anticipated—and found—heavy brain activity in the frontal lobes, which are responsible for concentration. But the scans also showed a near-total lack of activity in the area of the superior parietal lobe, located high in the back of the brain, near the skull. Termed the orientation area, it processes external stimuli and is believed by scientists to control information like our sense of self, both metaphysically and in the real world. For example, it helps control the ability to ride a bike close to other cyclists and not bump into them. During meditation or prayer "a lot of that information is blocked," says Newberg, "and you arguably lose your sense of self and experience feelings of oneness and connectedness with the world."[155]

Newberg isn't the only scientist starting to research and validate the effects of meditation on the brain. Writing for *Time* magazine, Lisa Takeuchi Cullen reported:

> One recent study found evidence that the daily practice of meditation thickened the parts of the brain's cerebral cortex responsible for decision making, attention and memory. Sara Lazar, a research scientist at Massachusetts General Hospital, presented preliminary results last November that showed that the gray matter of 20 men and women who meditated for just 40 minutes a day was thicker than that of people who did not. Unlike in previous studies focusing on Buddhist monks, the subjects were Boston-area workers practicing a Western-style of meditation called mindfulness or insight meditation. "We showed for the first time that you don't have to do it all day for similar results," says Lazar. What's more, her research suggests that meditation may slow the natural thinning of that section of the cortex that occurs with age.
>
> The forms of meditation Lazar and other scientists are studying in-

volve focusing on an image or sound or on one's breathing. Though deceptively simple, the practice seems to exercise the parts of the brain that help us pay attention.[156]

"Focusing on an image or sound or one's breathing" seems similar to the forms of meditation created by Nakamura Sensei, suggesting that Anjo Daza Ho and Muga Ichinen Ho might offer comparable advantages. Lazar eventually presented her completed studies at a meeting of the Society for Neuroscience in Washington, DC:

> They found that meditating actually increases the thickness of the cortex in areas involved in attention and sensory processing, such as the prefrontal cortex and the right anterior insula.
>
> "You are exercising it while you meditate, and it gets bigger," she says. The finding is in line with studies showing that accomplished musicians, athletes and linguists all have thickening in relevant areas of the cortex. It is further evidence, says Lazar, that yogis "aren't just sitting there doing nothing".
>
> The growth of the cortex is not due to the growth of new neurons, she points out, but results from wider blood vessels, more supporting structures such as glia and astrocytes, and increased branching and connections.[157]

Lazar's research, in a sense, is continuing the line of thinking started by Nakamura Sensei long ago, despite her contention that "yogis aren't just sitting there doing nothing." In fact, genuine meditation *can* be described as doing nothing, and science is proving its benefits, something Alison Motuk wrote of for the respected website *NewScientist*.

In her article she indicates that scientific studies point to tangible changes in the brain during meditation, including altered patterns of brainwaves and the synchronization of neuronal firing patterns. Significantly she also outlines the work of researchers at the University of Kentucky, who concluded that meditation evokes restorative advantages similar to deep sleep. Volunteers in their study gazed at an LCD screen and pressed a button once they saw a certain image appear. Most folks can do this in around 200 milliseconds, but the sleep deprived take a lot longer to perform this task. Their subjects were tested on this "psychomotor vigilance task" before and after 40 minutes of napping, reading, conversation, and meditation. A cat nap somewhat improved their performance, but it took everyone roughly an hour to get rid of their initial grogginess.

Meditation was the only activity which led to immediately better performance. Performance enhancement through meditation was even more spectacular after the volunteers went a night without sleep. None of the subjects had experienced meditation prior to the study.[158]

Nakamura Sensei would've been fascinated by studies like this, although he might have noted several variables weren't mentioned in some of the articles quoted. How skilled were the people engaging in meditation? What kind of meditation was used? And do results vary according to the system of meditation, since "meditation" can describe divergent practices?

Scientists are also analyzing the physiological effects of meditation on the brain itself, speculating that the meditative process may positively alter neural pathways. Until the late 1990s the majority of scientists believed adult brains had finished their development, thinking that learning requires the growth of fresh connections, but no new neurons were developing, and when those cells perished they disappeared permanently. However, current scientific belief holds that new neurons *can* grow. Perhaps adult brains are more flexible than prior theories allowed for.

This could explain why some studies have found the neural processes in the brains of experienced meditators are more coordinated, which could be connected to the elevated awareness cited by seasoned meditators. Such research is a significant first step toward a meeting of scientific and meditating minds. More and more, science is looking seriously at meditation's benefits and how they can help humankind in the new millennium. If that trend continues perhaps this century can signal an end of the split between science and spirituality.

In a somewhat similar vein, Harvard-trained neuroanatomist Jill Bolte Taylor suffered a stroke in 1996, leading to remarkable insights that may someday scientifically validate Nakamura Sensei's meditative experience of *munen muso,* "transcending thoughts and mental images." *The New York Times* wrote:

> On a December morning in 1996, Dr. Taylor woke up with searing pain behind her left eye, the beginnings of a hemorrhagic stroke. As the left side of her brain shut down, she began to feel disconnected from her body and entered an almost-euphoric like state. It took her a while to make sense of the experience, but as her right arm became paralyzed, it dawned on her that she was having a stroke.
>
> "How many brain scientists have the opportunity to study their own

brain from the inside out?," she said. "In the course of four hours, I watched my brain completely deteriorate in its ability to process all information. On the morning of the hemorrhage, I could not walk, talk, read, write or recall any of my life."

Her account of the experience of stroke is vivid, and at one point, she recalled, she felt like someone had taken a remote control and hit the mute button. "I was shocked to find myself inside a silent mind," she said.

What is so surprising about Dr. Taylor's story is that she experienced a sort of euphoria as she was left with only right-brain functions. She lost her sense of self, but she also shed the stress of her life and, as she puts it, "37 years of emotional baggage."

"Imagine what it would be like to be totally disconnected from your brain chatter," she said. "I felt a sense of peacefulness."[159]

Taylor wrote a book about this event and the differences between the right and left sides of the brain. While having a stroke isn't something to be happy about, her insights into the mind via this calamity may partially match the experiences of people in meditation. If a greater meeting of science and meditation takes place in the 21st century, both sides could obtain valuable information that if shared with humanity might have a transformative quality.

Researchers like those mentioned in this chapter represent something different from the traditional science vs. spirituality schism, in that they're examining meditation using logical scientific methodologies. True, they are a bit on the fringe, but it's a growing fringe, which will only become bigger if the attitudes of each of us comprising society shift from the conventional science vs. spirituality division. If our worldview transcends this divide then science may continue validating elements of disciplines like Shin-shin-toitsu-do. And Shin-shin-toitsu-do will allow the average individual to personally experience and experiment with parts of life that are scientifically verifiable (like the unity of mind and body or the interconnectedness of nature), but which most have trouble grasping through solely intellectual means.

Paradigm Shifts

Many major civilizations exist in conflict of one kind or another, to a greater or lesser degree. Likewise, much of humanity sees life in terms of conflicting opposites. This situation isn't new; it's at the root of much of the world's suffering, and little in the news leads us to believe genuine change is coming soon.

Nonetheless, changes in the viewpoint of societies have periodically occurred throughout history. They're known as paradigm shifts. These shifts also apply to science and its impact on culture. At the start of the 20th century such a shift occurred when science moved from traditional Newtonian physics to embrace relativity and quantum physics. Yet many imagine new discoveries in scientific truth are progressive steps in our collective understanding of life, culminating in a last step which totally comprehends reality. However, an honest appraisal of scientific history reveals subjective aspects relating to the birth of new scientific paradigms. The same can be said for social mores and morality that change as a culture is exposed to fresh knowledge and ideas, which causes a social paradigm shift.

Since human understanding of science is changeable, and since it can be influenced by subjective elements that give birth to new paradigms, Nakamura Sensei used scientific methodologies when applicable, but he didn't unblinkingly assume science has categorically resulted in us contacting a wholly objective reality. Tenzin Gyatso, the Dalai Lama and the de facto face of Tibetan Buddhism, has long engaged in dialogues with top scientists. He mentioned a similar realization in *The Universe in a Single Atom*:

> When I speak with open-minded scientists and philosophers of science, it is clear that they have a deeply nuanced understanding of science and a recognition of the limits of scientific knowledge. At the same time, there are many people, both scientists and nonscientists, who appear to believe that all aspects of reality must and will fall within the scope of science. The assumption is sometimes made that, as society progresses, science will continually reveal the falsehoods of our beliefs—particularly religious beliefs—so that an enlightened secular society can eventually emerge. This is a view shared by Marxist dialectical materialists, as I discovered in my dealings with the leaders of Communist China in the 1950s and in the course of my studies of Marxist thought in Tibet. In this view, science is perceived as having disproved many of the claims of religion, such as the existence of God, grace, and the eternal soul. And within this conceptual framework, anything that is not proven or affirmed by science is somehow either false or insignificant. Such views are effectively philosophical assumptions that reflect their holders' metaphysical prejudices. Just as we must

avoid dogmatism in science, we must ensure that spirituality is free from the same limitations.[160]

Nakamura Sensei held a similar viewpoint, respecting and using the scientific method, but also recognizing potential limitations and possible subjective elements in this method. He understood science is a system of investigation that works with elements of life which can be empirically seen and measured. This system is based on repeatability and universal verification, in that numerous scientists should be able to verify the truth of a hypothesis. It primarily focuses, therefore, on physical aspects of reality, but Nakamura Sensei also felt in certain cases nonphysical, psychophysical, and metaphysical elements could benefit from a scientific approach. This can be seen in some exercises and experiments in *The Teachings of Tempu*.

Nonetheless, our present scientific paradigm centers on empirical findings and experimentation relating to physical matter. Although this has lead to worldwide medical and technological advances, this way of looking at life cannot cover every aspect of life. Young and old still wonder, "Why was I born?" Past generations looked to organized religion for answers to existential questions like this, but with the advances of science and the cultural upheaval of the 20th century, church attendance is down, science is taught in every public school, and the world is left adrift—no longer wanting to be limited by old answers but not finding ultimate meaning in the current socio-scientific paradigm. Even though science has objectively inquired into the material realm with great effectiveness, humanity nevertheless must cope with a subjective internal environment filled with spiritual aspirations, sensations, values, and emotions.

If we ignore the medical and technological potential of science, we'll suffer. If we relegate the subjective realm and meditative experiences to the dustbin labeled "Unscientific and of no Consequence," we see only one aspect of existence, losing the richness and value of living. Most of us feel our lives are more complex and nuanced than is sometimes objectively valued by scientific materialism.

Nakamura Sensei looked for a comprehensive way of understanding the universe, a methodology embracing the objective inquiry of science and the subjective experiences of meditation, humanizing the former while grounding the latter in reality. The world's ready for a major paradigm shift that allows us to reap the profits of reason and technology without losing our "humanness." This is a complicated topic, but it is a hot topic nonetheless, and it's not going away soon. Shin-shin-toitsu-do, as a discipline which unifies mind and body, science and spirituality, East and West, has the potential to bridge the sometimes self-created gap between rationality and spirituality.

Transcending Object and Subject

It's convenient to define science as objective and meditation as subjective. Though I've written as much above, real meditation transcends subject and object, self and others, internal environment and external universe to unearth an absolute reality that's integrated and beyond duality. My earlier chapters on Muga Ichi-nen Ho and Anjo Daza Ho meditation hinted at as much, and now I'll expand on universal harmony.

Humankind has long wished for an end to war as well as personal and interpersonal conflict. But we never seem to get there.

To arrive at this state perhaps what's needed isn't merely the desire to end conflict, but rather personal discovery of a consciousness rooted in our absolute nature, which is beyond relative differences, us and them, rich and poor, strong and weak . . . all duality. Until each of us sees past such differences, perceiving the absolute, interrelated, and eternal nature of existence, conflict won't end for us. We may wish to stop fighting, we may create governments based on this worthy ideal, but if our basic consciousness remains in conflict, unable to perceive undivided reality that's more than a concept, we'll still struggle and fight. We may consciously espouse harmony, but our unconscious will bring forth the conflict within it. Most of humanity is deeply divided and conflicted—desiring peace while unable to recognize the undivided nature of the absolute universe.

We habitually relate to the world as if each person and thing we encounter has a separate, independent reality. This is relative perception, and while we can make a relative, artificial distinction between various entities, they're differing aspects of one whole. They aren't really self-enclosed nor are we, notwithstanding our inclination to think in terms of an individual, separate, and permanent ego. By examining the matter deeply and logically we can see how this illusion leads to attachment, prejudice, and conflict.

In *The Big Bang, the Buddha, and the Baby Boom* Wes Nisker writes:

As a Tibetan Buddhist text states, "All things are the illusory, magical display of the mind." Through very different methods of investigation, the quantum physicists arrived at a similar conclusion. They say that we participate in the creation of reality by observing it. When we aren't looking, there are just waves of energy—"probability waves"—and only when we try to measure or pin the process down does the world of particles and things make an appearance. The most widely accepted explanation of quantum physics, the Copenhagen interpretation, says, "There is no reality in the absence of observation."[161]

Nisker's ideas, while simply stated, can be a bit tricky. "Observation" and "measurement" in quantum mechanics have different meanings than in the colloquial context. They don't necessarily require that someone observe or measure a quantity or value of a system, certainly not directly. And despite the nearly complete acceptance of the observational truth of Einsteinian relativity and quantum mechanics there are regimes where old Newtonian mechanics and classical electrodynamics fully explain the system under measurement. For example, few physicists would argue that quantum mechanics or general relativity is needed to study the motion of a baseball thrown by a pitcher, and not many physicists would bother viewing an object as massive as a baseball as a probabilistic wave packet.

Simply put, science's interpretation of quantum physics is evolving, and how the quantum realm relates to everyday life hasn't been definitively determined. Even as some suggest that the Copenhagen interpretation's maxim, "There is no reality in the absence of observation," suggests the interrelationship of all things, others assert that we don't control what the spin of an electron or the magnetic moment of an atom will be by experimental measurement. Nonetheless new discoveries in medicine, psychology, and quantum physics may offer corollaries to meditation that are food for thought.

In a vein at least metaphorically similar to the Copenhagen interpretation, Indian mystic Krishnamurti challenged his readers to find a clear-cut division between "the observer and the observed," asserting this distinction was ultimately a construct of the mind. He wasn't the only one.

Author Adam Smith once interviewed famous physicist John Wheeler (1911-2008):

"That's some list: the mind, the quantum, and the universe," I said.

"All three," Wheeler said, "threaten the clean separation between observer and observed that used to be the essence of science."[162]

Wheeler of Princeton University was a colleague of Einstein, and he went on to explain:

"In the world of the quantum," Wheeler said, "the observer and the observed turn out to have a tight and totally unexpected linkage. The quantum principle demolishes the view we once had that the universe sits safely 'out there,' that we can observe what goes on or in it from behind a foot-thick slab of plate glass without ourselves being involved in what goes on. We have learned that to observe even so miniscule an object as an electron we have to shatter that slab of glass. We have to insert a measuring device. We can put in a device to measure position or a device to measure momentum, but the installation of one prevents the insertion of the other. We ourselves have to decide which it is that we will do. Whichever it is, it has an unpredictable effect on the future of that electron. To that degree the future of the universe is changed. We changed it. We have to cross out the old word 'observer' and replace it with the new word 'participator.' In some strange sense, the quantum principle tells us that we are dealing with a participatory universe."[163]

Wheeler, responsible for coining "black hole" and "wormhole," was awarded the Wolf Prize for physics in 1997. He seemed to indicate the observation of the process has turned out to be a component of the process. In my words, the observer is the observed, the personal is the universal, and nothing exists apart from everything else. Nisker further explains:

Overall, the findings and theories of modern physics lent credibility to the cosmological insight of the Asian sages, and helped to open the Western mind to Hindu and Buddhist psycho-physical practices as well. If the Asian sages had such a good intuitive sense about the vastness of creation and the structure of reality, then perhaps they were correct about nirvana and self-liberation as well. Ironically, Western science became one of our primary gateways to mysticism.

"As I look more deeply, I can see that in a former life I was a cloud. And I was a rock. This is not poetry; it is science. This is not a question of belief in reincarnation. This is the history of life on earth."

VIETNAMESE ZEN MASTER THICH NHAT HANH[164]

Our bones contain calcium phosphate, more or less "the clay of the earth." Evolutionary theorists proclaim that only after earthy landmasses appeared did living things grow legs. Body fluids are chemically similar to ocean water. Scientifically and spiritually, we're not separate from the earth, from nature, from the universe.

We might feel that moving from the realization that we're comprised of some of the same building blocks as the universe to Nakamura Sensei's assertion that we're one with the universe isn't scientifically well-founded. Yet this is indeed what he and others discovered via meditation. In the 21st century science may determine that universal harmony makes not only intuitive sense; it also makes literal scientific sense. With a positive meeting of science and spirituality, both scientists and meditators might someday state: "We are the universe; the universe is us."

But what about humankind's cultural and racial differences? Well, modern genetics indicates humans have nearly identical DNA structure. We're vastly more alike than different, and our "big differences" are largely the outgrowth of an impermanent ego and its byproducts of racism and nationalism. Scientifically and spiritually, we're connected. What's more, we're related to all living beings. Scientifically, mice have 90% of the same DNA as you, me, and the leaders of most nations. Spiritually, one of my Shin-shin-toitsu-do teachers mentions that in meditation he "feels the life of every creation." Nevertheless, while geneticists and physicists number among my students the majority of us aren't scientists or meditation masters.

So for most there's a disconnect between how they perceive the world and how things actually are. That primary conflict is the origin of countless other types of conflict.

Everything—physical or mental—exists in relationship to everything else, with no truly self-sufficient existence aside from artificial distinctions we make when speaking and writing. If parts of life were genuinely self-contained and independent, cause and effect would break down. A quick example: I'm typing these words using a keyboard, which connects to a computer, which causes letters to appear on my monitor. Each component acts on the others through cause and effect and their interrelationship. If the keyboard, computer, and monitor were truly separate, self-governing units, they could just as easily not respond to each other. Whereas we think of them as separate they really aren't; they exist in relationship to each other and everything else. So do we.

We understand this intellectually, but that doesn't lead to concrete change. Science has long indicated everything (at the very least conceptually) is linked to everything else through the cycles of nature. But people still relate to events and other social groups based on self-interest or hate. The interconnectedness of all creations is an idea floating around in our heads as opposed to something we deeply feel.

Thus, Nakamura Sensei indicated there's frequently a difference between saying or reading something and actually doing it. In Shin-shin-toitsu-do he offered meditation to personally experience the absolute, non-dual nature of reality. What we experience with our whole minds and bodies—firsthand and directly—is vastly more powerful and transformative than something we just read, hear, or think about. The difference between intellectually grasping a concept and feeling it in our depths is huge. Nakamura Sensei's genius rested in his ability to help others personally feel oneness of mind and body, self and others, the individual and the universe. If through Shin-shin-toitsu-do people *genuinely feel* in harmony with the universe, this experience is much more than another idea they've collected. It heralds a bona fide shift in awareness that's beyond relative differences and therefore beyond conflict. This state, if it's real and more than an idea, expresses constant harmony. If enough people exist like this—something which hasn't occurred during recorded history—then authentically new ways, governments, and methods of dealing with the earth and each other can arise in the new millennium.

Oneness with the Universe and the New Physics

Before the average person in either the East or West was aware of fresh directions in quantum physics, Nakamura Sensei was fascinated by German scientist Max Planck. Max Karl Ernst Ludwig Planck (1858–1947) was a Nobel Prize winner, and he's considered to be the creator of quantum theory and among the most important physicists of the 20th century. Aside from physics, Planck had a deeply spiritual inclination. His Christian worldview was, nevertheless, more or less pantheistic with an omnipotent, omniscient, compassionate but unknowable God permeating the universe, manifest by symbols, including physical laws.

Nakamura Sensei saw similarities between Shin-shin-toitsu-do, his experiences in meditation, and the newly emerging quantum physics. Yet few teachers of Shin-shin-toitsu-do today have followed up on this connection, a link that may be particularly significant in the 21st century and which I hope to clarify and update in this chapter.

Just as Nakamura Sensei's discoveries and principles occasionally challenge "common sense," so too does the microscopic world of quantum theory. In the new physics light can exhibit properties of both a particle and a wave; the uncertainty principle reveals that we can't know at the same time what an electron's doing or even where it's located;

the quantum idea of superposition indicates a very different way of looking at the universe from traditional physics, where things behave in a predictable and deterministic way. The new physics has also lead its proponents to consider new ways of looking at reality, which suggest parallels to the meditative consciousness evoked in Shin-shin-toitsu-do. This consciousness transcends the conventional functioning of the senses and perceives an infinite and absolute unity beyond time:

> "We go down and down," Wheeler said, "from crystal to molecule, from molecule to atom, from atom to nucleus to particle, and there is still something beyond both geometry and particle. In the end we have to come back to mind. How can consciousness understand consciousness? There's a paradox. Niels Bohr said we only made progress from paradoxes."[165]

In *Symmetries and Reflections* Nobel prizewinning physicist Eugene Wigner indicated that two sorts of "reality" exist: our individual awareness and a universal reality accounting for everything we think of as "not us." Yet Wigner (1902-1995) seems to assert that this second reality has as its primary function ease of communication and that it's only potentially valid, that the idea of an impersonal universe separate from our own consciousness is largely a concept.[166]

Well-known physicist and winner of the Enrico Fermi Award, J. Robert Oppenheimer (1904-1967) also elucidated two classes of reality, one rooted in time and history, while the other was beyond time—infinite and eternal.[167] Nobel laureate Werner Heisenberg wrote of "the objective world, pursuing its regular course in space and time, [and] a subject, mystically experiencing the unity of the world and no longer confronted by an object or by any objective world."[168] Heisenberg's statement parallels Nakamura Sensei's idea of forgetting ourselves in Muga Ichi-nen Ho meditation to merge with the object of concentration. Heisenberg was one of the founders of quantum physics, and these quotes show how quantum physics quite likely influenced Nakamura Sensei's eventual explanation of human consciousness, a consciousness that ultimately cannot be divided from the totality of life. In fact, at the end of this chapter I'll introduce Nakamura Sensei's related theory of two aspects of existence—genuine and transient—and his explanation of two types of self: genuine and transient. Perhaps Nobel Prize winning physicist Max Born was right in declaring, "The physics of one era is the metaphysics of the next."

The new physics was a textbook for a fresh spirituality for some folks in the 20th century. Baby Boomers, in particular, read in school about relativity, learning that matter and energy are united even as time and space are indivisible. And what about quantum paradoxes and nonlinear realities? Maybe these latest ideas suggested the universe existed in a nonmechanical but inter-reliant manner, a theory significantly dissimilar from what we perceived through our five senses. It even diverged from what society once held to be undisputedly true.

Sensing interdependence through meditation allows us to grasp the ultimate nature of reality suggested by both quantum theory and Shin-shin-toitsu-do.[169] Although the world doesn't really consist of endless independent objects and beings you might wonder why this is significant and how it relates to a different vision for humanity in the 21st century. If so, you're in good company. Tibetan Buddhism's Dalai Lama asked quantum physicist David Bohm (1917-1992) the same question:

> I once asked my physicist friend David Bohm this question: From the perspective of modern science, apart from the question of misrepresentation, what is wrong with the belief in the independent existence of things? His response was telling. He said that if we examine the various ideologies that tend to divide humanity, such as racism, extreme nationalism, and the Marxist class struggle, one of the key factors of their origin is the tendency to perceive things as inherently divided and disconnected. From this misconception springs the belief that each of these divisions is essentially independent and self-existent. Bohm's response, grounded in his work in quantum physics, echoes the ethical concern about harboring such beliefs that worried Nagarjuna, who wrote nearly two thousand years before. Granted, strictly speaking, science does not deal with questions of ethics and value judgments, but the fact remains that science, being a human endeavor, is still connected to the basic question of the well-being of humanity, So in a sense, there is nothing surprising about Bohm's response. I wish there were more scientists with his understanding of the interconnectedness of science, its conceptual frameworks, and humanity.[170]

As noted, the Dalai Lama believes scientists should avoid naïve materialism: assuming that scientific understanding destroys previously held spiritual beliefs. This is a sensible idea; one Nakamura Sensei also appears to have shared. However some scientists might note, as well they should, that the idea that new scientific paradigms question the independent existence of things and beings may turn out to be an over simplistic conclusion drawn from quantum mechanics. Consequently I'm not attempting to elevate the similarities between aspects of quantum mechanics and the philosophy of Nakamura Sensei to an exact equivalence. That said, I think Nakamura Sensei's advocated meeting of science and spirituality is important to consider if our world is to evolve in positive directions. I'm betting more than a few of you can see the wisdom of this idea.

Science is still coming to grips with the changes wrought by quantum theory. For generations traditional physics offered an explanation of life and the universe which seemed to work well with what the majority considered common sense. We had a mechanistic worldview with a clear distinction between the subject that knows and the object that's known. Yet according to scientists like Carl Von Weizsäcker the new physics imply the division between subject and object that most find reasonable is anything but, echoing meditative experiences down through the ages. Problem is, the only terms we have with which to describe quantum physics, and to a degree life as a whole, come from traditional physics, which is based on the complete determinability of measurable quantities, an idea possibly negated by quantum theory.

For centuries Asian mystics said they experienced unity with the universe during meditation and occasionally in their everyday lives. Even so, some wondered if this was wishful thinking or religious delusion. Now our up-to-the-minute understanding of science, particularly quantum physics, allows for conclusions relating to universal harmony that are similar to Eastern mysticism, at the very least on a metaphorical level. Regardless, the average person has a tough time making heads or tails of quantum mechanics, however valid it is, and they need to truly *feel* the interdependence of all creations as more than a concept. Without this bottomless oneness we'll continue acting as if we aren't in relationship with the whole, particularly when our senses appear to indicate we aren't connected to people in other countries and of other races.

Again, a difference exists between intellectually accepting an idea and behaving as if the idea is real. That's why sometimes even scientists (who should know better) react in ways that aren't rational. Knowing something intellectually involves thought, but intensely feeling something involves our entire being. It's on this level that Shin-shin-toitsu-do meditation helps scientists and non-scientists experience a reality transcending divisions, a universe in which harmony abounds.

A New Understanding of the Mind

Developments in science suggest another way of looking at the universe and life, and humankind clearly needs a paradigm shift to live up to our true potential. You'll soon note similarities between Nakamura Sensei's delineation of two aspects of existence and two types of consciousness and the above-mentioned theories of Oppenheimer and Wigner. It's a change in consciousness that many have been seeking, and though some feel quantum physics points to truths espoused by ancient Eastern mysticism, neither science nor religion has ushered in a different way of living devoid of longstanding problems.

Aware of this, Nakamura Sensei investigated science, psychology, and philosophy to find a fresh vocabulary for an original way of analyzing human consciousness and its impact on society. Although he elucidated these ideas decades ago, genuinely understanding them still evokes a new way of regarding ourselves and our universe in the new millennium. Central to this fresh understanding of the mind is reiseishin, the spiritual consciousness detailed earlier. Reiseishin is the meditative mind in harmonious action with the universe. Nakamura Sensei encouraged people to discover what their reiseishin was "telling them" in terms of how to live. It was an exhortation to find and follow the deepest, most essential part of ourselves, an awareness he insisted could be unearthed by genuine meditation.

As previously stated, reiseishin implies a spiritual mind that's one with the universe. This universal mind embraces emotion and reason; at the same time it transcends as well as harmonizes emotion and reason. It's the part of us which existed before birth, and it is thus more innate than feelings or logic. Reiseishin is a mind capable of recognizing its oneness with the universe. Nakamura Sensei wrote if we follow this part of ourselves, our actions are naturally in harmony with the universe. In following it we never take the wrong path.

This sounds great, but we're left wondering why few are aware of their universal mind. In *A Booklet on Anjo Daza Meditation* Nakamura Sensei recorded that we tend to lose ourselves in emotions and logical analysis. Likewise we are confused by the endlessly changing phenomena of the relative world. As the result, when our lives come to a crossroad we're at a loss as to what to do. Do we follow our feelings or reason?

When we face the infinite and regularly changing phenomena of the world we may lose sight of the absolute universe. The absolute universe is one, and it underlies everything in our relative world. Since it is one, it's both changing and unchanging, going beyond opposites and relative phenomenon. Since it is one, it's beyond conflict, existing in harmony with itself.

If we fail to acutely see and feel the absolute universe, if we fail to manifest rei-seishin, we cling to aspects of life that are dreamlike or at least ultimately unimportant. Sawai Atsuhiro Sensei calls these chimera "ephemeral delusions." An ephemeral delusion is something we cling to as real but which takes places momentarily and disappears. It has no permanent reality yet we mistakenly grow attached to it, thinking of it as extremely important. To quote Nakamura Sensei:

> The eyes see colors, the ears hear sounds, the nose smells odors, the tongue tastes food, and the body feels heat and cold. All of these phenomena are ephemeral—fleeting like mist dissolving in the morning sun. They're endless like waves hitting incessantly against a shore. Feelings such as joy, anger, sadness, pleasure, love, hatred, and desire rise up one after another as well. The mind also sees illness and death take place over and over again, along with birth and health. All of these things are impermanent, ever changing, and constantly alternating in the relative world.[71]

If we lose ourselves in relative phenomena we end up confused and in conflict. Logically such a mind transmits conflict and confusion everywhere. This conflicted mind, wrapped up in fleeting aspects of living, buries reiseishin beneath its turbulent waves making it difficult to see our real nature. This is why meditation is vital for stilling the waves of the mind and letting our reiseishin come to the forefront, so we can see the genuine self and genuine existence, terms used in some of the earlier Nakamura Sensei quotes in this book. But what is this genuine self, and how does it correlate to a genuine understanding of the universe?

Transient Existence and Genuine Existence

To answer this we must first consider the nature of the universe, since our genuine self and the universe are one and the same. Much of what we misguidedly think of as the absolute universe has no permanence. From an absolute standpoint in Raja yoga theory and in Nakamura Sensei's worldview, fleeting phenomena are "unreal." If we regard them as everlasting and important they become delusions. And we become delusional. Nakamura Sensei called the impermanent, relative nature of things *kaso*—"transient existence."

Though it's always intermingled, and hence impossible to truly divide, we can say existence has two aspects. One is the real, ultimate, and integrated nature of life—the absolute universe—which Nakamura Sensei called *jisso*, "genuine existence." It is the true, ultimate reality behind all relative phenomena. And kaso is the relative, transitory world of ever-changing, impermanent experiences and things. It's the world "on the surface," whereas genuine existence is always working beneath the facade. Recall that Nakamura Sensei compared water to the absolute universe (jisso) while snow, rain, ice, and hail belong to the relative world (kaso). They come and go, changing form but not essence. Water molecules, however, are constant.

If we thought seriously about this, we could at least intellectually grasp the distinction between transient existence and genuine existence. But we usually don't think this way.

Consequently we fail to realize that whatever we believe makes us happy or sad belongs to the fleeting, superficial aspect of existence. Transient existence is eternally appearing and disappearing back into absolute or genuine existence, so "happiness" based on impermanent phenomena is similarly short-lived and in flux. It's unreal even if we don't commonly realize this. Then we hope and pray that—just this once—we'll remain "happy." Yet depending on impermanent, undependable parts of life to give us permanent happiness doesn't make much sense. This may be the norm, but in this case the norm is delusional.

For this reason Nakamura Sensei emphasized transcending the senses via meditation. Raja yoga calls this *pratiyahara*, but it's commonly misinterpreted as blocking out sensory perceptions (especially during meditation). This is analogous to trying to run away from transient existence in favor of genuine existence, not realizing that ephemeral parts of life are actually expressions of the absoluteness of genuine existence. Clearly this approach is circular, and we end up chasing our tails.

Nakamura Sensei taught, instead, to simply and purely perceive the passing aspects of life without clinging to them. In this way the mind is undisturbed by their constant ebb and flow, growing eternally calmer. With this calm clarity we realize the true nature of existence, releasing attachments to momentary occurrences and material objects. We live through each experience fully and let it go. We enjoy everything our senses report, but we don't clutch after these sensations as they dissolve back into the absolute universe only to reappear in another form. Through experiencing transient existence without clinging to short-lived phenomena our minds grow peaceful, taking on a mirror-like quality reflecting genuine existence as it really is. In this mirror we discover a spiritual consciousness—reiseishin—that sees past transient existence to grasp the genuine existence of the absolute universe.

Nakamura Sensei described this well in *A Booklet on Anjo Daza Meditation*:

Once our reiseishin is active we see the actual nature of the universe includes, but goes beyond, opposites and conflict. With this realization our
minds are always bright. Anjo Daza Ho is a shortcut to letting go of attachments to relative, impermanent delusions. When we release our attachments
to thoughts, sounds, and sensations, experiencing them but not clinging to
them, then we'll know what our reiseishin is telling us. The universe itself
will guide us.[172]

In summary, Nakamura Sensei's recognized "two worlds" that are interrelated:

1. **Genuine existence**—the absolute universe, the totality of existence, the
   universal ki (jisso)
2. **Transient existence**—the relative world, the dualistic nature of existence,
   the ki of fleeting phenomena (kaso)

Transient Self and Genuine Self

Reality is beyond time, duality, distinctions, and even definition. We are the same.
But language needs distinctions and definitions. For easy communication we can
say there are two selves: the "genuine self" (*jitsuga*) and the "transient self" (*kaga*).
The genuine self is tied to and perceives genuine existence: jisso, the absolute universe
without distinctions and duality. This genuine self is the universe and vice versa. Most
people, however, are solely aware of their transient self, the part of themselves that's
born and dies like all transitory phenomena. This transient self is tied to and perceives
transient existence: kaso, the relative world of endlessly changing and impermanent
occurrences.

When we're in touch with our genuine self we transcend the five senses. If we only
recognize the transient self, we grow attached to whatever the five senses perceive.

To use language to discuss what's beyond language, we can also state there are two
ways the genuine self is manifested: *mui-jitsuga* and *yui-jitsuga*, the "unconscious genuine
self" and the "conscious genuine self." Moreover, we can say for the sake of description that the transient self also exists in two forms: *gyakudo-kaga* and *jundo-kaga*, the

"the dysfunctional transient self" and the "functional transient self." Nakamura Sensei created new terminology for a new way of looking at the mind, and he used these four important terms:

1. **The unconscious genuine self**—unconscious absolute self, unconscious eternal self (mui-jitsuga)
2. **The conscious genuine self**—conscious absolute self, conscious eternal self (yui-jitsuga)
3. **The dysfunctional transient self**—dysfunctional relative self, dysfunctional impermanent self (gyakudo-kaga)
4. **The functional transient self**—functional relative self, functional impermanent self (jundo-kaga)

What are these four aspects of the self? Here's a quick explanation:

The Unconscious Genuine Self

In the state of mui-jitsuga we have no consciousness, no desires, and no recognition of the existence of ourselves. Our five senses no longer function normally, and we exhibit a near vegetative existence. Such a trance-like condition is often mistaken for meditation, but it's really closer to being brain dead. It certainly can't be maintained in daily life.

When the genuine self is unconscious we arrive at a condition similar to sleep. The same thing happens if we faint and lose consciousness, when we've taken certain drugs, when we fall into a coma, or when we're near death. In these cases the genuine self exists beyond all attachments but it's unaware. Meditation results in a spiritual awareness (reiseishin) capable of recognizing the genuine self. Nevertheless, it isn't a trance, and in meditation we discover a genuine self that's fully awake.

The Conscious Genuine Self

In the state of yui-jitsuga we rise above the senses, going beyond attachments, and transcending thoughts. We experience a pure and right consciousness, which unites the body and mind. Yet we aren't in a trance, asleep, unconscious, or dying.

This genuine self exists in joy, united with the universe. It is completely conscious, realizing its oneness with the universe. Though it's beyond description, meditation leads to the conscious genuine self.

The Dysfunctional Transient Self

In the state of gyakudo-kaga we're attached to what at least one of our five senses desire, and we suffer from our attachments to what we desire. People in this condition are filled with complaints, rarely peaceful, and seldom content. They think pessimistically, and sadly the majority lives in this condition.

The Functional Transient Self

We experience the state of jundo-kaga when our five senses function with clear consciousness, untroubled by attachments, poverty, illness, or fear of death. We control ourselves easily and with determination. We're filled with positive ideas, even when life is difficult.

Practical Spirituality in the 21st Century

The above represents not only new terminology, but a new way of looking at existence and the mind. Consequently, not everyone finds it easy to initially absorb. And that's probably as it should be.

We readily comprehend what's gone before, what we're used to. Yet what we're accustomed to can only perpetuate itself. What we're accustomed to—for generations—is a conflict ridden world and a global populace suffering from its attachments to aspects of life which are dissolving from the moment of their birth. To arrive at a true shift in the worldwide paradigm we need a fresh viewpoint and fresh vocabulary to examine it with. Shin-shin-toitsu-do offers an innovative look at existence, the self, and the mind that perceives both.

Most folks are only aware of transitory parts of life and the transient self which experiences them. Meditators sometimes see past relative, impermanent phenomenon and reject fleeting aspects of life, focusing solely on an absolute, eternal self. This seems intelligent until we realize in one sense we're as ephemeral as every other portion of the relative world. Besides, as long as we're alive we must live in the relative world of passing things. Even if we refuse to acknowledge this world, it still exists, and it exists as a visible expression of the absolute: genuine existence.

Since we have a transient aspect to us it makes sense to refine this transient self, which allows us to live efficiently within transient existence, within the relative world. Your body and transient self may only be tools of a related genuine self, but even carpenters care for their tools, making sure they function effectively. Nonetheless, quite a few of us don't do this and that's whether we've heard of all of the above or not.

The majority is only aware of a transient self. However their transient self is dysfunctional because it clings to temporary things, constantly disturbing itself and regularly viewing life negatively as a consequence. Nonetheless, what most really want is a functional transient self, regardless of how we phrase this idea. Shin-shin-toitsu-do offers methods to understand what works and doesn't work in terms of the impermanent parts of ourselves—our minds and bodies. Using Nakamura Sensei's advice regarding diet, exercise, and other matters, we can keep our bodies in tiptop shape. By altering negative habits via autosuggestion and training the five senses we can also keep the brain and mind working well. For however long we live in the relative world of fleeting occurrences our tools can be fully functional.

All of this is significant, but what many don't appreciate is that a functional transient self ultimately comes from realizing a wholly conscious genuine self, which transcends the duality comprising our relative world of impermanent phenomena. It is this self that's beyond attachments to what the senses notice, and it's this self which sees past "us and them," sensing the absolute oneness of all creations. It is the genuine self which isn't born and doesn't die, that's the very essence of the universe. When we awaken to this the mind isn't disturbed by duality and the coming and going of ephemeral life. It becomes truly positive and still, seeing clearly what allows the transient self (which it uses as a tool) to function well. As Nakamura Sensei noted, meditation leads to this state:

> By sitting in Anjo Daza Ho every day we have a chance to be reborn as a person who can live in the relative world with a functional transient self.
>
> We live in the midst of many kinds of suggestions, especially in this modern age of mass media; some are positive, but many are negative. And all of us have what psychologists call "rapport," a habitual tendency to be affected by varied suggestions from outside of ourselves. If we receive positive suggestions we can more easily live well. But if we accept numerous negative ones, it becomes harder to live well, and our lives have a greater tendency to be degraded and miserable.

If we sit in Anjo Daza Ho positive suggestions easily enter our minds and negative ones are naturally kept out. This is because this method leads the mind to perceive calmness even in this turbulent world. If the mind is calm and wiped clean of the dirt and clouds of attachment, our consciousness functions well enough to choose between negative and positive suggestions, espousing only uplifting elements from the external environment.[173]

Using meditation we uncover reiseishin, grasping how our transient self and our genuine self correlate to the transient and genuine/absolute aspects of existence. We're not attached to the transient self, but we train it and maintain it, so we can use it effectively to live well. As we change the conscious and subconscious aspects of our minds to become more positive we grow in strength, giving us the capacity to shape and guide the direction of our lives.

That said, as meditation enhances our spiritual awareness, our reiseishin also let's us see directions or destinies we cannot change. Nakamura Sensei called this *tenmei*, the "directives of the universe." For example, we can't choose our parents before we're born. This is one kind of tenmei. Whereas we can change countless matters in life with the dynamic power of mind and body unification, certain factors cannot be altered. To think otherwise is to be in conflict with life itself. Nakamura Sensei explained:

> Tenmei stem from forms of cause and effect which create spiritual relationships in the universe. While we may not be able to figure out this complex web of eternal cause and effect, we can discover and respect the directives of the universe. Each of us has a unique relationship with the universe and a unique direction in life. When we discover what we're meant to do in life, living becomes easy. Anjo Daza Ho gives us a chance to realize the real nature of calmness, and in doing so to discover clarity of mind that can perceive tenmei.[174]

Through meditation we find a spiritual nature that isn't tied to any specific religion, but which lets us see the right direction to take at each moment. It's a path in harmony with our genuine self and the genuine nature of the universe. In *A Booklet on Anjo Daza Meditation* Nakamura Sensei wrote:

> We are never separate from the infinite and eternal life of the universe. With-

in this eternal process of existence is life and death. Regardless of whether we're alive or dead we are always part of this immense course of existence. Though we may change form between living and dying, we're never separate from the endless process of life that is the universe.

Before we were born we were in the womb of our mother. And before we were in her womb we were in the life of our father. Before we were in our father's life we existed in the great life of the universe. From this point of view we can conclude death is nothing but a return to our original state. We could perhaps also say death is what changes our present life into a new life. We return to the infinite and eternal life of the universe when we die.

So our minds must transcend both birth and death, being attached to neither. In a way, this is to go beyond rejoicing in birth and lamenting death. Thus we should ask ourselves if there's any real reason to fear death. We must never fear death without a reason. The moment we're born and the exact moment of our death are tenmei. To live with a peaceful mind, which I call anshin-ritsumei, we must discover, follow, and be contented with our tenmei.[175]

When we meditate we discover clarity of mind. When our minds become clear and calm, we sense our tenmei, what works best for us. Then good health and fortune come without seeking them.

Shinjin—*True Human Beings*

Nakamura Sensei regularly referenced shinjin: the "true human being." Through Shin-shin-toitsu-do he hoped to increase the number of these individuals worldwide, signaling a paradigm shift for civilization.

I'm pretty sure only homo sapiens are reading this. And in this context, you're all human beings. That's not what Nakamura Sensei was getting at.

Nor was he seeking to create "new life" like a horror movie mad scientist or a "new race" like certain World War II era experiments. He wasn't striving to engineer a new breed of human, but rather to give humankind tools to discover its real nature and potential, a potential already existing within us and which each individual must discover in their own way. As humans we have certain characteristics we share with material objects, plants, and animals. In other words, we have form, reactions, and emotions. We also have the inimitable faculty for refined reason, which the majority views as the inden-tifying trait of humanity. Nakamura Sensei didn't fully disagree, but he noted reiseishin is what ultimately makes us truly human, in that even monkeys and apes can learn to display abilities associated with reason.

Regrettably, scores of people he encountered were unaware of their spiritual nature and largely concerned with short-lived aspects of life. They were materialistic, but their materialism didn't buy peace of mind. They struggled to reason out parts of life that were infinite, using intellects unable to quantify infinity. Moreover, their reason was frequently overwhelmed by emotions and attachments to food, sex, money, and power, rendering them incapable of sound judgment. For Nakamura Sensei, individuals who couldn't think clearly from being blinded by emotions and obsessions, who cared only for momentary happiness—whether arrived at through food, drugs, or money—were living on a near animalistic level. This works fine for dogs and cats, but it's not so great for human beings, who have a distinctive direction in life.

He, consequently, distinguished between average people and shinjin—true human beings. True human beings, who're in touch with ultimate reality, display reiseishin: a spiritual consciousness which recognizes its oneness with the universe. This awareness is unearthed by a mind that's unconditioned by attachments to the past, especially to the relative, momentary parts of life. This mind exists in the present, in an instant transcend-ing time; it's unmoved by the waves of our relative world and hence capable of bona fide rationality as well as spirituality. It sees past "us and them," past conflict of every kind, resulting in a coordinated mind and body. In the end, true human beings grasp their true nature and realize their true potential via mind and body unification, artfully shaping their lives as a sculptor might clay.

We don't see many folks like this. Nakamura Sensei's true human being really represents a new human being, who can give birth to a genuinely new millennium, an era which isn't just a modification of what's gone before.

RESOURCES FOR FURTHER INSTRUCTION &
EQUIPMENT

Shin-shin-toitsu-do involves practicing with others and alone. In preceding chapters it probably became apparent that you'd need a partner to try some aspects of Japanese yoga with.

More to the point, our study of Shin-shin-toitsu-do must be sensible and aimed at ordinary life. Sitting motionless in a quiet room, with eyes shut, is relaxing and fine for meditation. It's rewarding to practice this way, but daily existence is far removed from such a setting. To more effectively discover unity of mind and body in life, Shin-shin-toitsu-do stresses meditation in action, learning to coordinate mind and body with the eyes open, and practicing with others. The easiest method to integrate mind and body is sitting motionless and alone. Coordination of mind and body within movement is harder, and maintaining this condition of unification in action and in relationship to others is still more challenging. The later represents many people's daily lives most closely, which is why we engage in group practice as well as solo meditation.

ONGOING STUDY

If you'd like to locate people to practice with, get additional information about Shin-shin-toitsu-do in English, or find out more about the Sennin Foundation Center for Japanese Cultural Arts, write or send e-mail to the address below. Visitors are welcome, but it's best to schedule an appointment before dropping by.

> The Sennin Foundation Center for Japanese Cultural Arts
> 1053 San Pablo Ave.
> Albany, CA 94706
> USA
> Website: www.senninfoundation.com
> Facebook: http://www.facebook.com/SenninFoundation
> E-mail: hedavey@aol.com

The Sennin Foundation also offers several blogs (web logs) on the Internet that pertain to Nakamura Sensei and his teachings:

Sennin Foundation Blog ~ http://senninfoundation.blogspot.com/
Nakamura Tempu & Japanese Yoga ~ http://nakamuratempu.blogspot.com/
Art of Japanese Yoga ~ http://artofjapaneseyoga.blogspot.com/
Japanese Yoga: The Way of Dynamic Meditation ~ http://japaneseyoga.blogspot.com/
Japanese Healing Arts Blog ~ http://japanesehealing.blogspot.com/

For folks fluent in Japanese, you can learn more about Shin-shin-toitsu-do by reading Nakamura Tempu Sensei's writings, some of which are listed in the Notes & References section of this book. They carry information about his teachings and the people devoted to what he created.

INTERNATIONAL JAPANESE YOGA ASSOCIATION

The purpose of the IJYA (Kokusai Nihon Yoga Renmei) is to make the practice of Shin-shin-toitsu-do (Shin-shin-toitsu-ho) available to people all over the world regardless of age, gender, or nationality. All members are treated equally and varying styles of Shin-shin-toitsu-do are accepted. The IJYA is a nonprofit organization.

Sawai Atsuhiro Sensei is the President of the IJYA, and the group's world headquarters is in Kyoto, Japan. The daily affairs of the association are handled by the author, who was appointed by Sawai Sensei as the IJYA International Chief Instructor and who handles the day to day running of the IJYA. The IJYA aims to make instruction in Japanese yoga inexpensively available to all interested parties, regardless of their level of experience and regardless of which Shin-shin-toitsu-do group they may (or may not) be currently affiliated with.

The goal is a worldwide coalition of friends that are interested in Nakamura Sensei's teachings, who work together to benefit each other and society, without conflict or organizational politics. For additional information about the IJYA, send e-mail to hedavey@aol.com.

Japanese Yoga: The Way of Dynamic Meditation

My book *Japanese Yoga* contains information about Shin-shin-toitsu-do stretching, self-healing, and forms of physical training that isn't covered in *The Teachings of Tempu*, which focuses primarily on meditation. The Sennin Foundation Center is offering new, signed copies of *Japanese Yoga*. It makes an excellent technical companion to the book you're reading. To order copies of *Japanese Yoga*, contact the Sennin Foundation Center.

MEDITATION BELLS AND BUZZERS

To practice Anjo Daza Ho you'll want a meditation bell (and/or a Shin-shin-toitsu-do style buzzer). This is the metal Japanese bowl-shaped bell referred to previously. When the edge of the bell is tapped with its accompanying wooden striker a melodious gong-type sound is produced. This bell, which is at times associated with Buddhist ceremonies, can maintain a long resonance. Try to buy a bigger bell, of top-quality metal, that will sustain its tone longer.

However, the buzzer used in Anjo Daza Ho isn't commercially available, and not everyone outside of Japan has easy access to a Japanese "bowl bell." To address this situation the Sennin Foundation Center produced CDs which feature alternating tones from both bell and buzzer. Appropriate silent spaces are included for meditation, and you can order these CDs by contacting the Sennin Foundation Center.

NOTES & REFERENCES

* Nishida Kitaro, *Fundamental Problems of Philosophy: The World of Action and the Dialectical World*, tr. David A. Dilworth (Tokyo: Sophia University Press), p. 237 (from the final essay in the volume, "The Forms of Culture of the Classical Periods of East and West Seen from a Metaphysical Perspective").

1. Nakamura Tempu, *Shokushu—Shuren Kaiin Yo* (Tokyo: Tempu-Kai, 1957), p. 46.

2. A yogi is a practitioner of yoga.

3. Changing names to commemorate key moments in one's life has a long tradition in Japan. While less common today, it is still practiced by some traditionally minded Japanese.

4. Hashimoto Tetsuichi, *The Sennin Foundation 25th Anniversary Commemorative Booklet* (Albany, Sennin Foundation Center for Japanese Cultural Arts, 2006), page 6.

5. Sawai Atsuhiro, personal conversation, 2006.

6. Much of the biographical material and quotes in Chapter One comes from *The Life of Nakamura Tempu*, an unpublished manuscript written by Sawai Atsuhiro. It is used with the kind permission of the author.

7. Nakamura Tempu, *Tempu Meiso Roku* (Tokyo: Tempu-Kai, 1988), pp. 76 and 77.

8. No author, "Imagery," *American Cancer Society* (n.d.), http://www.cancer.org/docroot/ETO/content/ETO_5_3X_Imagery.asp?sitearea=ETO.

9. Ibid, http://www.cancer.org/docroot/ETO/content/ETO_5_3X_Imagery.asp?sitearea=ETO.

10. Nakamura Tempu, *Shin Jinsei no Tankyu* (Tokyo: Tempu-Kai, 1947), p. 55.

11. Susan Donaldson James, "People Need Both Drugs and Faith to Get Rid of Pain," *ABC News* (Aug. 1, 2007), http://abcnews.go.com/Health/Technology/story?id=3433101&page=1.

12. Carmine Gallo, "Body Language: A Key to Success in the Workplace," *BusinessWeek Online* (February 14, 2007), http://finance.yahoo.com/career-work/article/102425/Body_Language:_A_Key_to_Success_in_the_Workplace.

13. Dr. Tedd Mitchell, "Health Smart: Depression and Heart Disease," *USA Weekend* (July 28-30, 2006), p. 5.

14. Susan T. Lennon, "Health Brief: Worrywarts Might Give Themselves Acne," *USA Weekend* (Feb 9-11, 2007), p.17.

15. No author, *USA Weekend* (July 14-16, 2006), page 7.

16. Nakamura, *Tempu Meiso Roku*, pp. 155-158.

17. Ibid, pp. 118-120.

18. Ibid, pp. 23-26.

19. Dr. Tedd Mitchell, "Holding Back the Years," *USA Weekend* (January 5-7, 2007), p. 7

20. Jorge Cruise, "Think Smart: Self-image matters," *USA Weekend* (March 17-19, 2006), p. 4.

21. Nakamura, *Tempu Meiso Roku*, p. 156.

22. Ibid, pp. 48-51.

23. Ibid, p. 48.

24. Ibid, pp. 59-61.

25. Ibid, pp. 31-36.

26. Ibid, pp. 100-108.

27. Nakamura, *Shin Jinsei no Tankyu*, pp. 207-208.

28. Ibid, p. 210.

29. Ibid, pp. 225-226.

30. Ibid, pp. 230-232.

31. Ibid, p. 230.

32. Ibid, pp. 173-174.

33. Ibid, pp. 174-175.

34. Ibid, p. 175.

35. Ibid, p. 176.

36. Ibid, pp. 179-181.

37. Ibid, p. 194.

38. Nakamura Sensei's exact recommendations for kumbhaka posture and breathing can be found in his books, particularly *Shin Jinsei no Tankyu*.

39. Jorge Cruise, "Think about it: Strong brains need exercise," *USA Weekend* (August 10-12, 2007), p. 6. ("Exercise enhances learning and hippocampal neurogenesis in aged mice." Gage, FH et al. J Neurosci. 2005 Sep 21; 25(38):8680-5.)

40. Nakamura, *Shin Jinsei no Tankyu*, pp. 282-283.

41. Nakamura, *Tempu Meiso Roku*, p. 70.

42. Brad Warner, *Hardcore Zen: Punk Rock, Monster Movies, & the Truth About Reality* (Boston: Wisdom Publications, 2003), pp. 7-8.

43. Jon Urry and Andy Barton, "The Comfort Zone," *Two Wheels Only* (August 2007), p. 61.

44. Nakamura Tempu, *Seidai na Jinsei* (Tokyo: Nihon Keiei Gorika Kyokai, 1990), pp. 335-339.

45. Urry and Barton, *Two Wheels Only*, p. 61.

46. Nakamura, *Shin Jinsei no Tankyu*, p. 166.

47. Sawai Atsuhiro (H. E. Davey and Kristen Doherty, editors), "The Life of Nakamura Tempu" (unpublished, n.d.), p. 7.

48. Nakamura, *Seidai na Jinsei*, pp. 383-384.

49. Ibid, pp. 362-363.

50. Ibid, pp. 379-380.

51. Ibid, pp. 385-387.

52. Ibid.

53. Ibid, pp. 387-388.

54. Ibid, pp. 388-389.

55. Nakamura, *Shin Jinsei no Tankyu*, pp. 112-114.

56. Ibid, pp. 117-119.

57. Ibid, pp. 122-134.

58. Ibid, pp. 134-135.

59. Ibid, p. 138.

60. Ibid, pp. 136-141.

61. Nakamura, *Shokushu Shuren Kai Yo*, p. 2.

62. John Roach, "Meditation Finding Converts Among Western Doctors," *National Geographic News* (February 1, 2006), http://news.nationalgeographic.com/news/2006/02/0201_060201_meditation.html. ("Mindfulness practice leads to increases in regional brain gray matter density." Lazar, SW et al. Psychiatry Res. 2011 Jan 30; 191(1):36-43. Epub 2010 Nov 10.)

63. Nakamura, *Seidai na Jinsei*, pp. 370-371.

64. Ibid, pp. 406-408.

65. Ibid, p. 408.

66. Ibid, pp. 409-410.

67. Lindsey Tanner, "Study: Unhealthy relationships may literally hurt heart," *Daily Republic* and *Associated Press* (October 9, 2007), p. A6. ("Work stress and coronary heart disease: what are the mechanisms?" Chandola T, Britton A, Brunner E, Hemingway H, Malik M, Kumari M, Badrick E, Kivimaki M, Marmot M. Eur Heart J. 2008 Mar; 29(5): 640-8. Epub 2008 Jan 23.)

68. Joel Stein, "Just say Om," *Time* (July 27, 2003), http://www.time.com/time/magazine/article/0,9171,1101030804-471136,00.html. ("Alterations in brain and immune function produced by mindfulness meditation." Davidson R. et al. Psychosom Med. 2003 Jul-Aug; 65(4):564-70.)

69. Nakamura, *Seidai na Jinsei*, pp. 410-411.

70. Ibid, pp. 411-412.

71. Ibid, p. 414.

72. Ibid, pp. 413-414.

73. Ibid, pp. 373-374.

74. Warner, *Hardcore Zen: Punk Rock, Monster Movies, & the Truth About Reality*, p. 75.

75. Ibid, p. 76.

76. Nakamura, *Seidai na Jinsei*, pp. 375-377.

77. Nakamura Tempu, *Anjo Daza Kosho* (Tokyo: Tempu-Kai, 1965), pp. 55-56.

78. Leeza Lowitz and Reema Datta, *Sacred Sanskrit Words* (Berkeley: Stone Bridge Press, 2005), p. 168.

79. Nakamura, *Anjo Daza Kosho*, p. 79-81.

80. No author, "Yogic Gaze . . . . (Trataka)," *Health & Yoga* (n. d.), http://www.healthandyoga.com/html/meditation/yogicgaze.htm.

81. Ibid, http://www.healthandyoga.com/html/meditation/yogicgaze.htm.

82. Nakamura, *Anjo Daza Kosho*, pp. 82-83.

83. Timothy Burgin, "Yoga Articles: Focusing on a Drishti," *Yoga Basics* (November 15, 2005), http://www.yogabasics.com/articles/index.html.

84. Nakamura, *Anjo Daza Kosho*, pp. 83-84.

85. Ibid, *Anjo Daza Kosho*, p. 89.

86. Nakamura, *Seidai na Jinsei*, pp. 401-402.

87. Ibid, pp. 395-396.

88. No author, "How to Meditate: Harnessing the Mind," *Life Positive: Your Complete Guide to Holistic Living* (n.d.), http://www.lifepositive.com/Spirit/meditation/how-to-meditate.asp.

89. Ibid, http://www.lifepositive.com/Spirit/meditation/how-to-meditate.asp.

90. Warner, *Hardcore Zen: Punk Rock, Monster Movies, & the Truth About Reality* pp. 70-71.

91. Fred Alan Wolf, "A Watched Pot Never Boils," *Forbes* (November 27, 2000), p. 93.

92. One should note that classical physics also assumes that nature is interrelated; that all matter exerts a force of some type on all other matter. (Classical physics would add that depending on distance and other factors, the force exerted may be too small to be measured, but it likely can affect *some* other matter.) Quantum mechanics makes the same caveat, but allows for the possibility of counterintuitive "nonlocal" phenomena, such as superfluidity and superconductivity.

93. Wolf, *Forbes*, p.93.

94. Wes "Scoop" Nisker, *The Big Bang, the Buddha, and the Baby Boom: The Spiritual Experiments of My Generation* (New York: HarperCollins and HarperSanFrancisco, 2003), p. 121.

95. Nakamura, *Anjo Daza Kosho*, pp. 100-103.

96. Nakamura Tempu, *Kenshin Sho* (Tokyo: Tempu-Kai, 1963), p. 114.

97. Ibid.

98. Ibid, pp. 114-118.

99. Marc Kaufman, "Meditation Gives Brain a Charge, Study Finds," *Washington Post* (January 3, 2005), p. A05. ("Long-term meditators self-induce high-amplitude gamma synchrony during mental practice." Davidson RJ, et al. Proc Natl Acad Sci USA. 2004 Nov 16;101(46):16369-73. Epub 2004 Nov 8.)

100. Ibid.

101. Pagnoni G., Cekic M., "Age effects on gray matter volume and attentional performance in Zen meditation," *NCBI* (July 25, 2007), http://www.ncbi.nlm.nih.gov/sites/entrez?Db=pubmed&Cmd=ShowDetailView&TermToSearch=17655980&ordinalpos=4&itool=EntrezSystem2.PEntrez.Pubmed.Pubmed_ResultsPanel.Pubmed_RVDocSum. ("Age effects of gray matter volume and attentional performance in Zen meditation." Pagnoni, G. Cekic M. Neurobiol Aging. 2007 Oct;28(10):1623-7. Epub 2007 Jul 25.)

102. Ibid.

103. Joel Stein, "Just say Om," *Time* (July 27, 2003), http://www.time.com/time/magazine/article/0,9171,1101030804-471136,00.html.

104. Ibid.

105. Nakamura, *Shin Jinsei no Tankyu*, p. 235.

106. Paul G., Elam B., Verhulst S.J., "A longitudinal study of students' perceptions of using deep breathing meditation to reduce testing stresses," *NCBI* (Summer 2007), http://www.ncbi.nlm.nih.gov/sites/entrez?Db=pubmed&Cmd=ShowDetailView&TermToSearch=17594225&ordinalpos=15&itool=EntrezSystem2.PEntrez.Pubmed.Pubmed_ResultsPanel.Pubmed_RVDocSum.

107. Nakamura, *Shin Jinsei no Tankyu*, p. 199.

108. Since Nakamura Sensei's time science has realized direct oxygen exchange between the air and skin accounts for a fairly small percentage of "breathing." Even more than the lungs, the circulatory system handles the majority of oxygen delivery to our cells. The diffusivity of oxygen and nutrients inside the body is extremely low, which is why we need the circulatory system in the first place. "Skin breathing" is worth considering, as Nakamura Sensei noted, but it primarily delivers oxygen to the top layers of skin cells before the oxygen is gone.

109. Nakamura, *Shin Jinsei no Tankyu*, p. 239.

110. Ibid, p. 245.

111. pH 7.35 – 7.45.

112. Jean Carper, "EatSmart: The risk in cold cuts," *USA Weekend* (December 30, 2005-January 1, 2006), p. 4.

113. Nakamura, *Shin Jinsei no Tankyu*, p. 251.

114. Ibid, p. 255.

115. Ibid, p. 263.

116. *Prevention* magazine editors, "11 Ways to Find Your Energy," *USA Weekend* (September 16-18, 2005), p. 7.

117. *Prevention* magazine editors, "24 sizzling tips to live it up," *USA Weekend* (July 14-16, 2006), p. 6. ("Water and food" Popkin, et al. http://www.ncbi.nlm.nih.gov/pubmed/16421349)

118. Nakamura, *Shin Jinsei no Tankyu*, pp. 265-266.

119. Tea is also a diuretic, especially caffeinated tea, and it can cause dehydration. Consequently if dehydration is a concern drinking water is better than drinking tea.

120. The Associated Press, "The jury is still out on green tea," *The Daily Republic* (September 17, 2006), p. D2. ("Recent advances on tea polyphenols." Kanwar J. et al. Front Biosci (Elite Ed). 2012 Jan 1;4:111-31, http://www.ncbi.nlm.nih.gov/pubmed/22201858 and "Medicinal benefits of green tea: Part I. Review of noncancer health benefits." Cooper R. J Altern Complement Med. 2005 Jun; 11(3):521-8. http://www.ncbi.nlm.nih.gov/

pubmed/15992239)

121. Ibid.

122. Ibid. ("Green tea consumption and the risk of incident functional disability in elderly Japanese: the Ohsaki Cohort" Tomata Y. 2006 Study. Am J Clin Nutr. 2012 Mar; 95(3):732-9. Epub 2012 Jan 25. http://www.ncbi.nlm.nih.gov/pubmed/22277550)

123. Nakamura, *Shin Jinsei no Tankyu*, p. 267.

124. Ibid, p. 269.

125. *Prevention* magazine editors, "11 Ways to Find Your Energy," *USA Weekend* (September 16-18, 2005), p. 8.

126. Nakamura, *Shin Jinsei no Tankyu*, p. 273-279.

127. Ibid, pp. 279-280.

128. E. Tan, "Free Radicals and Antioxidants, Disease Mechanism IV: Free Radical Damage," *HOPES: Huntington's Outreach Program for Education at Stanford*, http://www.stanford.edu/group/hopes/treatmts/antiox/k1.html.

129. Grant WB; Strange RC; Garland CF, "Sunshine is good medicine. The health benefits of ultraviolet-B induced vitamin D production," *Medscape Today*, http://www.medscape.com/medline/abstract/17156062.

130. *Prevention* magazine editors, "24 sizzling tips to live it up," *USA Weekend* (July 14-16, 2006), p. 7.

131. Nakamura, *Shin Jinsei no Tankyu*, p. 281.

132. See Einstein's E=MC^2, where E is energy, M is mass, and C is the speed of light.

133. Saran Arnquist, "Exercise prescriptions become more common," *Daily Republic* (November 27, 2005), p. A1.

134. Ibid, A7.

135. Nakamura, *Shin Jinsei no Tankyu*, p. 283.

136. Ibid.

137. *Prevention* magazine editors, "24 sizzling tips to live it up," *USA Weekend* (July 14-16, 2006), p. 6.

138. Nakamura, *Shin Jinsei no Tankyu*, p. 284.

139. *Daily Republic* wire services, "Exercise linked to lower risk of dementia," *Daily Republic* (January 17, 2006), p. A8.

140. Nakamura, *Shin Jinsei no Tankyu*, p. 287.

141. Ibid, p. 288.

142. Ibid, p. 296.

143. Ibid, p. 297.

144. Ibid, pp. 297-298.

145. Ibid, p. 202.

146. Ibid.

147. *Prevention* magazine editors, "24 sizzling tips to live it up," *USA Weekend* (July 14-16,

2006), p. 7. (This finding was based on NHANES (http://www.cdc.gov/nchs/nhanes. htm). Specifically, the findings reported at this conference: North American Society for the Study of Obesity's Annual Scientific Meeting, Las Vegas, Nov. 14-18, 2004.)

148. Ibid. (A meta-analysis of the effects of sleep deprivation on all types of mortality, cancer included, can be found here: http://www.ncbi.nlm.nih.gov/pubmed/19645960.)

149. Dr. Tedd Mitchell, "Holding Back the Years," *USA Weekend* (January 5-7, 2007), p. 7

150. Ibid.

151. *Prevention* magazine editors, "11 Ways to Find Your Energy," *USA Weekend* (September 16-18, 2005), p. 6.

152. Nakamura, *Shin Jinsei no Tankyu*, p. 290.

153. Ibid, pp. 291-294.

154. Associated Press, "More Japanese living a century," *Daily Republic* (September 18, 2006), p. A7.

155. Joe Lindsey, "The Science of Belief," *Bicycling* (November 2007), p. 81. (The experiment being described is in this excerpt: http://www.ncbi.nlm.nih.gov/pubmed/14620252.)

156. Lisa Takeuchi Cullen, "How to get Smarter, One Breath at a Time," *Time* (January 10, 2006), http://psyphz.psych.wisc.edu/web/News/Time_Jan06.html.

157. Alison Motluk, "Meditation builds up the brain," *NewScientist* (November 15, 2005), http://www.newscientist.com/channel/being-human/dn8317-meditation-builds-up-the-brain.html.

158. Ibid. (Here's the original study: http://www.ncbi.nlm.nih.gov/pubmed/20670413.)

159. Tara Parker-Pope, "When a Brain Scientist Suffers a Stroke," *The New York Times* (March 13, 2008), http://well.blogs.nytimes.com/2008/03/13/when-a-brain-scientist-suffers-a-stroke/?emc=eta1.

160. The Dalai Lama, *The Universe in a Single Atom: The Convergence of Science and Spirituality* (New York: Morgan Road Books, 2005), p. 38.

161. Nisker, *The Big Bang, the Buddha, and the Baby Boom: The Spiritual Experiments of My Generation*, p.124.

162. Adam Smith, *Powers of Mind* (New York: Ballantine Books, 1976), p. 368.

163. Ibid, p. 369.

164. Nisker, *The Big Bang, the Buddha, and the Baby Boom: The Spiritual Experiments of My Generation*, p.164.

165. Smith, *Powers of Mind*, p. 370.

166. Eugene Wigner, *Symmetries and Reflections: Scientific Essays* (MIT Press, 1970), pp. 197-98.

167. J. Robert Oppenheimer, *Science and the Common Understanding* (New York: Simon and Schuster, 1954), p. 69.

168. Werner Heisenberg, *Across the Frontiers* (New York: Harper & Row, 1974), p. 227.

169. Some might assert this is a "metaphorical reading of quantum mechanics' conclusions," while other scientists might feel it's more literal.

170. The Dalai Lama, *The Universe in a Single Atom: The Convergence of Science and Spirituality*, p. 51.
171. Nakamura, *Anjo Daza Kosho*, p. 22.
172. Ibid, p. 23.
173. Ibid, pp. 70-72.
174. Ibid, pp. 74-75.
175. Ibid. pp. 75-76.

During my research for *The Teaching of Tempu: Practical Meditation for Daily Life* I found the following books and articles especially helpful. Many of these books are (were) only available in Japanese:

Nakamura Tempu, *Anjo Daza Kosho* (Tokyo: Tempu-Kai, 1965)

Nakamura Tempu, *Ken Shin Sho* (Tokyo: Tempu-Kai, 1963)

Nakamura Tempu, *Ren Shin Sho* (Tokyo: Tempu-Kai, 1949)

Nakamura Tempu, *Seidai na Jinsei* (Tokyo: Nihon Keiei Gorika Kyokai, 1990)

Nakamura Tempu, *Shin Jinsei no Tankyu* (Tokyo: Tempu-Kai, 1947)

Nakamura Tempu, *Shokushu—Shuren Kaiin Yo* (Tokyo: Tempu-Kai, 1957)

Nakamura Tempu, *Tempu Meiso Roku* (Tokyo: Tempu-Kai, 1988)

Wes "Scoop" Nisker, *The Big Bang, the Buddha, and the Baby Boom: The Spiritual Experiments of My Generation* (New York: HarperCollins and HarperSanFrancisco, 2003)

Sawai Atsuhiro (H. E. Davey and Kristen Doherty, editors), "*The Life of Nakamura Tempu*" (unpublished, n.d.)

Adam Smith, *Powers of Mind* (New York: Ballantine Books, 1976)

Tohei Koichi, *Ki no Seiza Ho* (Tokyo: Ki no Kenkyukai HQ, 1974)

Tohei Koichi, *Ki no Toitsu Ho* (Tokyo: Ki no Kenkyukai HQ, 1974)

Brad Warner, *Hardcore Zen: Punk Rock, Monster Movies, & the Truth About Reality* (Boston: Wisdom Publications, 2003)

GLOSSARY

aikido: "the Way to union with ki," a Japanese martial Way

aiki-jujutsu: a traditional Japanese martial art

Anjo Daza Ho: Shin-shin-toitsu-do meditation on the declining sound of a bell

asana: the physical postures utilized in Hatha yoga; a seated posture of meditation

batto-jutsu: a type of Japanese swordsmanship generally similar to iaido

budo: "the martial Ways"

bushi: a classical Japanese warrior, similar to samurai

Dantei Anji: "Concluding Suggestion," employed in jiko anji

dharana: concentration in Raja yoga

dhyana: meditation in Raja yoga

Do: "the Way"

dojo: "place of the Way," a training hall utilized in Japanese cultural and meditative arts

fudoshin: "immovable mind," a condition of psychological and physical stability

gyakudo-kaga: "the dysfunctional transient self"

hanare-in: placing both palms open and upward in Shin-shin-toitsu-do meditation

Hanpuku Anji: "Repeating Suggestion," utilized in jiko anji

Hatha yoga: one of the forms of Indian yoga highlighting stretching via the application of yogic postures along with breathing practices

Hitori Ryoho: "Self Healing Methods" used in Shin-shin-toitsu-do; a.k.a. Hitori Massage

hsien: Chinese Taoist sage or mystic; see sennin

iaido: a form of Japanese swordsmanship

in: a hand gesture, generally symbolic in nature; a.k.a. mudra

jiko anji: "autosuggestion"

jisso: "genuine existence"

jitsuga: "genuine self"

judo: "the Way of gentleness and yielding," a Japanese martial sport

jujutsu: "the art of gentleness and yielding," a Japanese martial art jundo-kaga: "functional transient self"

kado: "the Way of flowers," Japanese flower arrangement

kaga: "transient self"

kane: a meditation bell; a.k.a. rin

Kan-I Jiko Ryoho: "Easy Self Healing"

Kanno no Keihatsu: exercises for developing the five senses

kappo: an old Japanese art of resuscitation

Karma yoga: the yoga of action, cultivating awareness of our actions and their aftereffects

kaso: "transient existence"

Katsuryoku no Iso Ho: "Method of Transferring Life Power," a healing art

kendo: a form of Japanese swordsmanship and martial sport

ki: "life energy," the absolute essence of the universe

ki ga nukeru: "the retraction of life energy"

kodo: "the Way of incense"

kokyu ho: "breathing exercises"

ku: "nothingness," "the void"

kumbhaka: an Indian word denoting the holding of breath; also employed in Shin-shin-toitsu-do to suggest a specific postural condition and/or breathing action

kunbahaka: Japanese transliteration of kumbhaka

Meirei Anji: "Commanding Suggestion," employed in jiko anji

mu: "emptiness," "the void"

mudra: a hand gesture, generally symbolic in nature; a.k.a. in

muga ichi-nen: "no self, one thought"

Muga Ichi-nen Ho: A visually oriented Shin-shin-toitsu-do meditation involving concentration on an external object

muga munen: "no self, no thought"

mui-jitsuga: "the unconscious transient self"

munen muso: "no thoughts, no mental images"

musei no koe: "the soundless sound"

nikusei ishiki: "physical consciousness"

orenai te: a Shin-shin-toitsu-do exercise involving ki projection through the arm

padmasana: half lotus position

prana: an Indian word characterizing "life energy"

Pranayama: Indian yogic breathing practices

Raja yoga: one of the forms of Indian yoga stressing meditation

reisei ishiki: "spiritual consciousness"

reiseishin: "spiritual mind," a universal mind

Renso Anji: "Associated Images Suggestion," employed in jiko anji

rin: a meditation bell; a.k.a. kane

ryaku-in: placing the palms upward in the lap, and forming a circle with the fingers, for Shin-shin-toitsu-do meditation

sado: "the Way of tea," tea ceremony

samadhi: the ultimate flowering of meditation in Raja yoga, resulting in spiritual realization and union with the universe; a.k.a. zanmai

satori: spiritual awakening

seiza: "correct sitting," kneeling with the legs folded beneath the hips, while resting softly on the heels

Sennin: a Japanese mystic, the Japanese equivalent to a yogi; see Hsien

Sennin-do: "the Way of the Sennin," generic for Japanese interpretations of Chinese Taoist yoga

Senjutsu: "the arts of the Sennin," generic for Japanese interpretations of Chinese Taoist yoga

sensei: "born before," teacher

shinjin: "true human being"

Shin Kokyu Ho: "Deep Breathing Exercise"

shinsei ishiki: "mental consciousness"

Shinto: "the Way of the gods," the indigenous Japanese religion

shin-shin-toitsu: "mind and body unification"

Shin-shin-toitsu-do: "the Way of mind and body unification," a.k.a. Shin-shin-toitsu-ho

Shin-shin-toitsu-ho: "the art or methods of mind and body unification," a.k.a. Shin-shin-toitsu-do

Shin-shin-toitsu no Yondai Gensoku: "Four Basic Principles to Unify Mind and Body"

shita hara: "lower abdomen," a natural center in the lower abdomen

shodo: "the Way of calligraphy"

shoku: "affirmations" for positively changing the subconscious

siddhasana: full lotus position

Sorin-in: placing the palms upward in the lap, and forming two linked circles with the fingers, for Shin-shin-toitsu-do meditation

sumi-e: "ink painting"

tanden: a lower abdominal center relating to coordination of mind and body, which has essentially the same meaning as shita hara

Taoism: indigenous Chinese spiritual path emphasizing oneness with the Way of the universe (Tao)

tenmei: "directives of the universe"

Toitsu-do: "the Way of unification," a.k.a. Shin-shin-toitsu-do

Trataka: a gazing meditation in Indian yoga that is similar to Muga Ichi-nen Ho

uchu-rei: "universal spirit"

wa: "harmony"

Yodo Ho: Shin-shin-toitsu-do health exercises/meditation utilizing rhythmic movement

yoga: an art, originating in India, for achieving union with the universe

yogi: a practitioner of Indian yoga

yuga ichi-nen: to focus the mind on one thought, but to still be self-conscious

yui-jitsuga: "the conscious genuine self"

zanmai: the ultimate flowering of meditation in Indian yoga, resulting in spiritual realization and union with the universe; the Japanese transliteration of samadhi

Zen: a type of Japanese Buddhist meditation

ABOUT THE AUTHOR

H. E. Davey is the Director of the Sennin Foundation Center for Japanese Cultural Arts, which offers instruction in Japanese systems of yoga, martial arts, healing arts, and fine arts. His introduction to the arts of Japan came via traditional martial arts. Since the age of five, he's studied *jujutsu* extensively in the USA and Japan. He has received the title of *Kyoshi* from the Kokusai Budoin, a Tokyo-based international federation. Kokusai Budoin defines Kyoshi as comparable to a "Master's Certificate" and equivalent to modern ranks of sixth- to eighth-degree black belt. He also serves on the Board of Directors of the Shudokan Martial Arts Association (www.smaa-hq.com).

In middle school Mr. Davey began Shin-shin-toitsu-do, a system of Japanese yoga and meditation founded by Nakamura Tempu Sensei. He's practiced in Japan and the USA under Nakamura Sensei's senior disciples, including Sawai Atsuhiro Sensei and Hashimoto Tetsuichi Sensei. Mr. Davey's also received extensive instruction in Nakamura Sensei's methods of bodywork and healing with ki ("life energy"), which he teaches. He is the only member of Tempu-Kai, an organization established by Mr. Nakamura, who is a full-time professional instructor of Shin-shin-toitsu-do. He's also a member of the Wakuwaku Honshin Juku in Osaka, an organization devoted to Nakamura Sensei's teachings that has given him their highest level of teaching certification. In addition, Mr. Davey is the Vice President of the Kyoto-based Kokusai Nihon Yoga Renmei (International Japanese Yoga Association). He has the most advanced grade of teaching certification in the IJYA and serves as their International Chief Instructor. He's furthermore received training in Hatha yoga and Pranayama breathing exercises in the tradition of Indra Devi.

Mr. Davey also studied shodo, or Japanese brush writing and ink painting, for 20 years under the late Kobara Ranseki Sensei, recipient of the Order of the Rising Sun. Mr. Davey holds the top rank in Ranseki Sho Juku shodo and exhibited in Japan for many years. He's received numerous honors in these exhibitions, including *Jun Taisho* ("Associate Grand Prize").

H. E. Davey's articles on Japanese arts and his artwork have appeared in numerous American and Japanese magazines and newspapers. He's the author of *Unlocking the Secrets of Aiki-jujutsu*, *Brush Meditation: A Japanese Way to Mind & Body Harmony*, *Japanese Yoga: The Way of Dynamic Meditation*, *Living the Japanese Arts & Ways: 45 Paths to Meditation & Beauty*, *The Japanese Way of the Artist*, and *The Japanese Way of the Flower: Ikebana as Moving Meditation*.

24002806R00171

Made in the USA
Charleston, SC
08 November 2013